MISSION TO THE MIDDLE CLASSES

MISSION TO THE MIDDLE CLASSES

The Woodard Schools 1848-1891

BRIAN HEENEY

Published for
the Church Historical Society
in association with the
University of Alberta Press

LONDON
S·P·C·K
1969

First published in 1969
by S.P.C.K.
Holy Trinity Church
Marylebone Road
London N.W.1

Made and printed in Great Britain by
The Camelot Press Ltd, London and Southampton

This work has been published with the help of a grant from the Humanities Research Council of Canada, using funds provided by the Canada Council.

Quotations from the Papers of the third Marquess of Salisbury, at present in the library of Christ Church, Oxford, are made by kind permission of the Marquess of Salisbury.

SBN 281 02326 3

TO

Goodith, Michael, Ann, Timothy
and Matthew
and in memory of
John

CONTENTS

ABBREVIATIONS

A.S.N.C.	Associate of St Nicolas College
S.I.C.	Schools Inquiry Commission
S.N.C.	St Nicolas College
Hurst	St John's Middle School, Hurstpierpoint

Schools are frequently referred to by place name (e.g. Lancing for SS. Mary and Nicolas School, Lancing).

PREFACE

This book is based on a thesis accepted for the D.Phil. degree at Oxford in 1962. To Dr John Walsh of Jesus College I owe an immense debt of gratitude, not only for his wise and ready advice, but also for his encouragement and friendship which did so much to make my years in Oxford unusually happy.

Of the many individuals who helped me with my research the following deserve special thanks: Dr G. F. A. Best, Dr G. Kitson Clark, Dr W. C. Costin, Mr B. W. T. Handford, Mr M. J. B. Otter, and Dr John Roach. I am conscious of my debt to the Woodard Corporation, and especially to the headmaster and staff of Lancing. Without the resources of the Bodleian Library and the libraries of the British Musuem, the Ministry of Education, and Pusey House, I would have accomplished very little. I am especially grateful to the librarian of Christ Church, Dr J. F. A. Mason, for helping me to make full use of the relevant material in the Salisbury Papers. I am also grateful to the Marquess of Salisbury for permission to reproduce portions of the correspondence between the Third Marquess and Woodard.

A Rockefeller Doctoral Fellowship and Canada Council Predoctoral Fellowships made possible the research upon which this book is based. Without substantial grants from the Humanities Research Council of Canada and the University of Alberta Press there would have been no book at all.

The preparation of this study has meant the desertion of my family for several months during two summers. My wife and children have suffered this neglect generously. Two Oxford families, the Walshes and the Heatons, have made these absences from my own family endurable by allowing me to become a temporary member of theirs.

Margaret Tyler and Bronwen Holden very kindly helped me with proof-reading and with the preparation of the Index.

Edmonton, Alberta.
February 1969

BRIAN HEENEY

INTRODUCTION

This book is about the life-work of a single-minded man.

Nathaniel Woodard left a vast correspondence (some 9,000 letters are preserved at Lancing College, and there are more in other collections);[1] virtually all of it is directly connected with the organization and development of SS. Mary and Nicolas College, the Corporation which he established as an Anglo-Catholic mission to middle-class England and as the national agent of middle-class schooling. There is very little in all the surviving letters and documents about Woodard's private friendships, about his children, or indeed about his wife. His biographer, Sir John Otter, devoted but nine pages, in his *Memoir* of several hundred pages, to Woodard's first thirty years. He was in fact a man whose life was almost wholly identified with his accomplishment after his thirty-seventh year. From that age he became simply "the Founder", a title by which he was known to all his colleagues and supporters.

Born on St Benedict's Day 1811, the ninth of twelve children, Nathaniel Woodard was the son of an Essex country gentleman of very narrow means. He was privately tutored, and although he early planned to enter the Anglican ministry he received a very indifferent education. Supported, it is supposed, by kind aunts, he matriculated at Magdalen Hall at Oxford in 1834. Although he managed to earn a Pass Degree in 1840, his academic career clearly suffered not only from inadequate preparation but also because of the domestic diversions and cares which resulted from his early marriage in 1836.

On 6 June 1841 he was ordained to the diaconate by the Bishop of London (Blomfield) and was given charge of the new district of St Bartholomew's, Bethnal Green. There he laboured strenuously to complete the building of a new church and to raise funds for a parochial school. In 1843 Woodard preached a sermon on Confession, which, despite his own earnest pleadings and those of parishioners, resulted in his removal from Bethnal Green by the diocesan, Bishop Blomfield. In the spring of 1846, after an uneventful curacy at Clapton, he was appointed assistant curate at New Shoreham in Sussex.[2]

Woodard's childhood and youth coincided with rapid changes in British industrial society. One aspect of that development, the increasing consciousness of class feeling, the growing corporate self-awareness of the "labouring poor" on the one hand and of owners and managers on the other, lay behind all Woodard's later activity. The late 30s and early 40s witnessed fierce conflict between social classes. Politics were directly related to this conflict; for the Chartist and Anti-Corn Law movements sharply polarized working-class and middle-class feeling.[3]

Woodard's years in Oxford and Bethnal Green were also the years of the Chartist and Anti-Corn Law agitations. The Chartists, although they caused immense worry to all men of property, failed at least in their immediate aims, and after 1848 the Chartist threat to order vanished as a national anxiety. In sharp contrast the agitation to abolish the tax on corn was supremely successful; and, by 1846, with the end of the tax on corn,

> not only had the phrase "middle class" established itself as a political concept, but those people who considered themselves as representatives of the middle classes were prepared to assert in the strongest possible language their claim to political leadership.[4]

Woodard, like his contemporaries, was accustomed to class conflict and to thinking in class terms. As a young man he observed the power and political effectiveness of the middle classes. When he came to Shoreham in 1846, the year of free trade triumph, he immediately began to teach a few middle-class boys in the vicarage. Two years later he launched a great educational scheme designed to attach middle-class power and energy to established institutions.

The early nineteenth century was a period of great educational effort by English churchmen. The National Society, founded in 1811, was designed to promote the education of the poor, and the decade after 1839 saw a great advance in this work. By 1846 nearly one million day scholars were being taught in 17,000 parochial schools.[5] Nor did churchmen direct their attention to the poor only. In the 1840s Thomas Arnold's work at Rugby began not only to influence the old upper-class boarding schools but also to inspire the foundation of new ones whose pupils were drawn largely from the families of rich manufacturers, traders, and professional men.[6]

Woodard was one of several churchmen who noticed that a large body of English children, the offspring of the people normally described as "middle class", were practically excluded from both parochial and public schools. It was Woodard's achievment, in the years after 1846, to rouse the Church to the educational needs of these children. As the parish was the basic unit in the structure of the schools for the poor, so the diocese, thought Woodard, would be the administrative unit of a nation-wide Church-centred secondary school system. Public boarding schools, so suitable and successful as agents for training the upper classes, would be adapted for the use of the less wealthy.

Woodard's first widely-circulated pamphlet, *A Plea for the Middle Classes*,[7] was directed at gentlemen-churchmen, who, for some years had watched the political and economic progress of the heavily nonconformist middle classes with dismay. Some of the men to whom the *Plea* was made had seen the need for Church action and already had made efforts to respond to the challenge.[8] The *Plea* was made to men who were acutely aware of the need to do something about the "condition of England", and aware too that the National Society's work of thirty years among the poor had not prevented social unrest.

Conditioned in these ways, Woodard's public responded enthusiastically. During the next forty years of his life Woodard was the effective symbol of the Church's effort to educate the Victorian middle classes. In his schools, built with astonishing rapidity at enormous cost, he attempted not only to provide a relevant education for a vitally important and growing segment of society, but also to attract the middle classes to Anglo-Catholicism and stable political Conservatism.

1

SCHOOLS FOR THE MIDDLE CLASSES

1

Nathaniel Woodard began his work at the end of a period of sharp class conflict, at a time when class consciousness in England was strong.[1] The two decades after 1848, during which Woodard's project developed and grew, were years of relative stability and quietness. W. L. Burn has described this mid-Victorian generation as the Age of Equipoise; and Asa Briggs has pointed to the softening of social antagonisms in a period during which "the word 'balance' was one of the key words . . . both in relation to politics and to society".[2]

Yet if the language of class lost much of its militancy in these years, nevertheless the fact of class remained. England was still an hierarchial society although the grades in the hierarchy were multiplying and the dividing-lines between middle and upper classes, as between middle and lower classes, were increasingly difficult to define.

This fact of class cannot be avoided in any study of mid-Victorian schools; for education at all levels was organized on class lines. To Nathaniel Woodard and his contemporaries secondary education meant middle-class education.[3] Before any useful study of Woodard's work can be undertaken, before his work and opinions can be compared with those of his contemporaries, it is essential to know about whom the mid-Victorians were talking when they spoke of the "middle classes".

Certainly money income was a dubious guide to social standing. It is clear that increase of income alone could not promote an industrialist into the ranks of the gentry; neither did poverty necessarily reduce the status of a "gentleman". Nevertheless, a large income enabled a man, despite his association with trade and manufacture, to send his son to one of the great public schools or to one of the new proprietary schools built to cope with increasing demand for upper-class education. By means of such institutions the newly-enriched family could, through its junior members, better itself socially and the family might, in the next generation, move into the coveted circles of "gentlemen".[4] On the other hand, inability to pay the price for such an education might cause a traditionally upper-class family to descend in the scale.[5]

At the opposite boundary of the middle class, income was an equally poor guide to social position. Some manual workers undoubtedly made more money than many clerks and others holding "respectable" white collar jobs. In 1860, for example, the average wage for cashiers in Manchester and Salford was no more than £100, and that for bookkeepers and clerks was only £60; nine years before, the average annual income of a male primary school teacher in Lancashire was £58 3*s*.[6] Yet we are told by a contemporary authority that some members of the working class were earning forty shillings a week and more in 1867, and, according to G. D. H. Cole, no less than 14·4 per cent of the income earners in the working class were being paid a weekly wage of from twenty-eight to thirty-five shillings in 1867.[7] Nevertheless, a large income did permit well-paid manual workers to adopt middle-class ways. E. J. Hobsbawm has shown that these aristocrats of labour were, in fact, much closer in culture and outlook to "small shopkeepers, independent masters, foremen, managers, and clerks" than they were to the lower strata of the labouring class.[8]

Woodard limited and arranged the clientele of his schools according to income. He would not normally permit a man with an income of over £150 to send his son to the "lower middle school" at the usual extraordinarily low fee.[9] Similarly the fees at his middle and upper schools were fixed according to an estimate of the amounts different classes of parents could afford. But he never attempted any formal grading on the basis of income.

The mid-Victorians commonly identified the middle classes with certain occupational groups. Thus, for example, in 1865 the *Guardian* referred to the middle classes as made up principally of farmers, retail dealers, and clerks.[10] Most contemporary definitions included this trinity of occupations, although a wide assortment of additional groups were frequently added. Some such lists excluded these highly paid manual workers who, as we have seen, might be taken to form a proper part of the lower middle class.[11]

Others, although they included the aristocracy of labour, left professional men and wealthy capitalists out of account. Indeed, as the century grew older, the line between the aristocracy and the upper middle class became progressively fuzzier. Many capitalists and merchants bought land and established themselves as country gentlemen, and certainly the cream of the professional class was accepted into upper-class society. "From above", wrote a contributor to *Blackwood's Magazine* in 1885, "the younger sons of the aristocracy have been dropping into the more active ranks of the middle class—'going into trade'. From below, the best men of the working class are still pushing up."[12]

To estimate the numbers of people whom the Victorians would have described as "middle class" is impossible.[13] However, Charles Booth, in his *Occupations of the People, 1841–1881*[14] did arrange the census figures in such a way as to illustrate the growing numbers in certain accepted middle-class occupations. Faced with the failure of the census to distinguish between trade and manufacture (and thus between dealers and makers) he made his own estimate of the number of dealers.[15] According to Booth, the number of people occupied in this essentially middle-class calling was over two and a half times greater in 1881 than it had been in 1841; during the same period the "employed or independent" population of England and Wales had not quite doubled.

The numbers employed in other work of a middle-class character also rose rapidly during the period of Booth's survey. The numbers employed in "commercial services" rose from 41,100 in 1841 to 67,500 in 1861, and to 225,300 in 1881. The numbers listed under "administration" in "Public and Professional Services" increased from 20,500 in 1841 to 64,000 in 1861, and 81,700 in 1881. In the "management" of the building industry the numbers doubled between 1841 and 1861, and had nearly doubled again by 1881. People employed in "education" more than tripled during these forty years. The older professions expanded too, although the percentage rise in "Medicine", "Law", and "Religion" was not as great as that in middle-class occupations as a whole. The only middle-class occupation which not only failed to keep up with the population rise, but absolutely declined during the latter part of the period, was farming. Furthermore, this remarkable rise in the number of people engaged in middle-class occupations continued after 1881.[16]

To Woodard, as to other mid-Victorian educators, the identification of the middle class with certain occupational groups was natural and reasonable. Furthermore he was well aware of the subdivisions within the middle class itself. It was clear to him, as it was to others, that the great range of occupations covered by the term "middle class" made necessary different schools offering education suitable to the different categories within that class. His first school was originally planned for "the sons of gentlemen of small incomes, solicitors, surgeons with limited practice, unbeneficed clergymen, naval and military officers."[17] The second school was for the central middle-class occupational trinity, "tradesmen, farmers, and clerks";[18] his third or "lower middle" school was for the "sons of tradesmen, small farmers, mechanics, and others of limited means".[19] In fact, though not in form, the Schools Inquiry Commissioners, appointed in 1864 to investigate the state of secondary education, adopted this occupational definition of the middle class, and divided their categories of secondary schools in a fashion almost identical to Woodard's.[20]

Mid-Victorians often defined "middle class" directly in educational terms. A typical middle-class parent required a certain type of education for his child: an education which differed both in quantity and in quality from that provided in the great public schools as it differed too from that provided in the many elementary schools of the country. Thus, for example, the Schools Inquiry Commissioners, in their 1868 Report, really described the elements in the middle class by stating the school leaving age of different groups of children requiring secondary education. The commissioners grouped parents of secondary schoolboys into three divisions. The first consisted of people whose sons remained at school until at least eighteen years of age; this group, which contained "bankers, manufacturers, and others of large mercantile business", sought and could afford an education of the sort provided for the sons of "gentlemen of independent means" and "professional gentlemen". Below this upper level was a large number of parents who wished their sons to remain at school until about the age of sixteen; this segment of society consisted, according to the Commissioners, of the "sons of tradesmen in considerable business, farmers, agents, managers, upper clerks". The third and largest group of parents of secondary schoolboys was that which consisted of people who could afford to permit their sons full-time schooling only to the age of fourteen; these people were described as "tradesmen in limited business, shopmen, clerks, upper artisans."[21]

If we exclude the "gentlemen of independent means", this classification corresponds well to the various definitions of middle class made on the basis of parental occupation alone. D. R. Fearon, the Assistant Commissioner whose report covered the metropolitan area, explicitly identified the families of such boys with the members of the middle class:

> Middle-class boys are boys whose general education ends between their 14th and their 19th years of age. . . . It will be convenient to divide them into three grades. . . . By the first grade is meant those boys who stay at school till they are in their 18–19th years of age. This grade is numerically small. It touches upon and is often blended and confused with the upper scholars. . . . By the second grade is meant those who stay at school till they are in their 16–17th years of age. *This is in every respect the most genuinely "middle" of any part of the class.* By the third grade is meant those who stay at school only until they are in their 14–15th year of age. The boys of this grade approach nearest to and are often blended and confused with the scholars of the primary and lower schools.[22]

The common understanding of middle-class schools throughout our period excluded those at which students remained until the age of eighteen, to which parents paid large fees and at which pupils associated with the offspring of "gentlemen"; also excluded were the mixed schools at which farmers' and tradesmen's boys were taught with those of labourers. Robert Lowe expressed a widespread view of middle-class education:

> What I mean [by middle-class education] is the education of a class that would not think of sending its children to primary schools supported by the State, and yet is not in the condition of life to think of sending its children to universities or public schools.[23]

Snobbery, independence, as well as the need for a broader curriculum and more extended schooling caused the middle class as a whole to reject parochial schools.[24] On the other hand, even if they desired the sort of education provided at Cheltenham, Marlborough, Rugby, and such places, they could not afford these schools; nor would they accept the rather degenerate classical teaching of many of the endowed grammar schools.[25] Consequently a great demand arose for schools described by the Schools Inquiry Commission as "second" or "third" grade (i.e. at which schooling terminated at 16 and 14 respectively). Those who created this demand and those who filled the wide variety of institutions which sought to meet this need formed the nucleus of the middle class.

2

As the middle classes grew in number during the middle years of the century the inadequacies of English secondary education became increasingly obvious. These inadequacies were of various sorts and contemporary assessments of their relative importance depended a good deal on the standpoint of the critic. Quantitatively at least, all agreed that provision for middle-class education was insufficient. In the mid-sixties, a writer in the *Saturday Review* expressed this common sentiment: "The upper classes have taken care of themselves, and the lower classes have been well cared for; but between these two fruitful regions lies a vast tract of howling wilderness and imposture."[26] Such a condition was not surprising in view of the constant increase taking place in middle-class occupations. It was confirmed in 1868 in the Report of the Schools Inquiry Commission: "In at least two-thirds of the places in England named as towns in the Census, there is no public school at all above the primary schools, and in the remaining third the school is often insufficient in size or quality."[27]

Probably of even greater importance than the deficiency in the number of schools was the doubtful quality of those that did exist. Particularly bad were most of the numerous private schools and "academies" which advertised not only their excellence but their economy in leading newspapers and journals. In 1857 a writer in *Chambers's Journal* asserted that he

> should almost blame more than the school speculators the parent who committed his child into such hands without making any calculations as to whether the other party in the bargain *can* be reasonably expected to fulfil his share of the contract. . . . That there is a great demand for these schools is evidenced by the number of advertisements . . . which appear daily in the provincial newspapers, as well as in *The Times* and other metropolitan journals.[28]

Some years before this was written, Woodard referred to

> these miserably imperfect schools which now abound all over the country; schools devoid of sound principle as of sound knowledge,

the conductors of which have no other object in view than to secure a scanty subsistence by the credulity of that class in society which is unable to judge of the requirements necessary to make a competent schoolmaster.[29]

Yet, if not educational successes, these private schools often proved to be commercially prosperous. This they did because the endowed grammar schools failed "to supply one of the great needs of the country—a good education for the lower section of the middle classes".[30] The Eldon judgment of 1805, which forbade any subjects of instruction but the classical languages in grammar schools, made it impossible for such schools to meet the needs of the expanding trades class for a relevant secondary education. Although this restriction was loosened somewhat by the Grammar Schools Act of 1840 and the institution of the Charity Commission in 1853, Latin and Greek remained the core of the curriculum at such grammar schools as retained genuine secondary status. Such a curriculum was wholly unsuited for the great majority of middle-class vocational and social groups, especially for those which were expanding most conspicuously.

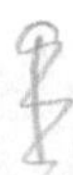

Radical educators had recognized this problem early in the century, especially as it affected the middle-class élite; and, by the 50s, it was widely accepted that a different or at least greatly broadened sort of intellectual training was required. In 1852 *The English Journal of Education* stated that "the greatest educational problem of the day, and the one which before all others demands solution" was the provision of a suitable education for middle-class children, based not on the dead languages or on abstract mathematics, but on "the living tongues and practical mathematics . . . their own language and physical science . . . [and] aesthetic training".[31] If the Schools Inquiry Commissioners' Report is accepted as a guide, this opinion must have been somewhat advanced; for in the 60s informed opinion still favoured language instruction as the basis of the middle-class curriculum, although natural science and English also occupied prominent places.[32]

Woodard was generally conservative in matters affecting the curriculum;[33] but his schools, together with a very limited number of other institutions, chiefly proprietary, were recognized by the Commissioners as providing the sort of education which the private schools through commercialism, and the endowed schools through reaction and neglect, failed to give to the middle classes.[34]

Many saw the need for an increase in the number of middle-class schools; at least as many saw an equal or greater need for change and improvement in educational standards and content. Early in the century the cry for educational reform had been raised by the same Radicals who led the campaign for Parliamentary Reform.[35] Thomas Arnold expressed the need in 1832;[36] Woodard did so continually after 1848. In 1861, at the beginning of a decade in which educational as well as franchise reform was much debated, *The Times* warned that

> The political centre of gravity is confessedly somewhere in the middle classes; they constitute the great majority of the ratepayers, the taxpayers and of the electors of Great Britain. . . . Yet . . . the great educational movement of the last fifty years which has done so much to elevate the labouring and artisan classes, and has affected . . . the highest classes of all has scarcely visited the intermediate region.[37]

In 1869 a clear note of urgency was sounded in the *Nottingham Daily Guardian*: as the middle classes participated increasingly in public affairs, especially at the municipal level, "the great importance, nay the urgent necessity of the improved education of such a class becomes more and more manifest".[38] "Before the English middle class can have the right or the power to assert itself absolutely," wrote Matthew Arnold in 1864, "it must have greatly perfected itself." The qualities it lacked, those of "largeness of soul and personal dignity," could be supplied by education in "great, honourable, public institutions similar to the *lycées* of France".[39] "These institutions", he wrote, referring to the French secondary schools,

> give to a whole new class—to the middle class taken at its very widest—not merely an education for whose teaching and boarding there is valid security, but something of the same enlarging, liberalizing sense, the sense of belonging to a great and honourable public institution, which Eton and our . . . great public schools give to our upper class only, and to a small fragment broken off from the top of our middle class.[40]

Many Victorian churchmen who recognized the need for middle-class education saw it principally as a religious enterprise. The middle classes needed schools to "form their moral taste and character".[41] Even more important, the Church needed mission stations among a section of the population largely given over to

Dissent and subject to Radical irreligion. Henry E. Manning, the future cardinal, warned the clergy of the Archdeaconry of Chichester in 1846:

> There is the great middle class. . . . I need not say what the Church is able to do for them; and what if the English nation is again to be folded in the English Church, it must do. I need not say what this middle class might do for the Church if it were drawn into its ministry and service.[42]

Even more vigorous and pointed were the remarks of a London clergyman ten years later:

> The classes she [the Church] has neglected have neglected her. She has failed to be their teacher and they have sought teachers for themselves. In the middle classes lies the strength of Dissent and the weakness of the Church of England. . . . It is the thriving shopkeepers who fill the pews of meeting-houses and are missing from our seats in church. . . . The orders of the Church are inaccessible to them from the expense of an academical education. . . . And the Church suffers beyond calculation. . . . Young men who would have heartily served her [are] forced into the position of rivals and opponents.[43]

Many churchmen who actually started middle-class schools in the years from Victoria's accession to the mid-sixties took this view: that the middle ranks of society, the most influential section of the population, were "opponents of the Church not from principle, but from want of understanding".[44] The function of Church schools for the children of such people was not only, or chiefly, to provide a good and suitable secular education, but to win back this critical element in society to the national religion.

3

Woodard was not the only churchman to take a practical interest in middle-class education; nor was the Church the first agency to do so in nineteenth-century England. Radicals had attacked the endowed grammar schools in the second decade of the century; in the 1820s Jeremy Bentham proposed a revolutionary middle-class curriculum, excluding religious instruction totally and displacing the classical languages as the basis of instruction. In 1832 University College School was opened in London and was conducted largely on Benthamite principles. The Liverpool Mechanics

Institution opened a "lower (or commercial) school" in April 1835, designed "to qualify the pupil to enter the workshop of the artist or mechanic, the office of the merchant, the accountant, or solicitor, the laboratory of the chemist, or the lecture-room of the surgeon". Boys were not expected to stay beyond the age of fourteen, and the fees were very moderate. Three years later a superior middle-class school was attached to the Institute for those children who had to begin work at the age of fifteen or sixteen, and whose parents could pay eight or ten guineas a year.[45] Such proprietary day schools multiplied; in Leicester, for example, "Dissenters and secularists" opened the "Proprietary School for the town and county of Leicester" in 1837.[46]

The years after 1840 saw a decrease in the number of new proprietary day schools and a swing towards public boarding schools set up on a proprietary basis. Most of these were in some sense connected with the Church of England, and were decidedly too expensive for all except the upper part of the middle classes. Throughout the early part of the century private schools of a new variety also flourished, the ancestors of the breed which Woodard and the Schools Inquiry Commissioners thought so scandalous later in the century.

But it was a group of Church of England clergymen and laymen who, in 1838, first set about the task of creating a national system of middle-class education. S. F. Wood, H. E. Manning, W. E. Gladstone, and other High Churchmen met in the spring of 1838 and succeeded in persuading the National Society to form a "Committee of Inquiry and Correspondence".[47] Among other things, this Committee was commissioned to

> consider with care the question of its [i.e. the National Society's] competency to act in a corporate character in the creation and support of schools for the education of the children of tradesmen and farmers and other persons standing in a similar relation to the class more usually designated "Poor".[48]

This committee, which contained many men besides those who agitated for its formation,[49] met regularly from 16 May 1838 until 14 May 1839. Its work was not confined to solving the problem of middle schools; indeed its practical achievement in encouraging the formation of Diocesan Boards of Education was of greater permanent significance.[50] But its perception of the need, its plans to fill the need on a national scale, and the disappointing yet significant results of its activities, make this committee important to a student of Victorian middle-class education.

The class to be aimed at was indicated by its representative vocations: farming and trade. The committee offered both a rural and an urban solution to the problem. It charged itself with an "inquiry preparatory to forming or taking into union middle schools in towns; and into the methods of instruction best adapted to them".[51] By August 1838 the committee's plans for urban schools had been settled, and proposed "local boards" in towns were designed to promote, not only the union of existing commercial schools, but also the establishment of new ones, and the examination of masters.[52] The aim of all such schools was to become self-supporting, and the suggested curriculum was extraordinarily "modern".[53]

At about the same time the committee was formed, the bishops of London and Winchester had founded an agency for establishing Church of England commercial schools in London; according to H. J. Burgess this project had been brought under the committee's jurisdiction by June 1838.[54] Almost certainly the "Metropolitan Institution for the Establishment and Improvement of Commercial Schools in the Metropolis and its Suburbs in Connexion with the National Church", opened by Dean Chandler on 28 January 1839, was the fruit of this venture.[55] So too, apparently, was the "East Islington Commercial School", opened by the Reverend R. Burgess in January 1841.[56] The fees at the Metropolitan School were fixed at 25*s.* a quarter and the curriculum excluded Greek and included "the elements of natural history and philosophy".[57] Dean Chandler hoped that similar institutions would be founded "not only among ourselves but in every other diocese in our land".[58]

For the rural middle classes, the Committee of Inquiry and Correspondence had a somewhat different proposal. It set about discovering

> in what manner higher branches of instruction may be engrafted . . . upon country schools in order to render them more suitable for the children of the classes analogous to those portions of the town populations for whom the middle schools are intended.[59]

The proposed curriculum for such superior National Schools varied somewhat from that of the town commercial schools, though it was equally modern.[60] Certainly some such schools were founded and the idea attracted a good deal of favour in later years; but it is doubtful whether the committee was directly responsible for any such institutions.

A third sort of middle school emerged from the committee's deliberations: the Cathedral school, primarily for training elementary schoolmasters, "singing men, and parish clerks", but also for a "specified number of pupils . . . who had no such ultimate views, and attended the school only to obtain that education which might prepare them for the future duties of life as Farmers, Tradesmen, or Mechanics".[61] The use of Cathedral institutions had been one of Manning's ideas.[62]

The practical consequences of the National Society's efforts in the realm of middle-class education did not balance the enthusiasm of the committee's members. "Unfortunately," wrote H. J. Burgess, "the National Society and its associated local boards could never quite free themselves from the fear that a successful middle school movement would divert funds."[63] Certainly the sum reportedly spent for both establishment and support of such schools in the five years after 1838 was modest,[64] and nothing like a movement comparable to that which, after 1811, covered England with elementary schools, developed.

Nevertheless there were some successful results. The 1841 Report of the Oxford Diocesan Board, for example, included the following paragraph:

> The board have now established Commercial schools at the following places, viz., Bicester, Newbury, Banbury, Reading, and Hungerford. At the first of these, which has now been opened a year and a half, there were, before Christmas, forty-one boys. At Newbury there were thirty-four.[65]

During 1841 a very successful and long-lived school was established at Cowley;[66] but the Oxford Reports of 1843 and 1845 show that a number of the original schools were closed down and that no new ones were opened. In 1843 the Winchester Diocesan Board "succeeded in establishing three schools for the agricultural and commercial classes".[67] In York, in 1846, a "Yeoman School" was founded in connection with the Diocesan Training College.[68] In the dioceses of Exeter, Canterbury, and Norwich local boards also managed to do something in the way of middle schools.[69]

The principal importance of the Committee of Inquiry and Correspondence lay not so much in its direct results as in the foretaste it provided, both of Woodard's much greater and more successful scheme, and of the recommendations of the Schools Inquiry Commissioners in the 60s. Ten years before Woodard published his scheme, Wood, Manning, and others had realized the need of the middle classes for a suitable education and had attempted to rally the Church to undertake the task on a national scale. Like Woodard's initial plan, the committee's scheme centred on the development of diocesan organizations; the object of both plans was to provide a national system of middle-class education run by the Church. Both insisted on self-support and both made provision for boys to advance through various grades of schools in pursuit of greater learning.[70] Indeed Woodard received substantial support from some of the members of the earlier committee. On the other hand, the committee was not at all concerned with the more affluent members of the middle classes; Woodard was. Also the committee's idea of a suitable curriculum for the sons of farmers and traders was very much less conservative than was Woodard's.[71]

The Schools Inquiry Commissioners followed the committee in recommending that the "farmers' school [should be] an upper department of the parish school".[72] In 1868 the Commissioners were acutely aware of the problem confronting the patrons of private schools: that of distinguishing good masters (and thus good schools) from bad.[73] This very problem faced the Committee of Inquiry and Correspondence thirty years before.[74]

The activities of the Committee of Inquiry and Correspondence and of some Diocesan Boards of Education help to explain the fertility of the ground in which Woodard planted the seeds of his project in 1848. But there were other ways too in which the Church had become involved in middle-class education before that date.

Something has been said about the growth of proprietary day schools. One such that was promoted by the Church was the Liverpool Collegiate Institution, opened in 1843; it consisted of three distinct schools corresponding to the economic divisions of the middle classes.[75] A similar school was opened in Leicester in 1838.[76] Another was the King's College School, founded in 1829, although, at least by 1869, it was far too expensive for any but the aristocracy of the middle class.[77] The same was true of the new boarding schools established in imitation of the old public schools.[78]

Two institutions may have shown the unrecorded influence of the Committee of Inquiry and Correspondence. Although they were not apparently Cathedral schools in the Committee's sense, there were two middle-class schools established in connection with Chichester Cathedral in the 40s. The first, opened in 1842, was for girls; and the second, started in 1844 "with the sanction and assistance of the bishop, the dean, and the parochial clergy", was for boys. Both were cheap day schools and the pupils from both attended services at the Cathedral.[79]

Another development, perhaps accidental, of one of the Committee's ideas occurred at King's Somborne, where the vicar, the Reverend Richard Dawes, encouraged the farmers and tradesmen of the neighbourhood to send their children to the National School and to pay a fee of from three to ten shillings a quarter for the privilege.[80] The school was opened in 1842. At Michaelmas of the next year there were 106 pupils; by 1847 the number had risen to 219.[81] In 1848 about one-third of the school consisted of the children of farmers and tradesmen;[82] the curriculum, which was common to all, included reading and writing, religious knowledge, arithmetic, English grammar, geography and history, algebra and Euclid and even natural science.[83] Dawes' school was well run and attracted a good deal of favourable attention. But it was not the only parochial school with middle-class students. Indeed, according to *The English Journal of Education*, several existed before 1842; among those who followed Dawes' example was Sir Robert Peel, who inaugurated such a school at Tamworth.[84]

4

It is clear that when Woodard began his work class descriptions of society were much used, and the term "middle class" had a real, though not a precise, meaning. Included in that class were the businessmen and manufacturers who had been the chief promoters of the Anti-Corn Law League; but included too were well-paid mechanics and "higher artisans".[85] The term covered those who occupied positions of increasing authority and prestige in the medical and legal professions, but it also embraced the smaller shopkeepers and tradesmen. In short, there were important distinctions *within* the middle class; the "class hierarchy was a fact, but the variations within a given class were scarcely less important".[86]

Most contemporary references included three occupational groups within the middle class: farmers, tradesmen, and clerks. From the 1840s to the end of the century tradesmen constituted the core of the middle class. At the beginning they were nearly always associated with farmers; towards the end, as the relative importance of farming declined, the rapidly growing army of clerks was often mentioned, and mention of the farmers was occasionally dropped.

This central middle-class group was distinguished and unified by its desire and need for an education different in extent and nature from that provided either for the "poor" or for the upper classes. On the other hand the "lower" and "upper" middle classes, below and above this rough occupational mean, often received different attention from educators, similar to and sometimes associated with that provided for the working classes and the aristocracy.[87]

Churchmen were among the first to seek practical solutions to the growing problem of middle-class education, and the Church's effort was important not only because it resulted in a number of scattered local efforts, but because, as early as 1838, it presented Victorian England with a reasoned national plan for the provision of middle schools. The plan of the Committee of Inquiry and Correspondence was not vigorously supported, and its implementation was fragmentary. Before ten years were out, the initiative had passed from the National Society into the hands of the poor curate of Shoreham.

In the years after 1848 Nathaniel Woodard succeeded in making the Church generally aware of the need for middle-class education; and he succeeded too in doing a great deal to meet that need. He built up an extraordinary organization; an Anglo-Catholic and a Conservative he attempted to penetrate and to undermine middle-class Radicalism and Nonconformity. Violently opposed by some, equally vigorously supported by others, he led a crusade to make the Church the educator of the nation.

The last quarter of the century witnessed important changes both in the social structure of England and in the provision of secondary schools. After 1867 the social equilibrium of the mid-century, with its complex but ordered hierarchical class structure, gradually changed. Society became both simpler and tenser. The labouring class, newly-enfranchized and better-organized in independent working-class organizations, became a powerful political force which evidently alarmed the middle classes. Meanwhile the growth of great industrial complexes and the development of large cities with middle-class suburbs resulted in the increasing separation of the middle and working classes both at work and at home.[88] As the social links between middle and working classes were loosened, important sections of the middle class became politically and socially associated with the old aristocracy. The monied upper middle class of the late nineteenth century was educated largely in the public schools or in expensive proprietary schools, so that "the educational process . . . made it impossible to tell at sight or by speech who was a 'gentleman' according to traditional aristocratic reckoning and who was not".[89] Furthermore, the Conservative party was transformed in the late nineteenth century. No longer only the party of the landed interest it became also the political expression of important sections of the well-off respectable middle classes.[90]

At the same time as the mid-Victorian alignment of classes shifted in the last years of the century the provision of secondary schooling radically expanded. As we shall see, a large number of individuals founded schools for the middle classes in the second half of the century. After 1869 central government agencies as well as local school boards also provided increasingly for secondary education, although the Royal Commission on Secondary Education which reported in 1895 described the situation as still "confessedly defective".[91]

Nathaniel Woodard's contribution to English education was made against the background of a particular class structure, a structure which remained relatively stable for the first twenty years of his experiment. Thereafter there certainly was change, and it may be that his analysis of the social position and educational need of the middle classes was somewhat dated by the time of his death in 1891. Nevertheless these changes were not immediately apparent to contemporaries, and they were neither even nor rapid. The Bryce Commission in 1895, like the Schools Inquiry Commission in 1868, conceived of secondary education as middle-class education, and classified secondary schools along very similar lines.[92]

2

PLANNING AND BUILDING

1

Considered simply as an achievement in school-building, fund-raising, and imaginative planning the life-work of the founder of St Nicolas College is well worth notice. The audacity of the vision, the magnitude of the buildings, the names of the trustees and supporters: all these contribute to a feeling of grandeur. But it is quite clear, as it was clear to the first observers of the scheme, that the genius of a poor and poorly-educated curate lay behind it all.

> This gentleman [wrote the *Morning Chronicle* in 1853] from all that we can learn, is not remarkable for his eloquence, nor for his great classical attainments, nor is he distinguished by what are commonly called accomplishments. Yet he is a remarkable man—he has a decided will, and large capacities for organizing and working a scheme. He possesses indomitable perseverance, a free, frank, and genial earnestness and honesty of purpose.[1]

If to this description were added the quality of imaginativeness and the capacity to link imagination with reality it could hardly be improved.

Within a few months of his arrival in New Shoreham, the new curate had demonstrated his capacity to deal with the educational needs of his middle-class parishioners. By 2 December 1846 he had obtained £50 towards the cost of a day school from a barrister friend, and was begging from no less a person than W. E. Gladstone:

> For the present [I] shall give up my own dining room for the use of the school. There will be appointed two masters, one a graduate, that the funds may be assisted by any sons of gentlemen, who living in the neighbourhood, might find it an accommodation. . . . The other master is quite competent to teach all elementary knowledge. The school will be directed by rules which I shall attend to myself. . . . I have already from 15 to 20 boys seeking admission, and three more sons of gentlemen.
>
> The expenses will, I suppose, be about £200 per annum.[2]

Very shortly afterwards he was able to tell J. B. Mozley of Magdalen College that he had secured between £150 and £200 and had "appointed Mr Christie B.A. of Queen's College Oxford as Master".[3] The modest day school opened on 11 February 1847 in Nathaniel Woodard's dining-room in New Shoreham.

In itself this little day school, which survived as a separate entity only until 1853 and never had more than a few dozen pupils, was of small importance. But in the planning and announcement of this first project were incorporated certain principles of organization which, when developed, were basic to the structure of St Nicolas College. Already Woodard hinted at a national and inclusive scheme linking class with class. Although the charge at his day school was listed as £1 per quarter, and the education provided was described as "good sound commercial education, together with the elements of Latin and French", his plans were not limited to the middle classes. He appointed a graduate master to lure "the sons of gentlemen to whom the sea-side may be an attraction"; these were to pay a higher fee and thus subsidize the cheaper education of their social inferiors.[4] Likewise Woodard sought to provide a means by which poor boys might receive an advanced education: "At each public examination [twice a year] the best boy in the parochial school will be elected into the grammar school, where he will receive his education free of expense."[5] The acumen which enabled Woodard to see the financial advantage of a graduate master with private pupils, and which made him start on a modest but soundly-based scale, was matched by his courageous and eloquent begging. This combination of qualities, applied in these ways, never left him.

In two other respects Woodard's plan for the small day school embodied seeds of the mature organization. The future distinction between the duties of pastoral and moral supervision and academic teaching was foreshadowed in the reservation of the construction of school rules and regulations, and the religious instruction, to the clergy of the parish.[6] Even more significant was his early conception of the school as more than a teaching institution:

> [It is to be] in addition . . . a sort of Christian brotherhood. The names of the children will be enrolled on the panelling of the School Room, from which they will only be erased . . . for certain specific crimes. While their names remain on those panels, they will always in

after life have a claim upon a common fund which the boys will at once commence by small quarterly contributions.[7]

Here was a seed, not only of a benefit fund[8] but also of the *Society* of St Nicolas College itself. By 1855 Woodard described the latter as designed to provide, not only middle-class schooling, but also

a certain number of centres of religious and intellectual enlightenment . . . which may act as barriers against infidelity, fanaticism, and the violence of wealthy oppressors, and at the same time elevate the taste of the population.[9]

While the work of the school was conducted by Charles Christie, and later by Henry Jacobs, Woodard himself divided his time between his duties as a parish priest and his educational plans. In March 1848 he wrote *A Plea for the Middle Classes*. Never published, but nevertheless widely circulated, this badly printed document was his manifesto. It was also the first of a long series of pamphlets and printed letters in which Woodard explained his plan.

2

There were three major stages in the articulation of Nathaniel Woodard's plan.

Apart from the hints which he provided in his first school at Shoreham, his first exposition of the scheme was in the *Plea*. Naturally enough it was fragmentary; indeed some of the fragments were rejected and replaced. The next step is to be found in a "Preamble" to his proposed Statutes, printed in 1855 or early 1856, but which exists only in proof.[9] After a long gap the final ideal form of the Society emerged in a *Letter to the Marquis of Salisbury*, published in 1869 and reprinted in 1883.[10] The *Draft Statutes*, drawn up by 1874, were an attempt to put the principles of the *Letter to Salisbury* into coherent and legal form.[11]

In the *Plea* the purpose of the scheme was clear and simple: "To provide a good and complete education for the middle classes at such a charge as will make it available to most of them." Woodard pointed to his little school at Shoreham as an example and defined his task as the expansion of that venture in such a way as to provide schools "suitable for the middle classes generally". He made no attempt to outline a national organization; on the other hand he did not restrict himself to the Diocese of Chichester or to the county of Sussex. The evils, political and social, to which he so eloquently drew the attention of his readers in the first part of the *Plea* were to be counteracted by providing schools, conducted by clergymen, for the sons of the middle classes. Although the offices of Trustee, President,[12] Headmaster, and Visitor were mentioned, no other and broader purpose was assigned to the organization.

The schools themselves were to be of two types—boarding and day—and were to be reproduced on two levels, corresponding to the strata of the middle classes themselves. Very little was said of the proposed day schools.[13] Boarding schools of the first level, for "the sons of the higher kind of tradesmen, professional men, and gentlemen of limited means", were to conform to "the rule of Winchester as it was at first", were to be staffed by clergymen, and were to offer board and education at £30 per annum. Those of the second level, "for the children of quite small traders and hucksters", were to provide board and education for £14 per year.[14]

By the union of the two levels of schools the whole would be rendered self-supporting, for the deficit incurred by the lower would be paid from the profits of the higher. Woodard expected a further advantage from this unity of organization: "The boys in any of the schools will be eligible for the scholarships or any other prizes which the whole scheme has at its disposal."[15]

In the years between the issue of the *Plea* and the printing of the Preamble, Woodard's vision broadened and changed in several important respects.

It became decidedly national in scope, geographically and socially. As early as October 1848 Woodard wrote to E. C. Lowe (soon to be his closest colleague)[16] that his plan involved extension into every diocese in England in which the bishop was friendly. Each diocese was to have a Provost at the head of a

> large religious society, with, where it can be obtained, the bishop as Visitor. The dependent schools in that diocese would be subject to the Provost of the Central School whose duty it would be to visit and regulate them. The Provost of each of the central schools will owe a defined obedience to a Principal who will be head of a school in the neighbourhood of Canterbury. Of this we hope the Archbishop will be Visitor.[17]

Although nothing was afterwards heard of the primacy of Canterbury, and although, after the Gorham judgment, Woodard seemed increasingly reluctant to associate his Society so intimately with the machinery of the Establishment, this diocesan part of his plan did not change for many years. In 1855, he could still write that the association was "to have a double action, one Diocesan, the other National";[18] and, in 1858, he pictured the hoped-for central diocesan colleges as comparable in dignity and importance to the cathedrals themselves.[19]

Socially Woodard's plan also expanded: his scheme became one for national, not simply middle-class, education, although his concern for the upper and lower elements of society was always ancillary to his first aim. By 1849 the original two levels of schools had become three.[20] The lowest remained, as before, for the sons of "very small tradesmen, hucksters, etc."; but the top level was divided between a superior stratum of schools for "gentlemen of limited means", and an inferior one for "tradesmen, farmers, and clerks".[21] In 1851 Woodard wrote:

> It will be readily seen that the two lower schools depend upon the upper one, and that it is necessary to have an upper one of some size to support those below; for in the upper one we train scholars and exhibitioners for the universities; support those who have taken their degrees, but are not qualified for a class; and help with money those schools which are too cheap to bear their own expenses.[22]

Though he never expected to set up schools for the lower classes, Woodard early sought to include them in his system by sending out men described as

> Senior Exhibitioners . . . as masters of day schools and parochial schools at half the cost of National school masters, which would relieve the parochial clergy of an overwhelming burden and at the same time make the Exhibitioners support themselves, and in a way unite even the lowest people in the kingdom with the one uniform system of teaching.

Nothing ever came of his dream; but Woodard, as we shall see, did devise one means by which working-class boys could share in the benefits of St Nicolas College.[23]

Perhaps the most important shift in these first years occurred in Woodard's idea of the purpose of the organization to which he had given birth. In 1848 the aim was simple: to provide good, cheap, Church education for the middle classes. But in the Preamble (1855) Woodard divided the plan into two parts:

> The *first* part contemplates the creation of large associations of clergymen and other educated churchmen. The *second*, the education and training of the people, especially those of the Middle and Lower classes by clergymen and other properly trained churchmen.[24]

Thus, by 1855, the primary element in his plan was not strictly educational, but the formation of these "associations" to draw the alienated middle classes back to the Church.

From the beginning Woodard had been convinced that the middle classes consisted largely of disaffected and neglected children of the Church of England. Although, he wrote, the Church had been responsible for baptizing the vast majority of this class, "once baptized, they are left to themselves".[25] According to Woodard, clergymen notoriously neglected their middle-class parishioners. Indeed, he wrote,

> in ninety-nine cases out of a hundred, a clergyman in London would find it impossible to gain an entrance to the family of his tradespeople, and where he did succeed it would put them out of their way and cause them pain and inconvenience rather than any pleasure.[26]

Woodard thought that the "mass of the middle classes are not members of the Church of England" in any active sense. He also believed that they formed the backbone of Nonconformity: "If the tradespeople, the farmers, the merchants' clerks, were not Dissenters, Dissent would be at a very low ebb." Even those who remained members of the Church of England "are yet so badly instructed . . . they feel no zeal for her".[27]

Woodard was certainly not alone in his feeling that the middle classes were remote from the Church. Archdeacon Manning, although he did not identify the middle class with Dissent, was aware that it was "not penetrated by the pastoral ministry" of the Church; Manning considered this failure "a critical feature of our times".[28] In 1843 the author of an article entitled "On Attaching the Middle and Lower Orders to the Church", ascribed this alienation to a failure to include the middle classes in the ranks of the clergy.[29] This exclusion from the clerical order (which was well recognized by Woodard)[30] persisted, and comment on it cropped up periodically in the Church press. In 1864 a correspondent of the *Guardian* remarked that

> during the last century and a half, while the clergy have been almost exclusively "class clergy" the middle classes have fallen away to

Dissent. Perhaps the middle classes would be more attached to the Church if they too could say of the clergyman, "He is one of us".[31]

In the mid-fifties another reason for the turning of the middle classes to Dissent was provided by the Secretary of the London Diocesan Church Building Society:

> They [the Dissenters] have more offices, deaconships, and visitors and tract distributors: and in these ways the chapels manage to employ their people very much better than the Church. This is an attraction to small shopkeepers and mechanics, who find they are looked upon as somebody in the congregation.[32]

Of course not everyone in the middle classes was a Dissenter. Horace Mann, in his Report attached to the Religious Census of 1851, although he allowed that "the middle classes have augmented . . . that strictness of attention to religious service by which . . . they have . . . been distinguished", yet concluded that not only "skilled and unskilled labourers", but also "hosts of minor shopkeepers and Sunday traders . . . are unconscious secularists".[33] Two years before, without the benefit of Mann's work, H. Dunkley had come to the same conclusion about the "aristocracy of the working classes".[34] In 1850 a writer in the *Guardian* suggested the establishment of an order of friars designed to conduct a great mission to "the middling classes—that extensive, increasing and powerful body", who were, in mid-Victorian England, "indifferent Churchmen, nay, positive aliens".[35]

In these circumstances Woodard laid more stress on his organization as a missionary society than as a strictly educational foundation in 1855. His proposed diocesan associations or societies, in addition to instructing the middle classes and providing "centres of religious and intellectual enlightenment", were to "forestall the evil day" of disestablishment so far as this was possible. If and when that day dawned, the Society would be

> a becoming machinery for filling up a void that will be seriously felt . . . educating the people in sound learning and true religion . . . able to succour the needy and defenceless . . . against want and oppression, and to resist the mad clamour of wealthy ignorance and the fury of political demagogues.[36]

In fact building and operating schools remained the chief function of the Society. Very soon the Public School ideal overshadowed the early proposal for "good and efficient grammar schools in populous neighbourhoods",[37] although provision was still made for opening or affiliating "day schools or small boarding schools".[38] The distinction between the pastoral and the teaching offices, already foreshadowed in the rules of the Shoreham Grammar School, soon took final shape: a chaplain was to be attached to each school, free from the tasks of discipline and secular teaching, independent of the Headmaster, and responsible only to the Provost.[39]

In Advent 1853, following a study of the subject by his colleagues, Woodard announced his plans for a Training School for "Commercial Schoolmasters" at the Hurstpierpoint second-level school. The object of this school was to provide, by training masters who were to be called "associates" on graduation, not only teachers for the Society's own schools, but also staff for day schools to which "very many persons—indeed the majority of the middle classes—can only afford to send their sons". "I am", wrote the Founder, "constantly applied to by clergymen and others to supply them with masters, and if we could meet that demand a great need in the Church would be met".[40]

Six years later Woodard wrote a paper in which he envisaged a College for Missionaries to be attached to Hurstpierpoint. Graduates of this establishment were to set up units of St Nicolas College in the colonies. The Founder's imagination excelled itself in his description of the fruits of this scheme:

> Our plan of settling Societies would bear some resemblance to that adopted by the Moravians. We should purchase land where it could be had cheap, but as near to the large towns as possible. The laymen of the Society might cultivate this for the general good, others would keep schools or work at trades, and others again would be clergymen, and place themselves in the hands of the Bishop. The architects or mechanics might build the college with their own hands, and would above all things provide for a chapel in which the service might be daily said as in our cathedrals at home.[41]

Little more was heard of this plan although Woodard was pressed to expand into the colonies.[42]

By 1869, in his *Letter to Salisbury*, Woodard was prepared to offer the public a complete outline of his plan. Five years later he had drawn up and printed draft statutes, defining the scope of the Society and its divisions and the duties and privileges of its officers.

For some years before 1869 it was clear that the diocesan scheme would be modified.[43] The final plan abandoned the diocesan basis altogether, and instead organized the country into five divisions, "one for the east, one for the west, one for the north, and one for the south, and one (the most important of all) for the Midland counties".[44] Each of these was to have a governing body, or Seniority, consisting of a Provost and twenty-four Senior Fellows, twelve of whom were to be resident and fully employed in the work of establishing public boarding schools on three levels, as well as day schools, in their division. In addition each division was to provide for at least twelve Fellows "not of the Seniority" who "shall be entirely occupied in the work of the Society either as Head Masters of Schools or as Masters of Forms . . . or as Chaplains, Stewards, Bursars, organizing Secretaries, or some kindred occupation productive of profit to the Society".[45] Probationary Fellows and Associates were also mentioned as members of the Society.[46] Each Division was to be subject to a Visitor; and all five, joined in a federal relationship, were to be governed by a Corporation consisting of the Provosts and Senior Fellows of the Divisional Societies.[47]

The distinction between Senior Fellows and Ordinary Fellows reflected Woodard's twofold purpose for the Society. The Seniority was not to be concerned directly with the work of education. In each Centre (or Division) its function was to plan and build schools; together, the Seniorities were to form the nuclei of the five central establishments, "small universities, acting directly on society, and by a liberal use of their powers . . . to be the right hand of the Church system all about the country".[48] The teaching task of each Centre was vested in the "fellows not of the Seniority . . . not to exceed twelve in number". This lesser body should be "held responsible by the Seniority and by public opinion for the success of the schools intellectually".[49] Clearly the Founder expected all these junior Fellows to be teachers themselves. It was true that Ordinary Fellows might be elected to the Seniority; it is not clear whether or not Woodard expected such Senior Fellows to resign their teaching posts. In any case the division, in each Centre, between the Seniority and the group of twelve teaching fellows demonstrates that a function broader than the comparatively simple task of instructing the middle classes was in the Founder's mind.

Two other matters stood out in Woodard's final outline.

The office of school chaplain, distinct and separate from that of the ordinary teacher and disciplinarian, and responsible in each Division, through the Senior Chaplain to the Provost, was defined.[50] In this respect the development of Woodard's thought was continuous from the very first. The second matter concerns finance. Clearly he lost confidence in the wisdom of allowing the higher schools to subsidize the lower ones. Although he refused to abandon the idea of mutual help, he denied that it was any part of his system "to make the Lower Schools *dependent* on the Higher. . . . No actual money is expected to be paid over from one to another." The Lower Schools were to be "baldly and nakedly self-supporting"; the help they derived from the upper schools was to be "more indirect than direct. . . . They train masters for them; they give them scholarships; they give credit and position to men who work in them."[51]

In his *Letter to Salisbury* Woodard estimated that the "shell of the plan" would cost £1,500,000, or £300,000 for each centre. By 1869 the outline of that shell was clear in his mind; he made no significant changes in it from that time to his death.[52] After two decades of work he had already spent a quarter of a million pounds. He was committed: "It must now go on and either be a succeess, or at least no contemptible fragment of what might have been a success."[53]

3

Woodard was remarkably successful in founding an organization which built and staffed public schools, and which provided a Church education for the middle classes on a large scale in widely-separated parts of the country. Because this proved to be a full time occupation for the Founder and his subordinates, the other broader and vaguer object of the Society suffered. But throughout his life Woodard never abandoned the hope of establishing associations in various parts of the country, each with a strong community life, and each with power to protect and popularize the Church.

In the South his last years were spent largely in building the home for such a centre at Lancing. The chapel of this first-level school was to be far more than a place of worship for the boys. It was planned as the "Central Minster"[54] of the Southern Division, "the centre chapel of a great Society, consecrated to a noble effort for the support and defence of Christian truth, as represented to us by the Church of our country".[55] This Lancing centre was to include a "great Public Library" to be housed in the room which, until 1875, was used as a temporary school chapel. In an appeal for books and donations, Woodard explained the purpose of this project:

> In the course of years, when the foundations of St Nicolas College are so firmly laid as to set free the Senior Fellows from ordinary school work, and a new phase of the teaching power of the Society as originally designed shall present itself to the country, a good library will be essential for the work in hand among our own members.[56]

But neither in the South nor in the Midlands was the Seniority filled during Woodard's lifetime; and, in the South, such Senior Fellows as were appointed remained teachers and other College officials. In the Midlands a number of "outsiders" were elected; but the time they gave to the Society was wholly devoted to raising funds and building schools. To some extent the ideal of a brotherhood was realized by the senior members of the Southern Society who gathered together at regular intervals in "octave meetings" for "purposes of devotion, business, and the exercise of a more extended hospitality".[57] But by and large the community life which so entranced the Founder was sacrificed to the educational needs of the middle classes and to the religious, social, and political ends which such education was designed to serve. The Reverend Edmund Field, for many years the senior chaplain of the Society, expressed disappointment at this sacrifice. It was because he had hoped to live as a member of a "religious brotherhood" that he had joined Woodard.

> Unhappily [he wrote] this hope has been disappointed, and it is on finding the devotional and ecclesiastical elements of the Society falling gradually more and more into the background that I have sought outside our body . . . the help and sympathy which I once hoped to find within.[58]

The year 1870 was the middle point in the story of Woodard's organization. From 1848 to 1870 Woodard concentrated his efforts chiefly to the development of a complete pattern of three levels of public schools in the South, all in Sussex and in the Diocese of Chichester. After 1870, extension of the Society's work into the Midlands, and eventually into the West, took first place. Naturally enough it was in the South, the home of the Society, that its greatest success and most perfect form was achieved.

On 1 August 1848, five months after issuing the *Plea*, Woodard opened the "Shoreham Grammar School and Collegiate Institution" (soon known as SS. Mary and Nicolas Grammar School), to provide "an education for the upper portion of the Middle Classes—sons of gentlemen of limited means, clergymen, professional men, etc." at the rate of £30 per year for board and education.[59] Thus was formed the nucleus of his upper school, soon to drop the "upper middle class" designation.[60] Until the summer of 1857 it was housed in the vicarage and other buildings in New Shoreham. Despite lavish expenditure on new buildings at Lancing, its growth was slow.[61] Constantly hampered during its early years at Lancing by its anomalous position in a scheme otherwise devoted to middle-class education, its most famous early headmaster, R. E. Sanderson,[62] experienced great difficulty in attracting masters and pupils in competition with the many other public and proprietary schools of the same class.[63] In 1871 he wrote to Woodard in an outburst of frustration:

> As to the school not filling . . . the reason is . . . this school is below all other schools of its rank and cost in the material machinery which the parents of boys, rightly or wrongly, consider essential to a well-ordered school.[64]

Subsequently the school did make modest progress.[65] But that the promotion of an upper school did not prove a real advantage, financial or otherwise, in the general scheme is demonstrated by the total absence of this element in the organization of the Midlands Division.

No sooner was his first establishment under way and an adequate staff appointed,[66] than Woodard began to work on the second part of his scheme:

> I have determined not to wait any longer for buildings for my cheap school, and therefore am getting ready the old Custom House at Shoreham and am willing now to receive boarders of the lower class at £18 18*s*. per annum. . . . The first boy arrives tomorrow.[67]

To this second-level school for "tradesmen, farmers, and clerks" the Reverend E. C. Lowe, already a teacher at the upper school, was appointed headmaster. Christened St John's Middle School, in January 1850 it moved to a temporary home at Hurstpierpoint, where it finally settled in its own building in June 1853.[68] This structure (for which Woodard had collected £5,000 by January 1850 and on which nearly £55,000 had been spent by 1878)[69] was the first permanent school building of the Society. It housed Woodard's first genuinely middle-class boarding-school, and was "the scene of the first attempt to ascertain if a Public School could be given to the middle classes, at a price within their means, could be made acceptable to them, and be itself self-supporting".[70]

The experiment was an undoubted success. In 1850 seventy-two pupils were registered in the school; within a year this number had increased to 106, and, by 1859, over 200 students were resident. In 1871, a year before Lowe resigned the Mastership to become Provost of the new Midlands Division, the number had increased to well over 300 students.[71] Throughout the 50s the basic fee for board and education remained at eighteen guineas; during the 60s, when a third school offering very cheap rates was in operation at Shoreham, the cost at Hurst was gradually raised until it settled, in the 70s, at thirty-three guineas and remained at that figure until the Founder's death.[72]

At Hurst Woodard commenced his first Training School for Commercial Schoolmasters.[73] The number in this department was always small, but it was regarded both within and without the Society as a most important part of the whole scheme.[74] At Hurst too was founded a school for servitors. Fulfilling an important practical function as well as forming a bridge between the middle and lower classes, these boys numbered fifteen by 1871.[75] Those on the Foundation were charged £5 per annum; any number over eight had to pay double that sum.

By 1858 the skeleton of Woodard's plan for the South was two-thirds completed. Both the upper and the middle schools (first and second levels) were successfully launched and accommodated in permanent (if only partially built) homes. During that year, in the old Shoreham buildings recently vacated by the upper school, the Provost opened a self-supporting third-level school, to be known as St Saviour's, "for the sons of small shopkeepers, farmers, mechanics, clerks, and others of limited means", in which he charged each pupil only thirteen guineas a year for board and education.[76]

There can be little doubt that this part of his plan was both the most popular and the most successful of all. It also provided the widest scope for the Founder's administrative and organizing genius. By 1855 Woodard was developing committees to raise money for this third-level school; after the school opened this work was intensified, and by 1864 (in which year the first stone of permanent buildings was laid at Ardingly) he was writing of the school as intended "for 1000 boys".[77] Although he never achieved such an immense school, the structure, finally opened on 14 June 1870, contained potential accommodation for 450 boys and was built for £15,000.[78] One way by which the Provost achieved such economy was to become his own contractor: "We have been our own builders and agents, we have made bricks on the ground, used our own sand . . . and by one means and another . . . have saved quite 30 per cent on the estimated cost".[79]

This third level school remained almost unbelievably cheap throughout Woodard's life, and it was soon as big as the state of the buildings permitted. In 1859 the basic charge was thirteen guineas per annum, and the temporary buildings at Shoreham contained 114 boys.[80] By 1871, when the school was accommodated in its new buildings at Ardingly, the charge for board and education had risen to fifteen guineas, and over 350 boys were resident.[81] In 1886 the numbers were over 420 and the basic fee was still listed as fifteen guineas.[82] Included in these figures, but each paying a much smaller fee, was a group of "servitors", accepted on the same basis as those at Hurst.[83] Like the superior schools this third level or "Lower Middle Class" school was entirely self supporting and was continually advertised as such.

Thus, by 1870, the threefold pattern of public schools for the middle classes had been established by the southern society. At Lancing was SS. Mary and Nicolas Grammar School, the first-level school; at Hurstpierpoint St John's Middle School (second level) was located; the Lower Middle or third level school, christened St Saviour's, was now established at Ardingly. All three schools were equipped with chaplains; senior members of the staff were Fellows of the Society and met the Provost at regular Chapter meetings and at occasional Octave meetings to conduct the business of the united body.

Two developments occurred in the South which had no place in Woodard's scheme. In 1850, he attempted to establish a "Military and Engineering" school, for those who wished their sons to enter the military or engineering professions or the service of the East India Company.[84] Notable chiefly for its curriculum and for its comparatively high fees,[85] this establishment at Leyton was one of the Founder's rare failures. It had disappeared by 1858.[86] The gap was filled by a new section already added to Hurst, styled an "Engineering and Surveying School", also expensive,[87] and which was later called the "Special School". This never had more than a few pupils.[88]

The second addition to Woodard's basic plan was the affiliation of a girls' school which eventually became an important feature of the scheme despite the Founder's lukewarmness to female education.[89]

St Michael's was founded at Hove in 1844 by Miss Mary Anne Rooper. On her death, in 1855, Woodard undertook to help her successor, Lady Caroline Eliot, to establish the school on a permanent foundation at Bognor.[90] Not until 1864 was the property conveyed to the Trustees of St Nicolas College; at the same time the Provost was made Patron of the Lady Wardenship.[91] Under Lady Caroline's successor, Miss Frances Wheeler, St Michael's developed along lines parallel to the Sussex boys' schools. By 1871 it consisted of three levels under one roof, corresponding to Lancing, Hurstpierpoint, and Ardingly;[92] but by 1886 the two inferior divisions had been eliminated.[93] The school, never large in the Founder's lifetime, was always described, not as a *part* of St Nicolas College, but as "allied" to it.[94]

As early as 1851 Woodard had turned his eyes northward, and had seen the need for middle-class Church schools in the Midlands.[95] But the pressure of work in Sussex, and the need to raise huge sums of money for the southern schools, prevented him from taking any action until the 60s. By 1864 he was in correspondence with several Midlands clergy; and late in 1866 Sir Percival Heywood offered him a site at Denstone, Staffordshire, and £1,000 towards the construction of a "second Hurst".[96] Throughout 1867 rapid progress was made, and on 22 October 1868 the cornerstone of "St Chad's Middle School" was laid by the Marquess of Salisbury. In August 1872 the formation of the "Society of St Mary and St John of Lichfield . . . in federal relation to St Nicolas College, Lancing" was announced, and the Reverend E. C. Lowe, D.D., headmaster of Hurst, was chosen by Woodard as Provost.[97]

Several features in the development of the Midlands Society are worthy of special notice. As no upper school or "centre" was founded, the attention of this Society was entirely devoted to middle-class education.[98] Under the aegis of Lowe, in some respects a greater and certainly a more liberal educator than Woodard, it early and enthusiastically founded a girls' school, and later, at Dewsbury, established the first and only day-school for the middle classes of the Woodard Corporation.

On 6 August 1873, one year after the appointment of the new Provost, Denstone school was opened to receive 200 boys, and Dr Lowe was formally installed.[99] Already the buildings had cost about £25,000; by 1888 (in which year the buildings, with the exception of the Hall, were complete) £60,000 had been spent on this school alone.[100] The school was a replica of Hurst (including a middle grammar school, a training school for masters, a servitors' school, and a Special department), although the fees were somewhat higher.[101] Growth in numbers was steady if not spectacular: in 1874 there were about 100 boys; by 1890 the figure was 245. It was never filled to its full capacity of 400 during the Founder's lifetime.[102]

As in the South, so in the Midlands, it was the Lower Middle, or third level School which proved an immediate success. In 1871 Woodard, who had been made a canon of Manchester in 1870 on Gladstone's recommendation, was busily forming a committee in his cathedral city to raise funds for a school "in a locality accessible from Manchester, from the great towns of the north, and from the Midland counties generally".[103] A great many sites were investigated; but not until 1877 was a suitable one discovered at Ellesmere, in Shropshire, on Lord Brownlow's estate. In the interim Woodard had received promises for "near upon £10,000".[104] By the end of 1878 the Ellesmere site had been paid for and in the following year construction began on the newly named St Oswald's School.[105]

This school, on which by 1882 £18,371 had already been spent, was opened in September 1884 for a limited number of pupils.[106] In the first term eighty-one boarders were registered; by August of the next year Dr Lowe reported that there were "156 boarders and a few day boys—four beds only remain unfilled".[107] In February 1886 the number had risen to 173 (including three Probationer Associates, three day boys, and ten servitors), and

Provost Lowe "begged Mr Bullock [the headmaster] to reduce this next term".[108] Although the agricultural depression delayed the completion of the dormitories, and 170 boys was listed as the maximum possible number of residents, there were 172 pupils in the school in 1890. The fee for board and education at Ellesmere was eighteen guineas—three guineas higher than at its southern counterpart, Ardingly.[109]

Such was the enthusiasm for St Oswald's, Ellesmere, that within three years, Woodard accepted a site at Worksop, given by the Duke of Newcastle, for another Lower Middle School.[110] The foundation stone was laid in 1890; but the school was not opened until after Woodard's death.

Even before his transfer from Hurst to the Midlands, Dr Lowe showed a determination to educate girls as well as boys.[111] Indeed, although they received very little support from the Founder, local supporters in the Midlands had suggested a middle-class girl's school as early as 1867.[112] In 1872 a house was bought at Abbots Bromley and opened as St Anne's school with accommodation for twenty-five girls in 1874. It was an upper or upper-middle school, and the fees ranged from twenty-eight to forty guineas.[113] In 1881 a cheaper establishment, called "St Mary's Lower Middle School", was opened in the same village with accommodation for thirty boarders at a charge of £21 per annum.[114] By 1886, in enlarged buildings, St Anne's had sixty-six students, and St Mary's thirty-eight; in 1890 these numbers had risen to seventy-two and fifty-eight respectively.[115] Meanwhile the Dean of Bangor, in 1886, had written to Woodard inviting him to establish a girls' school in his diocese. As a result St Winnifred's was set up in Bangor, under the direction of the Midlands Division, as an upper-middle school "for the daughters of Clergymen and professional men of limited means, and the agricultural and commercial classes generally". In 1890 this school had twenty-five pupils and charged twenty-five guineas a year for board and education.[116]

Woodard started his educational work for the middle classes with a day school at Shoreham. In the *Plea*, the establishment of day schools had a distinct place; even in the *Letter to Salisbury* the hope of establishing these on a nationwide basis had not been abandoned. But enthusiasm for the public school system, and the immense exertion involved in making it available to the middle classes, pushed the projected day schools into the background.

It was left to Dr Lowe to establish in the Midlands the only day school actually founded by the Society. Supported by a strong local committee, and acutely aware of the possible incursions of the rival schools of the Church Schools Company,[117] he opened St Augustine's Grammar School in Dewsbury in May 1884. For the "sons of professional men, tradesmen, and others" the education provided cost five guineas a year for boys under twelve and £7 10*s*. for older boys.[118] At first this venture was a success; with fifty-four students on the books Lowe could write on Christmas Day 1885 that "Dewsbury has paid salaries, rates, and rent, and has £15 to the good".[119] In the same year the Wheelwright Foundation, a "charity founded in 1725 by John Wheelwright for the benefit of Dewsbury and two other places", offered St Augustine's a grant of £10,000. But, as the Charity Commissioners would not permit the offer to be accepted unless the Society adopted a conscience clause, it was refused.[120] Subsequently the Foundation endowed the Wheelwright Grammar School, built in 1889 in the same town. Although it lasted for another decade, St Augustine's finally succumbed to the competition of its heavily-endowed neighbour and closed in 1899.[121]

By the end of the 70s work was in progress in the South and in the Midlands. After 1872, although he still kept a firm grip on all major decisions, the Founder left the ordinary work of the Society of SS. John and Mary of Lichfield to Dr Lowe, and himself concentrated on fitting out and completing his schools in the South and attending to his duties as a canon of Manchester. But in 1879, presented with an already-built boarding school at a bargain price, he extended the Society's operations into yet another part of the country.

In November 1879, he reported his new venture to the Marquess of Salisbury:

> The County School for Somerset, called the Taunton College School Limited, has collapsed. The school was founded about ten years ago, and received its scheme from the Schools Commissioners, including a Conscience Clause, and thereby acquired the proceeds of an old grammar school founded . . . by Bishop Fox. . . . I was written to . . . urging me to purchase it and save it from one of the competing parties—the Baptists and the Papists. The buildings are fine and stand on about 15 acres of freehold land close to the town of Taunton. The company have spent about £25,000 upon them. . . . I

> made . . . the mortgagee an offer of £8,000 which was accepted for the whole thing as it stands, including 15 acres of land, the right to buy back 7 acres adjoining it a fixed price, the buildings, furniture, a large library of valuable books, and last but not least Lord Taunton's bust. Here therefore we take our point of departure for constituting our centre for the West, and thus giving . . . the foundation of three out of five of our Educational Divisions for the entire Kingdom.[122]

Some question arose as to the level of the school in the Woodard scheme; in the end it was opened on the model of Hurst in October 1880 and christened "The King's College".[123]

Suspicion of the successor of a failure, and the hard times which affected fund-raising all over the country, badly reduced the local support on which Woodard had counted. Inexperienced teachers also reduced its appeal to parents.[124] Certainly the number of boys was few; of the forty under instruction in October 1882, no fewer than twenty-two were day scholars; by 1886 the number had risen to fifty-nine (including one Probationer Associate), but in 1890 it was down to forty-four.[125] The cost of board and instruction was thirty-four guineas; for day boys the charge was nine pounds. Although it was designed as the first school of a new Western Division, Woodard kept the King's School under his personal supervision until his death.[126]

Nathaniel Woodard died on 25 April 1891. Although he never succeeded in creating the instrument of national middle-class education, he left a magnificent legacy which, even to him, must have seemed "no contemptible fragment" of a success. By 1891 thousands of people, men and women from all ranks of society, but particularly from the middle strata, owed their education to his exertions. In 1890 eleven schools, representing an investment of hundreds of thousands of pounds, were in operation. In the South were SS. Mary and Nicolas, Lancing; St John's, Hurstpierpoint; St Saviour's, Ardingly; and St Michael's, Bognor. St Chad's, Denstone; St Oswald's, Ellesmere; St Anne's and St Mary's, Abbots Bromley; St Winnifred's, Bangor; and the day school at Dewsbury all functioned in the Midlands. King's College, Taunton, was established in the West. In these institutions dozens of teachers (many of them qualified through the Society's own training scheme) had about 1,350 pupils under instruction.[127]

4

As in planning and organizing the schools, so in raising funds to build and support them, Nathaniel Woodard himself played the leading role. Every penny that he was given was spent on endowment, largely in the form of buildings, but also to found exhibitions, scholarships and fellowships.[128] To acquire the hundreds of thousands of pounds necessary for the realization of his plans, Woodard made efficient use of a number of different devices.[129]

Many of Woodard's most stalwart and permanent contributors were gained through personal acquaintance and friendship. Several of the men who gave largely of their fortunes and their time to the cause had known Woodard even before he circulated the *Plea*: R. C. Carpenter, the architect who designed Hurst, knew Woodard in his college days;[130] A. J. B. Beresford Hope who was a trustee, a munificent contributor, and an indefatigable speaker at meetings, made his first contribution on 31 December 1847, enclosed in a letter which indicates previous acquaintance;[131] William Cotton, pillar of the National Society, church builder, and a man long interested in middle-class education, made Woodard's acquaintance as early as 1841 and remained a strong supporter until his death in 1866.[132] It is possible, even probable, that others of his important supporters knew the Founder in his Bethnal Green and early Shoreham days;[133] in any case, there is no doubt that Woodard's personal influence on such men as Henry Tritton and Lord Robert Cecil was enormous and was a very important factor in their munificence to the scheme.[134] This personal appeal remained important throughout Woodard's life. Its inevitable absence during the early days of expansion into the Midlands brought repeated calls for his presence from those who were trying to organize the work there.[135] But as the scheme developed, other means than that of personal approach had to be employed.

Of these none was more extensively used than the written word. To many important people Woodard issued hand-written appeals.[136] But it was by means of printed papers of various sorts that he drew the attention of thousands to his cause.

The *Plea for the Middle Classes* was his first attempt at mass circulation; it was highly effective and brought offers of help and contributions from an impressive list of notable men.[137] From 1848 on there issued from Woodard's pen and those of his associates a stream of pamphlets, circulars, subscription lists, invitations to fêtes and meetings, reports, appeals, and sermons.[138] Many of these are of trivial importance historically, although some of the seemingly most insignificant (e.g. invitations to corner-stone laying ceremonies) often produced results of the greatest practical value.[139] But in the more substantial pamphlets and circulars the religious, social, and political facets of Woodard's appeal were eloquently expressed.

Another technique frequently employed for rallying support and raising funds was the public gathering. Two types of such gatherings can be distinguished. The more distinctive took place at a site or in a building owned by the Society, and normally centred around some event such as a school opening, chapel dedication, stone-laying, or annual festival. The pattern of these meetings was fairly uniform, although they varied greatly in size. Woodard would begin by writing to a number of notable figures, both clerical and lay. Having chosen a date on which a sufficient number of these could and would attend, he would then issue printed invitations, together with an exact timetable of the day's activities. These usually included an early celebration of the Holy Communion in parish church or school chapel, a later service at which a sermon was preached,[140] frequently followed by a procession, and nearly always ending with a luncheon, often for hundreds of guests,[141] at which numerous speeches were made and toasts proposed.

Woodard's luncheons were grand affairs, attended by a variety of dignitaries. One such gathering at Denstone was thus noted in the *Staffordshire Advertiser*:

> Luncheon was served in the great hall of the College at one o'clock . . . 400 guests were seated in comfort at the tables. Some 200 visitors . . . took luncheon in a room below. In the large hall Canon Woodard presided, supported by the Lord-Lieutenant of Staffordshire and Lady Wrottesley, the Marquess of Salisbury, the Earl of Shrewsbury, Earl Nelson, the Lord Bishop of Winchester, the Lord Bishop of Lichfield, the Lord Bishop of Chichester, the Lord Bishop of Lincoln, Lord John Manners, Lord R. Cavendish, the High Sheriff of Staffordshire, etc. The band of the Staffordshire Yeomanry . . . was engaged for the occasion.

The reporter went on to quote from Lord Salisbury's speech:

I have been a trustee for many years, and have been invited to many of these celebrations; and after some sixteen years of experience I have learned the duties of a trustee. . . . The definition of a trustee is that he is a luncheon-eating animal.[142]

Care was taken at such luncheons that each guest was given a subscription form, so that his opportunity to contribute was not confined to the collection plate. The marvellous efficiency with which Woodard organized these gatherings, the numbers which attended, the standing of the speakers and prelates present, and the amounts of money collected were matched only by the publicity they received in the newspapers, both local and national.[143]

Of smaller interest, but of no lesser importance, were the more ordinary public meetings held in large centres in rented or borrowed premises. The pattern of these, whether large or small, was the same: important people on the platform made speeches and submitted resolutions to a gathering drawn to the meeting by good advertising and expected to contribute before leaving. The most important of these meetings were those in London and Oxford; but similar ones in Manchester, Shrewsbury, Cambridge and other places took the same general shape and had comparable results.

On 24 June 1861, in St James Hall, Piccadilly, Lord Brougham chaired a meeting attended also by the Archbishop of York, Lord Lyttelton, Lord Redesdale, and other highly-placed individuals. Whether or not this gathering resulted in any large increase in subscriptions is impossible to ascertain; certainly the actual collection was small and did not cover the expenses involved.[144] But it did draw the attention of the public to St Nicolas College. The *Guardian*, for example, devoted a leading article to an assessment of middle-class education, concluding that "Mr Woodard and his staff will receive the credit of having turned the first sod and gathered the first fruits of a noble harvest by their toil".[145] The Oxford meeting, held in the Sheldonian Theatre, was notable chiefly for an eloquent speech by Mr Gladstone and the interruptions of the violent Protestant C. P. Golightly.[146] It resulted in the establishment of an Oxford Committee, which included the Vice-Chancellor and ten heads of houses, and which went to work to raise subscriptions.[147] A second London meeting on 20 June 1865, this time with the Archbishop of Canterbury in the Chair, produced only £131 7*s* 6*d* in subscriptions; but, we are told, it "caused numerous enquiries respecting the schools from all quarters".[148]

Woodard did not depend on spontaneous contributions at such affairs. He was careful to follow up those who attended and expressed interest; within a month after a meeting at Manchester in 1872, for example, Woodard sent around "the begging box" in the form of a circular letter soliciting donations or subscriptions.[149]

Partly to assist in the preparation and follow-up of public meetings, but chiefly to mobilize regular support in the form of annual subscriptions, Woodard made considerable use of committees. In the South the work of these was confined to raising funds and generating enthusiasm for the third-level or "Lower Middle" schools, described as early as Advent 1855 as "the chief work which the Society has at heart".[150]

In that year a Central Committee was formed in London, with Lord Robert Cecil as Chairman and the Reverend Robert Gregory, the future Canon and Dean of St Paul's, as Honorary Secretary; its purpose was to find money with which to buy property and erect a building for a Lower Middle School in Sussex, and also to assist in the establishment of local committees in various parts of the South.[151] Soon after its formation an office was opened in London, and the Reverend Charles Eagleton, formerly a teacher at Leyton, was made part-time secretary. Before long it became clear that this arrangement was far from effective. Even by November 1856 Cecil pointed out that the members of the Committee were busy men

> not fit for canvassing; we should not know how to set about it. . . . We must be content with being screens for the labours of more active men. . . . The printed appeals do nothing it is clear; neither do parochial meetings. There is nothing left but a house to house canvass. So that the whole question resolves itself into this one. Have you an agent fitted for such a work?[152]

On Eagleton's resignation the following year Gregory put his parish temporarily into the hands of others, and for several months became a full-time travelling secretary. Despite extensive travel and a good deal of correspondence, the results of his efforts were disappointing.[153] In fact, it was not until after the great London meeting of June 1861 that the Committee began to do really effective work.

In 1864 Cecil resigned the Chair (although he remained on the Committee) and his place was taken by Lord Richard Cavendish, with J. G. Talbot as Honorary Secretary and M. J. Lomax as paid Assistant Secretary. Under this direction the Committee devoted itself anew to its task. Local committees were established at Cuckfield, Lewes, and Bognor; the already-existing ones at Brighton and Hurstpierpoint were reorganized and enlarged.[154] Similar groups were established in and around the metropolis.[155] Lomax applied himself assiduously to his task: he visited local committees to stir them up and to collect arrears, sent out letters of collection to subscribers, and solicited local vicars to preach on and devote collections to the Lower Middle School Fund. By 1876, two years before its dissolution, the London Central Committee had been responsible for raising a total of £24,950.[156]

In 1878 Woodard decided to discontinue this committee which had "lost by death or by the high political engagements of many of its members so much of its original vigour"; he intended to

> constitute in its place a national committee to be directed by one or more paid secretaries. . . . The object . . . will be to establish a settled annual income for building lower middle schools in those parts of the kingdom where they are most needed.[157]

There is no evidence either that this committee was formed or that its object was achieved.

Of the other committees established in the South those at Oxford and Cambridge (both of which came into being after large public meetings) had the most impressive memberships, although there is no record of the amounts of money they raised.

In 1871, a year after his appointment as a canon of Manchester, Woodard had established a Central Committee there with no less than ninety-one members;[158] but the antipathy of Bishop Fraser, who thought Woodard's system excessively "monarchical" and "sacerdotal", and the long delay in discovering a suitable site for a Midlands Lower Middle School, seem to have weakened its effectiveness.[159]

Certainly by 1884, Provost Lowe no longer regarded Manchester as the centre of fund-raising in his division. In that year, convinced that "the day of large meetings and munificent donations is passing away",[160] he proposed to form a local Association . . . in each Diocese of the large Midland district. . . . Of such Association a Fellow of Denstone College [the informal name used for the Society of SS Mary and John of Lichfield], resident in the Diocese where the Association shall be formed, will be Chairman, assisted by two secretaries with such other Churchmen as will unite with them under him.[161]

By the following autumn a Central Committee of five had been set up at Denstone, chairmen (all non-resident Fellows of the College) had been appointed for the local committees in Lichfield, Southwell, Chester, Hereford, Peterborough, Bangor, and Ripon, and the Extension Fund into which contributions from these centres were paid, had a total of well over £5,000.[162] Whereas the committees in the South sought to raise funds for lower middle schools only, the new Midlands organization collected money for the completion of existing buildings and the extension of the several types of schools.

Most of the money used to build the Woodard schools came from the general public and was sought out in the ways described above. But, in addition, the Founder had two internal sources of revenue which were of some value.

The first, a modification of the early idea of mutual help among the schools, took the form of a "Reproduction Fund". In 1881, the Reverend Henry Meynell, a Fellow of Denstone, described the working of this Fund as follows:

The schools of St Nicolas College are not only self-supporting but reproductive; from every boy's payment a sum is set aside for building purposes. Denstone College, for example, when furnished and full, would be able to give £2,000 a year from its earnings towards the building of St Oswald's at Ellesmere or other schools.

In this way the Southern schools gave £1,000 towards the construction of Denstone, and another £1,000 in aid of the Ellesmere buildings.[163] In a similar manner a capitation charge was laid on all the boys in the three Sussex schools and paid into the Lancing Chapel Fund; in 1873–4 this amounted to one guinea for each boy at Lancing, five shillings for each at Hurst, and two shillings apiece for those at Ardingly, and the total raised in that academic year was £230 9*s* 3*d*.[164]

Towards the end of his life the Founder began to solicit the aid of the old boys of his Southern schools. From 1875 on, Henry

Martin Gibbs, an old boy of Lancing, regularly gave very large sums; he started by establishing two scholarships at a cost of £2,000, completing the upper quadrangle at Lancing, and helping to furnish the chapel crypt.[165] Encouraged, no doubt, by this example Woodard issued a pamphlet in 1884 entitled *To the Past and Passing Generations of Lancing Boys*, in which he invited them to form an association for the extension of the Lower Middle Schools throughout the kingdom. Each member of the Association was to be an annual subscriber of from five shillings to five guineas. In 1885 he sent the pamphlet, with a covering letter, to the Old Boys of Hurst and Ardingly, inviting them to join in this work. Martin Gibbs wrote in June 1885 that there were seventy members of the Association and £142 in the bank. Progress soon slowed down, however, and the accomplishments of the Association were very modest.[166]

5

A final word must be said about the Founder's role in his own organization.

The single-mindedness which led him to devote himself and his own income entirely to the Society he founded,[167] resulted in a tendency towards autocracy which often must have rankled with his colleagues and supporters. Although he vested the property of the Society in Trustees in 1855, he refused to deliver his statutes until 1880, and even then reserved the right "to alter or amend or annul such statutes and rules as are found not to work satisfactorily".[168] In practice he retained absolute control over the whole Society during his lifetime; and, even as early as 1856, objections were heard on this ground.[169]

In the Midlands the objection was raised most strenuously; Lord Lichfield announced in January 1867 that "he was not prepared to support a scheme which was to spread over the country to provide schools for the middle classes which depended solely and entirely on the management of any one individual".[170] After the publication of the *Letter to Salisbury*, the Bishop of Lichfield and Bishop Abraham tried, without success, to persuade Woodard that the government of the Corporation (with which final authority was to rest) should be more broadly based and in closer union with the Church as a whole.[171] There was a strong suggestion that the lack of a constitution and the autocratic position of Woodard was responsible for the drying-up of support at Oxford.[172]

Whether or not it was a serious drawback to the spread of the Society, Woodard's autocratic tendency, manifested in concern and interference with the most minute details of school management, certainly strained Dr Sanderson's good temper:

> The moment I begin to contemplate . . . [a minor change in the domestic arrangements of the school] I am met with the objection that the Provost will not consent. . . . I write to ask you whether . . . the hands of those . . . who care for . . . the school's welfare more than anything else on earth are to be tied as if they were children. . . . If the Provost cannot find time and leisure to attend to these details, either he should give more freedom to the Headmaster, who is more than 40 years old, has lived 6½ years at Lancing, and only labours for the welfare of this school, or else he must recognize this fact, that as he can't trust him with any freedom, he must not hold him responsible for the inevitable failure of the school.[173]

On some occasions the peremptory tone of Woodard's missives to senior members of his teaching staff must have taxed the patience of the recipients.[174]

But despite this quality, the great body of Woodard's supporters and colleagues, and particularly those who knew him best and longest (among whom Sanderson was prominent), were intensely loyal. Partly, no doubt, this was due to his stimulating, even magnetic, personality. More likely it was the result of real attachment to the aims of the Society of which Woodard was the founder and ruler, and on whose practical ability the achievement of those aims so largely depend.

3

PUBLIC SCHOOL CATHOLICISM

1

The Oxford Movement originated (according to Cardinal Newman) in a sermon of political protest; it blossomed in a series of theological tracts; it reacted against liberal ideology and the Erastian spirit; it moved a new generation of clergy to rediscover the high seriousness of its calling and the necessity of discipline in the Christian life.

As the first leaders of the Movement disappeared into the bosom of a less ambiguous Church or retired into country parishes or Oxford colleges, a second generation took their message into less rarefied corners of England. These new men either caught the message at the universities during their student days or were infected at second-hand. It was they who, still leaning on Dr Pusey, did battle against Gorham and the Privy Council on behalf of the independent authority of the Church and the integrity of her doctrine. They fought the battle of the Athanasian Creed; they defended the prohibition against marriage with one's deceased wife's sister. Drawing out the implications of Tractarian theology men of this new generation used treasures long neglected by the English Church: the sacramental system, colourful ceremonial, the religious life, retreats, medieval music, and architecture. With these weapons in their armoury, the Ritualists began their work: W. J. E. Bennett, Bryan King, Charles Lowder, A. H. Mackonochie and others in the slums of London; Upton Richards in the more fashionable congregation of All Saints, Margaret Street; a community of priests at St Saviour's, amidst the proletariat of Leeds. Edward Monro of Harrow Weald began to articulate a developing Anglo-Catholic tradition in pastoral theology, and a group of High Church Evangelicals, of whom G. H. Wilkinson was the most prominent, mixed Evangelical enthusiasm with Catholic doctrine to produce Anglo-Catholic parish missions in many

English towns and cities.[1] Through the agency of the Camden Society, and its successor the Ecclesiological Society, the principles of the Catholic Revival were enshrined in church buildings throughout the kingdom. Music too was affected by the Movement. Plainsong was revived; hymns were composed by some, translated and popularized by others.

It is hardly surprising that a movement which so pervaded the life of the English Church should have deeply affected the attitude of churchmen in the contemporary discussions and controversy about the education of the people. With the exception of Charles Marriott, the first Tractarian leaders did little to apply their theological principles to school problems.[2] As in other fields, so in education, the responsibility for applying Tractarian principles devolved upon men of the second generation.

In his history of the National Society, H. J. Burgess has described how George Anthony Denison, Archdeacon of Taunton, led the "High Church–Tractarian coalition"[3] in the violent debates which racked the National Society annual meetings in the late 40s. Centred on opposition to the so-called "management" and "conscience" clauses, he championed the unity of education (religious and secular) and the Church's right to teach on her own terms without state interference. As Denison was the embodiment of Anglo-Catholic protest against the secularization of primary schools, so Nathaniel Woodard was associated throughout the Church with the effort to extend Tractarian principles into secondary education. Indeed, on the Archdeacon's own enthusiastic admission, Woodard's permanent achievement was of far greater value to the Catholic cause than was his own. In 1879 Denison, by this time one of the keenest adherents of St Nicolas College, wrote to Woodard:

> It adds . . . interest to recall, that, whereas 1847 was the first year of my attempt to save the Church schools, ending as it has done, in utter defeat; 1848 was the year in which you set yourself to begin the great work which has been so signally blessed.[4]

But if Woodard was the chief apostle of Tractarianism to secondary education, he was not the only one. Nor, indeed, was he the first. Mention has already been made of the parts played by Manning and S. F. Wood in the effort to extend the National Society's work to include the children of middle-class parents.[5] In the great expansion of the public school system which followed the coming of the railway age and Arnold's reforms at Rugby other founders besides Woodard were affected by Anglo-Catholicism.

William Sewell's St Columba's (founded in 1843) and Radley (founded in 1847) were both connected with the Oxford revival. Like Woodard, Sewell laid great stress on "religious training, carried on . . . in full accordance with the principles of the Prayer Book" as the mainspring of reformed public school life. At St Columba's "full Mattins and Evensong were sung daily. . . . The feasts of the Church were strictly observed, and also the fasts". At Radley, "rumours of compulsory fasting played their share in the constant allegations of Romanism. . . . Even before the first term started four Irish harvesters came to the House on a Sunday asking if Mass was to be celebrated that day".[6] Bradfield, founded by Thomas Stevens in 1850, had a "character for High Churchism" which "militated against the increase of the school". Bradfield's historian notes that Stevens "was always trying to tear off the label of Ritualism which people were always trying to fasten on the school".[7] In 1851 a small public school at Harlow, called St Mary's College, was founded by the Reverend Charles Goulden; ten years later it was described as "one of those institutions which have sprung from the recent revival in the Church of England".[8] All Saints School, Bloxham, bought in 1859 by the Reverend P. R. Egerton, was intended to inculcate "the clear, distinct systematic teaching and practice of the Church".[9] Its life was marked by frequent chapel services, and the Chaplain was "strong on the point that the blessing of sacramental confession was part of the Catholic heritage of the Church of England".[10] Similarly, St Edward's School, founded at Oxford by the Reverend Thomas Chamberlain in 1863, was closely associated with the Anglo-Catholic movement.[11]

It is impossible to tell whether or not many small commercial schools were affected by the activity of local Puseyite clergy. But in at least one there is clear evidence of such influence. The Reverend William J. Butler of Wantage (founder of the Sisters of St Mary) wrote to Woodard in May 1848, asking "for a good man as Master of a middle school". "In a singular manner", he went on,

> the power over it has fallen into my hands, and I am very anxious not to lose the chance. . . . We have Morning and Evening Service daily

and weekly Communion, and three or four clergy, so that an earnest man might look for the comfort of Church privileges and brotherly sympathy in his work.[12]

One institution, certainly of Anglo-Catholic origin, though of doubtful secondary status, deserves mention because of the interest it aroused in Tractarian circles. Founded in 1846 by the Reverend Edward Monro, St Andrew's College at Harrow Weald was described by Thomas Mozley as designed "for the transmutation of raw ploughboys into sweet choristers and good scholars".[13] Keble preached the sermon at the opening of the school, and the addresses at the anniversary celebrations a year later were by two lesser lights of the Movement: Henry Wilberforce and W. Dodsworth.[14] The first rules of the school had about them a strong flavour of Anglo-Catholic romanticism:

All who are members . . . shall in all things obey and serve to the best of their power, Christ's Holy Catholic Church, and the Bishops and Governors placed over them by her; and shall daily attend her services and observe her appointed seasons of fast and festival. . . . The scholars shall attend and assist in all ministrations of the Church in which the priest may find need of them. . . . The scholars shall devote a portion of each day to the relief of Christ's poor, and those afflicted by God with sickness, by carrying food to their respective houses. . . . The scholars will devote a portion of each day to the attainment of such knowledge as shall fit them to be useful and faithful members of the Holy Church of which they are children. . . . The divisions of such work shall be as the superiors shall direct, between learning from good books, the care of cattle and the tillage of the ground.[15]

The school was small, and by 1851 had assumed a somewhat more conventional form. In that year, according to the *Guardian*, boys "taken from all classes" were enrolled, and the routine put much stress on useful knowledge:

The boys have their workshop, their glass-staining, their printing-press, their band of music, their debating society, their trials by jury, their concerts, their own magazine, their cricket club—they 'keep pace, in short, with the "spirit of the age" '.[16]

In these various ways, and no doubt in others too, attempts were made to infuse Anglo-Catholicism into the realm of secondary education. Some ventures, like that at Harrow Weald, or St Mary's, Harlow, were small and relatively short-lived. The success and extent of Tractarian-inspired commercial schools of the sort Butler controlled is shrouded in obscurity. Though some of the men who drew the National Society's attention to the needs of the middle classes were Anglo-Catholics, the committees and Diocesan Boards which carried out their recommendations were in no sense party bodies, and the schools which they started could hardly have been seminaries of Puseyism.[17]

The group of public schools, independent of St Nicolas College, which owed their origin to Tractarian followers and Anglo-Catholic sympathizers was a relatively stable element in the later Victorian scene. But the religion taught and practised in some of these schools was far from full-blooded Anglo-Catholicism. Sewell of Radley "was studiously moderate in his churchmanship and frequently inveighed against aberrations in the direction of Rome (the confessional and what he called 'ecclesiastical man-millinery' were singled out for condemnation)".[18] At Bradfield "no boy . . . was urged to go to confession, nor had they ever the opportunity of fasting communion".[19] Bloxham and St Edward's, Oxford, were quite clearly Anglo-Catholic. But both were repeatedly offered to Woodard, and Bloxham actually became a member of the Corporation shortly after Woodard's death.

Not one of these ventures could compare in size and success with St Nicolas College. None of them exhibited the application of Tractarian principles to school life more faithfully, and some far less completely, than did Woodard's scheme. The theology and piety of the Anglo-Catholic Revival, to which Woodard himself was firmly attached, permeated his Society, produced a novel type of public school religion, and carried the message of the Oxford Movement to thousands of Victorian boys and girls most of whom were sons and daughters of middle-class parents. To examine Woodard's own religion, to discover how he introduced into his foundations a type of religion utterly alien to the Arnoldian public school, and to relate how he and his associates met the storm of opposition which his efforts aroused, are the aims of the remainder of this chapter.

2

Throughout his life Nathaniel Woodard retained a firm grip on all facets of the life and organization of his schools. His dominion was nowhere more evident than on the religious side of that life. It was no mean feat to maintain public confidence and, at the same time, to create and sustain in his schools an unyielding Anglo-Catholic ethos in an age when the successors of the Tractarians were generally suspect, blocked from ecclesiastical preferment, and frequently subjected to persecution. Its successful achievement was the result of a combination of tact and courage which was rare among Woodard's Tractarian and Ritualist brethren. Indeed his refusal to throw off the bonds of tact, and his determination to build and run his schools as institutions for the whole Church, and not merely for a small party, led to accusations of lukewarmness and half-heartedness by Catholic zealots.[20]

But Woodard's moderation was not the consequence of doubtful devotion to Anglo-Catholic principles; nor did he ever sacrifice any essential part of the Catholic system of belief or practice to the demands of expediency. His refusal to join the more colourful Ritualist crusades was the result of his acute sense of his primary responsibility for the success and permanence of his schools. The tension between the aim of success and that of loyalty to Tractarian principle was evident in nearly all his correspondence relating to religion in the schools.

The available evidence which bears on Woodard's early religion is not extensive. Certain it is that he was an intensely religious youth, and that he early felt a vocation to the ministry of the Church. In middle age he wrote that "in 1827 when I was preparing for my first Communion I went and told my sins which pressed upon my conscience to a very Low Church clergyman in London, who urged me to do so, and who had hundreds of others applying to him".[21] Woodard was sixteen at the time of this experience. Three years later he composed a "Covenant of Works" in which he pledged his life to the service of God, and begged him to "keep my soul fixed upon Thee and make me to die daily to this world, and give me to look upon it only as a howling wilderness through which I have to pass ere I get to the promised land".[22]

His correspondence for the few years prior to his arrival at Oxford reveals that he leaned for advice, not only on clergymen of pronounced Evangelical views, but also on the famous quasi-Dissenter, Rowland Hill.[23] Despite the experience of 1827 (which he later described as his first confession) and a statement to Bishop Blomfield that he was taught George Herbert's "Sacred Poems" as a boy,[24] there is no evidence to suggest that his youthful religious enthusiasm contained any distinctively High Church element.

Woodard arrived at Oxford in 1834, one year after Keble's Assize sermon and the publication of Newman's first Tract. He remained there until 1840. Of the stages in his conversion to the Tractarian viewpoint we know nothing. But it is certain that he emerged from Oxford a convinced disciple of Keble, Pusey, and Newman. Shortly after Woodard's ordination, his old Evangelical mentor, the Reverend Thomas Mortimer, wrote:

> You know, with all my regard for you, I have but too great cause to apprehend danger when I see how completely you drink down every cup of doctrine or duty which the Oxford Tractarians put into your hand. Oh Woodard! I tremble lest amid all this cry of "The Church, The Church" your ministry should be devoid of that saving unction and power which attends the faithful exhibition of Christ crucified.[25]

Yet Woodard never belonged to the Romanizing wing of the Movement. During the crisis of 1845 he was serving a curacy at Clapton. While Newman teetered on the brink Woodard was in correspondence with Frederick Oakley, the former minister of the Anglo-Catholic Margaret Street Chapel who followed the future cardinal to Rome in the autumn of that year. Although the letters indicate close friendship and sympathy and show Woodard's acute distress at his friend's state of mind, there is no suggestion that he ever contemplated taking the same course. On 29 July Oakley wrote: "I hope . . . your anti-Roman . . . prejudices are melting. I make little doubt of seeing you a Jesuit yet."[26] But on 8 November, a month after Newman's conversion and shortly before Oakley's own, Woodard could write: "I hope I have never led you to believe that my faith in the fundamental constitution of the English Church was shaken."[27]

This faith was never shaken. A year later, after Woodard had begun work at Shoreham, another Romanizing acquaintance wrote: "I cannot but envy the confidence you seem to have in the Church of England which my reading rather tends to shake."[28] Many years afterwards, applied to on behalf of a person who wished to see him about her doubts concerning the Church of England, Woodard described his work as a confessor to those drawn to the Roman obedience in the forties: "Twenty years ago I could have been of use to her as I was to many people under similar circumstances, having all the books ready to hand, and giving infinite trouble in every case; but now I am . . . rusty."[29]

When the Vicar of Shoreham, the Reverend William Wheeler, seceded to the Roman communion, Woodard rose to the defence of the English Church with characteristic vigour;[30] and in the Preamble to the Draft Statutes of his Society, composed in the mid-fifties, he referred to the Church of England as "the last hope for retaining pure religion in the world".[31]

But Woodard's loyalty to the Church of England was combined with a strong conviction of its Catholic nature and a firm belief in practising and teaching its Catholic heritage. On no point was this belief stronger, and on no issue was scandal more certain to arise, than on that of Confession.

It was a sermon on this subject, preached at St Bartholomew's, Bethnal Green, in May 1843, that caused Woodard to lose his first charge. The sermon was forwarded to the bishop (to whom complaint had been made) who found that it taught "the necessity of auricular confession, one of the most pernicious abuses of the Church of Rome". Certainly, some of the expressions Woodard used were, at the very least, indiscreet; Bishop Blomfield quoted him as speaking of "giving man a share in the pardon of sins"—of God's having "appointed a priesthood to act as his vicars on earth". One sentence was particularly offensive: "A sincere penitent is positively bound by the terms of the Gospel to apply to God's vicegerent upon earth for redemption of sins."[32] Woodard tried to retrieve himself without denying his strong advocacy of the practice. He denied that he believed auricular confession to be "necessary to salvation",[33] and he assured the bishop, that, "though I preached that sermon, yet my practice is, and always has been, to make the people avail themselves of the public services for absolution".[34] But Bishop Blomfield remained unconvinced. He admitted the provision made by the Church for the clergy to receive confessions from those who could not quiet their consciences by any other means before communion or in cases of sickness. But he believed Woodard's doctrines to be "at variance with those of the Church of England" and therefore declined to place him "as incumbent in the new church which is about to be consecrated".[35]

The bishop's discipline succeeded in making Woodard somewhat more circumspect in the expression of his views; but it did not change them. Both Marriott and Keble gave him advice on the matter of confession;[36] and Woodard himself certainly heard the confessions of both masters and boys in his schools.[37] But as time passed and the cares and distractions of building-up his organization pressed heavily upon him, he seems to have done little of this work. In 1868, Lady Shrewsbury asked him to hear her sister's confession. He was reluctant, not because his convictions on the matter had changed, but because, he wrote,

> I am utterly secularized by my present engagements and am accordingly unfit for the higher duties of the Church. . . . If you could see me with my numerous heavy buildings, with architects, lawyers and others, with masses of workmen, and daily and hourly demands upon me for payments of all sorts of bills, you would think me very unfit to be a confessor. I should doubt if William of Wykeham was able to hear confessions or if he were he must have been very unequal to the duty. It is at all times a most serious matter and requires special gifts. . . . To do justice in such cases a clergyman should be perfectly calm and unruffled, and his mind should be well stored with remedies for every kind of case. If I were to hear your sister's confession, and were unequal to the office, I might do her more harm than good.[38]

It happened that public recognition of Woodard's Catholicism focused on his advocacy of sacramental confession. But his opinions on other matters were not less Anglo-Catholic. Closely connected with his view of confession was Woodard's firm belief in the authority of the Church and in the need to express that authority in dogma and in an enhanced view of the office of priest. In 1846 he wrote: "Church after church, parish after parish, is now being taught . . . that the sacred principles of the Faith and the divine institution of the law by which it is shielded are to bow and give way to human opinion".[39]

On one occasion he analysed the ills of the Church for the benefit of a bishop:

> What inclines people to doubt her [i.e. the Church of England's] authority is her having no dogmatic system and no test for the simplest doctrine. . . . She did good and great work in rescuing us from the

oppression and unjust tyranny of the Bishop of Rome, and she entered her protest against certain popular errors, and for the rest she left us where she found us. I would even presume to suggest whether on the question of private confession her design was not to do this when we find the most enthusiastic of the Reformers—Bishop Latimer—lamenting its disuse. My own hope is she did, as I can scarcely see how unruly minds are to be taught authority in any other way. . . . It is . . . the want of rule or authority in our Church which drives so many to leave her.[40]

He considered it part of the duty of his Society to defend "the rights of the priesthood, with all its responsible duties . . . at all hazards",[41] and he criticized the bishops for their failure to do so. As a result of that failure "the English people (i.e. not one in a thousand of the body of the Church) do not believe in a priesthood".[42]

Erastianism, understood as "the view that neither the Church nor the Bible was the final authority in religious belief, but the State",[43] was one of the principal dangers against which the Oxford reformers reacted. There is no doubt that Woodard shared the Tractarian appreciation of this threat. In 1846, he expressed doubts about the wisdom of an established Church in which "the worldly-wise precepts of politicians will constantly clash with divine truth".[44] He fully shared in the general alarm occasioned by the Privy Council decision in the Gorham case, and wrote his mind to Archdeacon Julius Hare:

If the Court thinks it can thrust Puritanism and German theology down the throats of the people of England, it will certainly find its mistake. . . . To whom are the souls of the people of this country committed, and who will have to answer for them? Is it the Queen? Or is it the Church, and especially the clergy? . . . A firm and determined struggle is now entered upon for the defence of the truth of God, and, by God's help, we will clear our Church or perish.[45]

It was Woodard's increasing fear that this struggle would end with the "apostasy of the English people from the Faith of our Fathers"[46] and the denigration of the Established Church. Dismay at this prospect made him insist, against strong pressure from the Bishop of Lichfield and others, that his Society should be as independent as possible from the official organization of the Church.[47] When it was proposed in the 70s that the Athanasian Creed should be omitted from the Prayer Book, Woodard, in company with Liddon and Pusey, thought the crisis had come.

> Now [he wrote to Salisbury] the doctrine of the Church is to be altered by law, and we [St Nicolas College] shall in that case find ourselves daily more and more out of harmony with the State religion. . . . If it [the Creed] should go after a use of twelve centuries, the old Church of England will cease to be.[48]

This danger passed, but Woodard remained on the alert:

> If I felt that the Church of England could not and dared not teach with authority, without asking the State, I should leave her and go to a Church that was free.[49]

Although the main part of his working life coincided with the great ritualist persecutions and prosecutions, with the activities of the English Church Union and of the Church Association, and with a general, if painful, advance in ceremonial in the Church of England, Woodard himself took surprisingly little active interest in these matters. Yet Bishop Blomfield, in dismissing him from Bethnal Green, wrote that "Mr Woodard seemed inclined to go too far" in matters "of rubrical observance and ceremonial additions to the Form of Common Prayer", and Woodard placed himself among the "persons labouring to restore the ancient ritual of the Church".[50]

Certainly Woodard did sympathize with those who suffered in the Ritualist battles. One instance of such feeling is evident in his relationship with J. M. Neale, the ecclesiologist, hymn-writer, founder of the Sisters of St Margaret, and Warden of Sackville College, an alms house at East Grinstead. Neale was inhibited by Bishop Gilbert from officiating in the diocese of Chichester for sixteen years because of his ceremonial and decorative changes in Sackville College chapel. In 1856 Mrs Neale asked Woodard to intercede with the bishop on her husband's behalf.[51] Whether Woodard was effective as a mediator is doubtful; for the inhibition was not withdrawn until 1861. But that he did try, and that his efforts were appreciated by Neale, is clear.[52] Later on, in 1881, when the Reverend S. F. Green, vicar of Miles Platting, in the diocese of Manchester, was imprisoned in Lancaster Castle for his use of vestments and incense and for contempt of court, Woodard showed full sympathy with the prisoner. He made a contribution towards the work of Green's nuns at Miles Platting, and he wrote to the unfortunate victim throughout his eighteen months in gaol.[53] The Green episode did nothing to improve Woodard's opinion of James Fraser, the Bishop of Manchester, whom he described as "a radical, a heretic, and a conceited tyrant".[54]

But Woodard was not an advanced Ritualist himself, and he did not take a leading part in the ceremonial revival. Indeed he sometimes expressed a sentiment not far short of contempt as he observed the activities of the new generation of Ritualists.[55] He must, in fact, have seemed old-fashioned and stubborn to some of the younger Anglo-Catholics. In 1865, for instance, he refused to communicate at All Saints, Margaret Street, on the ground that the clergy there consecrated unleavened bread:

> The wafer you used failed to convey to my taste the natural accidents of bread; and . . . it could not possibly be given in the oblation for the domestic use of the priest if there were any left unconsecrated.[56]

Certainly Woodard refused to risk the success of his schools by a dispute on a trivial point of ceremonial, or, indeed by the imprudent actions of his more advanced clerical colleagues.[57] Yet he was not wholly indifferent to such things. "I am . . . unprepared", he wrote Lowe in 1854, "to reduce the services and the furniture of the Church to the unreal and slovenly condition which we see around us."[58]

But in most ways, Woodard's Anglo-Catholicism was far from being old-fashioned. He took a lively interest in the Gothic revival, and sought to incorporate its principles into his buildings; he also fostered the revival of plainsong in his school chapels. Above all, like the Ritualists who brought the Tractarian message into the slums of London and Leeds, Woodard devoted his life to putting Tractarian theology into practice. His vocation was to apply it to education, and particularly to the education of the middle classes.

3

"Our work", wrote Woodard in 1883, "chiefly consists in creating corporations for teaching the middle classes the truth, and guarding them against compromises".[59] By truth he meant religious truth; and that he equated with the teaching implicit in the Prayer Book, expressed in the services of the Church, interpreted according to the thought of the Catholic revival.

In Woodard's view, the achievement of this aim involved changes in the public school approach to education. Of that approach generally he was a great admirer;[60] and "for the system of moral training", he wrote, ". . . we naturally turned our eyes towards the best models of our public schools".[61] But for Catholic-minded Woodard, woolly doctrine and slack religious discipline were dangers against which the existing public school system failed to guard.

To stave off the first hazard, Woodard rooted the actual religious instruction of his scholars firmly in the Church Catechism, the three Creeds, the Bible, and in an English *Primer* especially drawn up for use in the schools.[62] The aim of all religious instruction was Confirmation. No one was exempt. Whatever the persuasion of a boy's parents, they

> would have it plainly pointed out to them that when a boy was 14 or 15 he would be confirmed, if, of course, he was considered fit for confirmation; and that inasmuch as the school is founded for the distinctive purposes of the Church of England, . . . the authorities would not be at liberty to break down that system; so that if they do not like the system they must withdraw their boys from it.[63]

Dr Lowe recalled that, when he was headmaster of Hurst,

> there were eleven divinity classes, which were arranged with reference to the Confirmation which the Bishop held annually for the school. Boys who had been confirmed and were in the sixth form of any department came to me. The boys who were candidates for the next confirmation attended the chaplain; the rest, according to age, were divided among the masters.[64]

No doubt this fixed focus for all religious instruction does something to explain the impressively large classes confirmed annually in the schools; for example, at Ardingly in 1883 the candidates numbered "no less than 94 boys of the school and six of the servants—or a total of 100 persons from this one Christian household".[65]

It is somewhat surprising to discover that Dissenters sent their sons to the Woodard schools. Yet during the years 1863 and 1864, there were at Hurst alone twenty-two boys who were the sons of *bona fide* Dissenters.[66] Later on, Ellesmere astonished Provost Lowe with "the favour it finds with Welsh Nonconformists, I presume from its cheapness for it does not hide Church dogma under a bushel".[67] On Whit Tuesday, in 1885, out of thirty-five candidates presented to the bishop for confirmation at that school, four were from Dissenting families.[68] Not only did a number of Nonconformists sent their boys to the schools, but at least one Dissenter contributed generously to the Society's revenue.[69]

At first sight these facts seem to conflict with Woodard's rule that "no Dissenter, as a Dissenter, has a right of admission".[70] Actually, the Provost modified this exclusiveness in a significant way, and by so doing permitted the children of Nonconformists to enter the school, though they could not be exempted from the usual rules governing religious instruction, baptism and confirmation:

> We do not consider everybody who goes to a meeting-house a Dissenter, and as all people belong to the national Religion till they declare themselves otherwise, we receive them as such, prepare them for baptism who have not been baptized, and otherwise fulfil the duties of national clergymen.[71]

The importance of the Founder's convictions about the "duties of national clergymen" as they affected his thought on education will be discussed later.[72] But those convictions had a profound effect too in the narrower sphere of school religion. For however great was Woodard's devotion to the Anglo-Catholic cause, and however determined he was to promote Tractarian teaching and practice in the schools, he was equally determined that his schools should be Church schools in a national sense. As we have noticed, St Nicolas College was designed to provide *the* national system of middle-class schools.[73] Clearly this would be impossible were the Society to be branded a "party" propaganda organization which not only Dissenters, but the vast majority of Churchmen, clerical and lay, would refuse to patronize and very likely violently oppose.

Woodard was not unaware of the inherent conflict between his championship of Anglo-Catholicism and his ambitions for St Nicolas College. He was constantly on his guard lest the Society be made the instrument of a party to the ruin of its wider objects. To prevent this he sedulously cultivated support from ecclesiastics who were known to differ widely from his Anglo-Catholic friends. Thus the chief supporters of the College included not only Keble, Pusey, Marriott, Gregory, and Denison, but also the liberal

Archdeacon Julius Hare, Archdeacon James Garbett, Bishop Connop Thirlwall, and Bishop Gilbert of Chichester, who at the time Woodard began his work, and for many years afterwards, held J. M. Neale under inhibition. To keep such men on his side, and, at the same time, to maintain the instruction and practice of "the truth" as Woodard understood it, was no simple task.

The actual religious instruction in the schools did not, apparently, arouse any serious opposition. Dissenters had no reason to expect more favourable terms and no reasonable churchman could have taken exception to the ends of such instruction: baptism and confirmation. The content of the religious teaching required no defence and can, therefore, be assumed to have inspired no serious challenge. It was not in the realm of religious teaching but in that of practice and pastoral supervision that Woodard was most clearly at variance with the liberal Arnoldian tradition and most obviously advancing Anglo-Catholic principles. In this sphere the tension between Woodard's "party" and "national" aims was severe.

"A present palpable defect in the working of our public schools", wrote Woodard in 1851, "determined me on appointing one or more chaplains to each of our large schools, whose duty should be to attend to the spiritual welfare of the boys".[74] The appointment of these men, who were to be "quite independent of secular teaching",[75] directly responsible to the Provost, and governed by printed Directions to Chaplains (Appendix A) marked a new departure in public school religion. Thomas Arnold, of course, had emphasized the religious purpose of public school life. He "was a staunch supporter of clerical headmasters, compulsory chapel, and lessons in scripture",[76] and he used the school pulpit with great effect. But he did not attempt to direct, individually and systematically, the religion of his boys. Woodard, in company with other Anglo-Catholics, considered such individual attention and control essential.[77] Through his chaplains the Provost sought to direct the spiritual life of each of the boys individually, to ward off the temptations of youth, and to provide for the institution of sacramental confession.

In a pamphlet directed to the clergy of the Diocese of Chichester, Woodard dwelt particularly on the first two purposes of this office. He pointed out that chaplains were appointed in the schools

> because we think that a greater degree of confidence will be inspired by a clergyman who has nothing to do with *teaching* and *punishing*; and because in after life, these children will love us more for having taken care of their souls than for anything we may have taught them either of technical religion or of science.

His most frequently repeated argument concerned the moral dangers to which public school boys were exposed, and the assistance which a chaplain could give in warding off these temptations. Had the old public schools been so equipped, they "would have been far less immoral". He developed his case:

> The people of this country have a very undeserved *reputation for chastity*; when, notoriously, the whole land is drenched in the sin of uncleanness and most of our youth grow into life familiarized and reconciled to living in the most deadly sin.

In the sort of pastoral supervision provided by his chaplains, acting under their Directions, Woodard saw the chance to save his boys from this "source of misery and desolation".[78]

The chaplain was to be "a friend to his boys, interviewing each one in private at least twice a quarter",[79] advising and directing each concerning his "religious duties" and conduct, and giving blessing on each occasion "to those children who show a proper disposition and who have evidently been trying to exercise themselves in religious habits" (Appendix A). Certainly the Provost himself was satisfied that the system worked at Lancing:

> The evidence of all the masters who come here from nearly every public school in the country confirms me in the belief that this is the most moral school in England. The state of a school of 100 boys, many of whom are nearly men, without the semblance of an act of gross immorality, is, I am told, unknown in England.[80]

The most distinctive and explosive provision in the Directions for Chaplains was that which concerned the hearing of confessions. Two sections of the Directions were devoted to the manner in which chaplains might receive the confessions of boys. In neither of them was there any mention made of restricting the administration of this rite either to those preparing to receive the Holy Communion, or to the sick: the only two provisions for the practice specifically mentioned in the Book of Common Prayer. Evidently in 1848 Woodard took the view, expressed publicly by Anglo-Catholic leaders in 1873, that "the command to priests to hear confessions set down in two offices of the Church cannot be construed into a command not to receive confessions on any other occasions".[81]

Yet Woodard did impose an important restriction: he required the prior consent of the penitent's parents or guardians. He also insisted that confession should be a purely voluntary discipline. Adherence to these restrictions permitted Woodard to "deny that Confession and Absolution is any part of our plan",[82] and to assert that "it is quite contrary to our system to urge or advise boys to go to confession".[83] Statements of this sort were made to allay the fears of the Society's influential moderate supporters and to substantiate Woodard's perfectly honest assertion that he had "no thought of making this [his educational project] a party matter".[84] Dr Lowe, in commending the Society to the whole Church in his booklet *St Nicolas College and its Schools*, took the same line about the practice of confession.[85]

But none of these statements or restrictions, nor the rule which permitted only the chaplains and a limited number of other masters to hear the confessions of boys, could alter the fact that specific provision for the rite was an unusual thing, even in a High Church public school.[86] Even Lowe, who himself heard confessions and was certainly sympathetic to the practice, pointed this out to the Provost:

> You recognize the practice in some measure, and define in a way peculiar to S.N.C. the mode of action allowed to the clergy generally. In the presence of this fact I think it would be hard to say that Confession is a question which has no special bearing on the College.[87]

"Systematic confession" was not urged; nor was confession ever taught as necessary or compulsory. But its availability was brought forcefully before the boys' minds. The Reverend Edmund Field, Chaplain of Hurst, "always taught publicly and privately in the schools that private confession is not of *absolute* necessity".[88] He described his approach to the subject when preparing a boy for confirmation:

> In going through the Communion service, I dwelt upon the first exhortation as containing the Church's directions with reference to the work of preparation. In doing this I pointed out to him under what circumstances Confession is recommended, and left it entirely to his own conscience to determine how far it was necessary or

desirable in his case without attempting to exert any undue influence over him.[89]

From the communications received by Woodard himself from schoolboys whom he had prepared for Confirmation in 1849, it is clear that he was equally meticulous in emphasizing the Church's provision in this respect.[90] There is evidence too, that the books used in school confirmation classes stressed the availability of sacramental confession. The headmaster of the new school at Taunton noticed this in 1881, and wrote to Woodard:

> I understand that you have sanctioned the use of two little books (by Crake) *Simple Prayers* and *The Bread of Life*. Does this sanction extend to the whole of them? For Confession seems led up to in them beyond what I believe to be your views as to its being exceptional rather than a general rule. They also lay great stress on the necessity for its being full and complete.[91]

All this indicates that, although Woodard was careful not to permit any notion of compulsion, nor to exert any overt pressure on the boys, he was equally careful to bring the possibility and even the advisability of sacramental confession before them. In this, he followed the method recommended by H.P. Liddon:

> If . . . men preach the nature of sin, the reality of absolution, and the liberty of coming to confession granted by the Church of England, people will ask to come, just as they will do for medicine when they are sick and in pain.[92]

How many boys actually went to confession? The evidence is rather skimpy. In January 1857 Bishop Gilbert asked Edmund Field for a record of the number of boys admitted to confession, either by himself or others, at Hurst and New Shoreham after March 1853.[93] According to Field,

> between 60 and 70 boys have made formal confessions during the last three years. . . . Some of these have come with more or less frequency to confession since resorting to it for the first time. . . . The form of absolution used has been that in the service of the visitation.[94]

Considering that there were over 250 boys in the two schools in 1857, this might not seem a large number of penitents for a three-year period. But it must be remembered just how unusual sacramental confession was in the 1850s, and also that boys before confirmation age were not normally received at confession.

Field made a similar return to the Bishop in 1861. He had received forty-one Hurst boys at confession between October 1858 and November 1861; of these thirty-one had confessed only once, six had been twice, and four "more frequently". The total number of boys under his pastoral care at Hurst during these two years was 531, of whom 167 were communicants. Of the communicants, 105 had been confirmed at the school since 1858. "These confessions", he stated, "have been made, in the great majority of cases, at the time when boys have been confirmed and received the Holy Communion for the first time . . . about the age of 15." For seven or eight months during these years, Field had also acted as chaplain to Lancing and to the new Third school at Shoreham; during that period, seven boys from the two schools had made their confessions to him.[95] At the end of November 1861 Field wrote that he had admitted thirteen new penitents among the boys at Hurst in that year alone, as well as "others . . . who had come before". This number, he confided to Woodard, was "altogether less than in other years".[96]

These figures tell us nothing factual about the years not examined by Field, nor about the schools with which he was not connected. But there is no reason to suppose that the instances of confession dwindled in the ensuing years, or that they were either more or less numerous at other schools of the Society. Certainly Woodard did not give way to the assaults of the attacking Protestants; if anything, he tended to loosen the restrictions contained in his Directions to Chaplains. In 1873 he wrote to the Bishop of Chichester:

> I did at first require the chaplains to write to parents before a boy was allowed to come to Confession, and I have little doubt that this practice is still in existence. But I had no legal right thus to restrict the laws of the Church, and I am not putting the restriction in my statutes. . . . The Church of England has no wish to repel penitents.[97]

The provision of independent chaplains, acting as advisers and confessors, was the most novel and controversial aspect of the practice of religion at the Woodard schools. But there was, of course, much more to school religion than this. In the Provost's attitude to chapel services, extra-liturgical devotional exercises, ceremonial practices, and retreats, as well as in his supervision of the religious proclivities of his masters, the tension between enthusiasm for promoting Anglo-Catholic ideals and the duty of maintaining schools acceptable to all reasonable churchmen was evident.

In the chapels themselves, Woodard strictly forbade any but Prayer Book and official college services.[98] During most of his lifetime the boys evidently attended full Morning and Evening Prayer;[99] every Sunday and Saint's day there was a Communion Service and a sermon was preached.[100] But a good many opportunities were offered for extra-liturgical devotion; it was in these private services that the Catholic aspirations of Provost and masters found an outlet.

A complete account of such devotions at Hurst appeared in a *Report of the Committee . . . on the Religious Ceremonial of St Nicolas College*, compiled by Field, Lowe, and two other Fellows in 1857.[101] Held in "the oratory or in the schoolroom", they included services of "Preparation for, and Thanksgiving after Holy Communion" translated from the Roman Missal, and "morning and evening prayers . . . founded on those published by the Rev. W. Butler of Wantage". At the service of Thanksgiving a collect "commemorating St Lawrence" was used; and at the services of evening prayer it was "usual to commemorate the Black Letter Saints". During Advent and Lent, some of the masters and boys met before Morning School for "mutual private devotion"; such meetings were spent largely in meditation.

Certainly the atmosphere created by such exercises, by the regular services, and by the presence of devout clerical masters and assiduous chaplains, must have had some influence on the boys. In 1871, Field reported to the Provost that "when the chapel is lighted in the evening throughout Lent for private devotion, as many as 40 or 50 boys go to it".[102]

The ceremonial used in the College chapels during the 1850s was of a sort, which, in other places, made incumbents the objects of litigation. The *Report* of 1857 listed many points of furnishing and ceremonial generally regarded as "advanced": coloured altar frontals; burses and veils; credence tables; bowing towards the altar; the use, by celebrants, of black stoles with embroidered crosses; adoption of the eastward position at the Holy Table when celebrating the Communion service; candles on the altar, lighted on the greater festivals; the use of cassock and surplice by celebrants, and of surplices by the choir; flowers on the altar; the mixed chalice. But, whereas in the country generally, the period between 1857 and 1868 saw "a great growth of ritual" among High Churchmen,[103] the use of St Nicolas College was, if anything, simplified. For example, the use of the mixed chalice was forbidden in 1858 on the recommendation of Bishop Samuel Wilberforce and to "avoid possible interference from the visitor and consequent complications". This prohibition was still in force as late as 1872.[104]

Woodard's own relative indifference to ceremonial, and his increasing antipathy for Ritualists, was shared by Dr Lowe.[105] Consequently, neither the Founder, nor the new Provost of the Midlands, was willing to risk a "party" battle on this subject. During the 70s and 80s eucharistic vestments were used increasingly in ritualistic parishes; but, in 1878, Woodard wrote to Lord Salisbury: "Neither have you nor have I any doubts . . . about the legality of the vestments. We think it imprudent to use them and we plead custom."[106]

Even in 1886, by which time prosecutions promoted by the Church Association were very much on the wane, Lowe had doubts about admitting the use of the mixed chalice in the Midlands; for the first time in that year he permitted the use of coloured stoles by clergy in his school chapels.[107] The regulations on ceremonial issued that year for the guidance of "the Chaplains, Clerical Fellows, and other clergy ministering in the Chapels of the College of SS Mary and John of Lichfield" show practically no advance on the custom outlined in the *Report* of 1857.[108]

Woodard was prepared, indeed forced, to fight the battle of Anglo-Catholicism in order to preserve his chaplaincy system. He also approved extra-liturgical devotions of a decidedly Catholic sort, provided they were carried on outside the chapels. On the other hand, he exercised great prudence in his government of the services held in the school chapels, and in the ceremonial accompaniment of such services.

The same prudence prevented him from allowing a group of High Churchmen to hold a retreat at Hurst during the summer vacation of 1858. In reply to the request he expressed sympathy and friendship with the clergy involved;[109] but he nevertheless refused them the use of the school:

> If I followed my own sense of the demands of friendship my course would be clear, but I have to take into consideration that Hurst is a small country village, with all the weaknesses of country villages, and

the importation of twenty clergymen, strangers, to keep a retreat in our buildings . . . might lead to the most absurd report. Now this would be an evil, and yet not one that I should fear or be influenced by if it only affected ourselves. But we shall be useless as a Society if we cannot get boys to be educated by us; and any excitement alarms the mind of the middle classes and retards our work. . . . I regret to write with an appearance of cowardice to men who deserve so well of us all.[110]

The conflict in Woodard's mind between his Catholic sympathies and the need for moderation, showed itself very clearly in his dealings with his masters. There is no doubt that very nearly all the masters were Anglo-Catholics.[111] To have them such was undoubtedly one of Woodard's objects. In 1880 he interviewed R. H. Quick, subsequently a well-known educator, then a candidate for the headmastership of Hurst. After the interview, he wrote the following report to Lowe:

[I] found him most agreeable. I was consequently all the more disappointed to hear from his own lips that he is not a Churchman in our sense, but candidly avowed that F. Maurice was his model. . . . This makes it impossible for me to entrust Hurst to him. . . . I grieve to think how difficult it is to find a solid man of the old Tractarian school.[112]

Men of the "old Tractarian school" he wanted and needed to forward the Anglo-Catholic aims of his foundation. He did not want extreme Ritualists, for he knew that nothing would do more to undermine public confidence in his undertaking than the latter. Yet because the required type was dying out, he was forced to accept Ritualists; and a good deal of his and Lowe's energies were devoted to curbing their excesses. Thus at Hurst, in 1860, the youthful Sabine Baring-Gould[113] and another young man named Bond were described by Lowe as

in some irritation at my having told them that before Easter I shall wish their cassocks discontinued. . . . They are talking nonsense about joining an Anglican Benedictine order to be set up in Lincolnshire . . . where they are to *wear* (of course the first consideration) a dress like the blue coat boys (only black!!) and to have incense. It is vexatious that people should, even under the irritations of Lent, talk such nonsense and let their minds be distracted from the grave duties of this place. Bond is so ignorant he is dangerous. He has very much the idea that his mission here is to bear witness against the prudence or

> the cowardice of his seniors. . . . He reads Roman books, and, I think, wants a good overhauling.[114]

Of actual Romanizers there were few, although George Bampfield, one of Woodard's earliest masters, actually seceded to Rome, and, in 1856, tried to entice others to follow him.[115] Woodard, in a letter to Bishop Gilbert, stressed that "a primary object" of the Society was "to keep people from Romanizing, and this we have done by offering them all the advantages of the Church of England".[116]

Woodard was at his most imperious when curbing the masters' and chaplains' religious enthusiasm. He prevented Field from preaching at Bryan King's parish of St George's-in-the-East;[117] and, fifteen years later, Field (then the Senior Chaplain of the Society) felt it necessary to excuse and explain his attendance at a meeting of the English Church Union.[118] After the exposé of the *Priest in Absolution* (a guide for confessors published under the auspices of the Society of the Holy Cross) in the House of Lords in 1877, Woodard discovered that at least two members of S.N.C. were also members of the Society of the Holy Cross: Field and Lewington, chaplain of Ardingly. Woodard demanded their resignations from the offensive Society, and apparently issued a general order prohibiting masters to join any such "party" organizations.[119] Both the offenders obeyed the Provost's command. But Field, the senior of the two, did not hesitate to disagree with Woodard's action:

> I think it deserves consideration whether, in the vain hope of conciliating those who make one surrender a ground for demanding others, it is worthwhile to alienate many with whom, after all, our sympathies really lie.[120]

Some years later, faced with an order from Woodard to sever his connection with a new Sisterhood near Worthing, Field again raised a similar objection:

> I do not see how we are to attract to our service men who are really devoted to the Church . . . if the price we have to pay is abstention from all sympathy with the Church movement of their day.[121]

There were, in fact, approved ways in which the masters could show their "sympathy with the Church movement of their day". In 1875, Sanderson proposed that the clerical masters of Lancing should undertake charge of a mission in "lower Lancing"; he pointed out that such activity "would exalt and hallow a great deal of our social tone . . . and . . . promote a graver feeling of ministerial responsibility".[122] In the crisis over the Athanasian Creed, Woodard was so disturbed that he organized a petition, signed by the Trustees, Fellows, and chaplains of S.N.C., to be presented to both houses of Convocation in 1872;[123] indeed, on this occasion the Provost departed from his own rule and joined a public committee for the defence of the Creed, organized by the English Church Union.[124]

In the Midlands, Lowe tried to establish a "Guild of the Holy Child Jesus and His Servant St Nicolas", organized with a Superior, Masters, and Brothers, for the promotion of the work of Church middle class education. The "suggestions for the constitution of the Guild" were drawn up in a way imitative of other and more exciting High Church clubs.[125] No doubt Lowe was trying to channel off some of the guild-enthusiasm which had such an attraction for Victorian Anglo-Catholics.[126] Whether he succeeded or not is not known.

Another outlet for the masters' religious enthusiasm was provided by the formation of guilds for the alumni of Hurst and Ardingly in London. In 1870, the chaplain of Ardingly wrote to Woodard:

> I hope to spend part of each holidays in London looking after Old Boys. I have found that some of the most regular of our communicants at school have ceased to communicate since they came to London . . . A Guild, I think, will give encouragement to many.[127]

Four years later, Field set up a similar guild for Old Hurst Boys, "binding its members . . . to little more than praying daily for those connected with the place and attending annually a Celebration, after which we might have breakfast together".[128]

When Lowe was headmaster of Hurst, he took a lead in this concern for the religious welfare of alumni. Every year he sent all his Old Boys a letter during Lent, in which he not only described the state of the school and its prospects, but exhorted his readers to attend to their religious duties. Prominent in his annual advice was a sentence of this sort:

> If with any, conscience is burthened . . . let such remember that the Church "who is mother of us all, is free" and that we find our

> birthright . . . in release from all scruple and doubtfulness, from guilt of sin, from the pain of remorse and from the apprehension of judgement; all which is given to us in absolution at the hand of the discreet and learned minister of God's word to whom we open our grief.[129]

The elements of architecture and music had an important, if secondary, bearing on the religious life of St Nicolas College. A good portion of Woodard's correspondence was with his architects, and Woodard frequently referred to his buildings as "part of our educational scheme".[130] As was inevitable in the heyday of the Ecclesiological Society, his buildings were Gothic and expressed the medieval religion so idealized by Anglo-Catholics.[131] In particular Woodard was careful to endow each of his schools with a majestic chapel. In a paper about Lancing Chapel, written in 1885, he exhibited clearly the romantic side of Tractarianism:

> This Chapel is so constructed, and is built on such a scale, and with such materials and artistic design that, be the worshippers in it who they may, be they the sons of the greatest lords and heirs to large estates, or be they the children of toil and industry, they may alike rejoice that the system in which they have been educated and taught to worship the God and Saviour of the world has shown itself equal to the highest effort of reverence and devout acknowledgement of His mercy and His sovereign power.[132]

As the revival of Gothic architecture became intimately associated with the Catholic revival, so renewed interest in Gregorian plainsong became a mark of advanced churchmanship. As in architecture, so in music, Woodard carefully adopted a pattern designed to increase the effectiveness of the chapel services. Advised by his friend Thomas Helmore, one of the leaders in the plainsong revival, he would allow no other music whatever.[133] Under pressure from Lowe and some of the masters at Hurst, he laid down the principles which governed his musical choice.

> I have heard no evidence yet which carries conviction to my mind that Gregorian Tones represent only a rude and imperfect form of music. . . . If there be a sacred harmony which is the inheritance of the Church, my desire is that our Church should partake of it. . . . Before we abandon the pleasing and sacred dream which seems to unite us with the Choir above, I shall wish to hear all that can be said . . . in England . . . and to send a competent man or two to Belgium to find out what is there known on the subject.[134]

We have noticed that Woodard's original plan involved a Society of Fellows with a corporate life analogous to that of a religious community. We have seen too that the pressure of strictly educational work caused this part of his plan to break down.[135] In accordance with his general view of a female education,[136] the Provost also attempted to establish a convent-like framework for St Michael's at Bognor.

An undated pamphlet, printed after St Michael's had been conveyed to the trustees of S.N.C., contains the outline for a "Society of St Michael's", to consist of a Lady Warden, twelve "canonesses", and twenty-four "companions".[137] None of these ladies was to be a regular teacher in the school. Each of the canonesses should spend four months in residence every year, assist in the administration of the school, and observe the religious offices of the Society. These offices were to include the daily services in chapel, Communion on Sundays and Holy Days, and "the canonical hours in the Oratory". Every canoness, whether in residence or not, was daily to "recite the 'Short Office of the Holy Ghost' in private", and to observe the fasts of the Church. A "distinctive dress" would be worn by these women while in residence at the school, and a medal at all times.

There is little evidence in the Woodard Papers which bears on this unusual arrangement. In 1875, Frances Wheeler, the Lady Warden, wrote Woodard suggesting that the Rule should be slackened somewhat, and that the ladies should be called "Companions of St Michael".[138] Bishop Kirk observed that the "order of canonesses . . . continued to govern the school under successive provosts of Lancing until 1920", when it was discontinued because of its unnecessary complexity.[139] No similar monastic element appeared in the Midlands girls' schools.

Just what effect the religious instruction, close pastoral supervision, and devoted attention to worship and prayer had on the pupils of the Woodard schools is hard to assess. But if vocations to the ministry of the Church are any indication of success, there is some evidence that it was achieved. Of the sixty boys at Lancing when the corner stone was laid in 1854, fifteen attained to the priesthood;[140] and at the Advent ordinations in 1882, Chaplain Field was delighted to discover that "not less than 16 [ordinands] had in one way or another belonged to S.N.C., four as masters and twelve as boys. Every school was represented".[141]

Among the boys at Lancing in 1854 who took Holy Orders was Charles John Corfe, future first bishop in Korea (1889–1905).[142] Twenty years later, Mark Trollope, third bishop in Korea (1911–30) entered Lancing. Not only did Lancing contribute two of the first three bishops of this strongly Anglo-Catholic missionary diocese; it also provided, in Leslie Brooks, the architect and builder of the diocesan cathedral, appropriately dedicated to St Mary and St Nicolas.[143]

Sam Brooke, who came to Shoreham in 1855, and left Lancing for Oxford in 1862, has left a few comments in his *Journal* on the religious life of the college from a boy's point of view. He seems to have been well satisfied, and even to have approved the stark fare on Good Friday, when dinner consisted of "rice and bread and cheese".

> The observance of Good Friday [he wrote in 1861] is especially strict, but, I think, not unwholesome. The extreme sadness which the day wears here is specially observable, and there is a sort of calm and holy quiet peculiarly agreeable in my opinion.[144]

Brooke stood up for the authorities of the college when they were subjected to Protestant attack.[145]

It is hard to say, of course, whether Brooke was typical in his receptivity. But whatever the impact of the Society's religion on those who came under its care, there is no doubt that, in one way or another, it made a deep impression on churchmen at large.

4

The great majority of Woodard's substantial supporters were either Anglo-Catholics themselves or else men with strong High Church sympathies.[146] But Woodard proclaimed his Society to be the instrument of the whole Church for the education of the middle classes. Not surprisingly, many leading men of the Church, and a good proportion of the rank and file, were unhappy about the religious practice countenanced, and even encouraged, in the schools. Especially were they uneasy about the institution of sacramental confession. But not all such people were outspoken in their opposition; much less did many of them join in the several violent rows which marked the Society's early relationship with the Protestant wing of the Established Church.

Some of the men who supported Woodard, and continued that support despite the most malicious rumours and attacks, were themselves far from being Anglo-Catholics. A. T. Gilbert, Bishop of Chichester from 1842 to 1870, was an old-fashioned High Churchman, and very suspicious of the Tractarians. At first Bishop Gilbert was doubtful about the new curate's ambitious project.[147] But Woodard's enthusiasm, and the undoubted need for Church middle-class education, won him over; on 29 March 1848 he accepted the office of Visitor to the new Society and made the first of many money contributions.[148] Without Gilbert's support, and his staunch defence of S.N.C. against the attacks of extreme Protestants in the 50s and 60s, Woodard's plan might well have collapsed.

Yet the Bishop's support was far from uncritical. In his official capacity as Visitor he subjected the College's religious practices to thorough and impartial examination.[149] In particular, he was extremely careful on the subject of confession. He wrote to Woodard in 1851:

> Your benevolent undertaking . . . has been damaged in its prospects far more than you have yet allowed yourself to think by the confessions and absolutions which have been permitted at Hurst. . . . With a small section of churchmen you may not yet have lost, nor be very likely to lose, confidence. But you must not form from them your estimate. . . . I have every desire to promote your undertaking and to defend you from all unmerited attacks. That I may be able to do so, I must feel that I cordially approve of all your proceedings.[150]

None of the bishop's investigations caused him to withdraw his approval. But he was constant in his warnings against extremism. In 1853 he refused to ordain three masters to the priesthood on the ground that he could not be responsible for any priest "of whom I have reason to believe that he will hear confessions and use absolution without regard to our Church's evident limitations of the practice".[151] Some years later he still insisted that

> nothing . . . can prevent your complete success but the incubus of suspicion about confessions and absolutions; but that weight will drag your institutions down unless it be thoroughly shown that it does not correctly attach to them.[152]

As with the Bishop, so with the Archdeacon of Lewes, Julius Hare, strong and consistent support and sympathy were tempered with privately-expressed, but persistent, feelings of uneasiness about the "party" aspect of religion at S.N.C. A Broad Churchman and a genuine liberal, Hare early came forward as a champion of Woodard's scheme:

> I do not think . . . that you would find me shrinking from any amount of odium, so long as that odium is incurred by conduct which seems to me guided by the rules of Christian wisdom. . . . On the other hand . . . it would seem to me very reprehensible to peril such a good work as you are engaged in by any . . . peculiarities. . . . I am utterly opposed to all our Romanizing tendencies, and to all the decriers of our Reformation. Some of the names among your chief supporters might suggest fears that your scheme may have a leaning toward that side: but for that very reason I have been the more desirous to come forward and throw whatever weight my name and influence may have on the opposite scale.[153]

Hare's influence was considerable; and Woodard did not hesitate to use it in emphasizing the "non-party" nature of his undertaking and in wooing other Broad and Low Churchmen.[154] The best way to kill "party" practices at S.N.C., thought Hare, was to encourage men of different Church views to support it actively.[155] James Garbett, Manning's successor as Archdeacon of Chichester, shared this constructive approach: "One thing", he wrote, "is quite clear . . . such co-operation must have a modifying and controlling influence. . . . For myself, I have never offered more than a negative opposition."[156]

Pressure of this sort, exerted from the inside, was employed not only by men of distinctly different churchmanship, but even by some of Woodard's more moderate High Church supporters. After a particularly stormy meeting at Brighton in 1856, both Lord Robert Cecil and Lord Carnarvon privately pressed Woodard to renounce the use of sacramental confession; Cecil, indeed, desired from the Provost a public "point-blank disclaimer of any approval of Auricular Confession".[157] On this point, as we have seen, Woodard remained firm, although he always couched his public utterance in the most moderate and Anglican language.[158]

In 1851 Woodard was offered friendly advice on the subject of fasting:

> If the boys fast the greater number of English parents will say that they are to be made Roman Catholics or Puseyites or some such thing. Winchester has been half ruined by . . . such a suggestion, and

your school will not escape the same imputation, unless the fasting, except on Ash Wednesday and Good Friday, is abolished and heard of no more.[159]

Woodard apparently accepted this counsel. In 1857 he wrote: "No boys are required to fast at any time in our schools. . . . Two days only in the whole year are they required to use humbler food; on Ash Wednesday . . . and on Good Friday."[160] There is little doubt that internal criticism among his genuine supporters did have a moderating effect on Woodard, even though he refused to compromise any Anglo-Catholic principle which he regarded as essential.

A second group of Woodard's critics consisted of those who denied their support to St Nicolas College because of its religious peculiarities but who were unwilling to join in the fanatical Protestant attack. People of this sort must have been numerous, especially, perhaps, in the county of Sussex where Woodard always resented the paucity of contributors.[161] Lord Chichester, a Low Churchman, was unable to regard Woodard's Society as deserving the support of the whole Church. Yet he saw no objection to its existence as a "party" organization:

I am not amongst the "bigots" who have opposed your proceedings, for I have always considered the work itself to be essentially good and useful. . . . I see no reason why a member of the Church of England may not legitimately promote an educational institution upon principles peculiar to one section of the Church . . . [but] I suppose few persons would feel disposed to support a religious institution when the peculiar element in it is in the opposite direction to their own views.[162]

A similar attitude, adopted perhaps from motives of prudence rather than principle, lay behind the non-support of the Archdeacon of Nottingham:

Certainly in the public mind your schools are identified with the "High Church Party" to an extent that, as a no-party man, I should not myself desire to be identified. In Nottingham itself there is a small knot of very high churchmen, a small knot of very low churchmen, and a considerable number of those who work on the old reformation principles. I am not prepared, as Archdeacon, so to identify myself with either extreme as necessarily to repel the other.[163]

Probably much smaller, but inevitably far more vocal, were

the groups of Protestant churchmen who felt obliged not only to refuse their support to Woodard, but to attack the College as a principal agent of Anglo-Catholic propaganda and conversion. Vigorously supported by the *Record*, the *Rock*, and local newspapers, these people maintained a constant warfare against Woodard's activities throughout the 50s and 60s.

During most of these two decades the extremists engaged Woodard in guerilla warfare, designed to wear away his support and to excite suspicion among the protestant-minded middle classes. In 1850 "An Observer" wrote a letter to the *Brighton Herald* entitled "Puseyism at Shoreham", violently attacking the "reign of priestcraft" which Woodard allegedly was attempting to establish in his schools, and ending with the dictum that "to swear fidelity and receive wages from one Church, while enforcing the doctrines of its antagonist, is the basest and most dangerous dishonesty".[164] In the following year a good deal of suspicion was aroused concerning Woodard's views on confession,[165] and the rural deanery of Lewes collectively expressed doubts about Woodard's fitness for his task.[166] Seven Sussex clergymen published a letter to Woodard in the *Sussex Express*, in which they attacked the schools and pointed out that the "system" followed by Woodard had "been the means of perverting to Romanism more than one hundred members of your own University, and among them the late Archdeacon of Chichester, one of the first and most able supporters of the College at Hurstpierpoint".[167] This and similar insinuations made in the local press[168] were augmented in 1853 by the accusation of a former master, the Reverend J. W. Hewett, that "systematic confession is zealously encouraged in the Society".[169]

Protestant opposition reached its first climax on 2 December 1856, at a public meeting called to stir up support for the schools in Brighton. As usual, Woodard had invited a number of his prominent supporters to be present; these included the Bishop of Chichester, Lord Robert Cecil (in the chair), the Earl of Carnarvon, and Beresford Hope. The reporter from the *Sussex Express* described the scene on their arrival:

> Before the time for the commencement of the proceedings had arrived, the Assembly Room, which will hold nearly 2,000 persons, was crowded in every part . . . and many persons who could not

obtain admission to the room occupied staircase and stairs. At an early period of the meeting it became evident that it was about equally divided between the friends and opponents of the movement. . . . The latter portion had been invited to attend by various placards which were extensively circulated throughout the town some days previously, addressed to the "Protestants of Brighton", "Protestants of England", "Protestant Parents" etc. Many members of a body which has met fortnightly in the Town Hall, Brighton, for several months past, entitled the Protestant Defence Association were present. Mr Paul Foskett who is one of the most active members . . . occupied a seat close to the platform. . . . The first [of the official party] to ascend [the platform] was the Bishop of Chichester, who was received with cheers, hisses, groans, whistling, catcalls, and every other description of discordant noise.

The speeches of Woodard's supporters were constantly punctuated by cries of "We'll resist Puseyism", "No Popery", "Go to Rome", "It ain't religion", and other noises described as "cheers, hisses, and great confusion". After three hours of disorder, during which Foskett and others of Woodard's opponents had been allowed to address the mob, the Provost and his supporters finally gave up and left. As they went down the platform steps, "Mr Foskett turned his eyes to the ceiling, and, waving his hat, exclaimed 'Thanks be to God who giveth us the victory', then called for three cheers, which was enthusiastically responded to."[170]

After this performance it was clear that Woodard's scheme was a "party" matter. The *Record*, an organ of the extreme Evangelicals, denounced Woodard for not answering "yes" or "no" to a questioner who had asked if he believed in auricular confession; the *Record*, of course, took the Provost's silence as an affirmative. But that paper's liveliest vituperation was reserved for old Bishop Gilbert:

A more melancholy exhibition of amiable imbecility than is presented in the whole administration of Dr Gilbert never has been witnessed. . . . He has allowed himself to become a tool in the hands of others more subtle and decided than himself.[171]

Despite the attempt of a deacon-landowner of the county to prolong the attack inaugurated at Brighton,[172] its intensity inevitably fell. But that the ultra-Protestant attack had already achieved some success was proved by an incident the following year. In 1857, Woodard and Lowe planned to vote for the local Liberal candidate. Shortly before election day, the candidate's agent, R. W. Blencowe, wrote to Woodard:

> We are happy to think that you and Lowe will vote for Dodson. Every vote will be wanted. But will you both have the kindness not to say one word about your intention of doing so. The enemy is watching your movements and ours, and you have no idea how the opposite party has practised on the people by calling you Jesuits, Roman Catholics, Puseyites and what not. When you vote . . . will . . . you not . . . vote until late in the day. . . . We know what will be done if you should vote early. The poor voters after you will be intercepted and turned back.[173]

The second crisis in the ultra-Protestant campaign against Woodard occurred during and after the great Oxford meeting of 22 November 1861. The meeting was organized to mobilize University support for St Nicolas College. The Vice-Chancellor (Dr Jeune, Master of Pembroke) took the chair; he, Mr Gladstone, and Bishop Wilberforce made speeches warmly supporting Woodard's efforts, and an influential committee was subsequently set up to canvass Oxford.[174]

But even at the meeting there was an indication of impending trouble. As people arrived at the Sheldonian Theatre they were handed pamphlets on which two charges against the school were printed. The most important stated that "confession is encouraged among the boys"; the subsidiary indictment was that "crucifixes are distributed among the boys leaving the schools".[175]

The handbill and its contents were ridiculed by the speakers at the meeting. But the author of the pamphlet, the indefatigable anti-Puseyite C. P. Golightly, engaged Dr Jeune and the Bishop of Rochester (J. C. Wigram) in correspondence, and, early in December, printed the charges afresh, together with an affidavit from one Sarah Leggat of Brighton, affirming the second and subsidiary charge. He went on to describe "strange reports . . . of beads being distributed . . . as well as crucifixes, and of a room called the Confessional . . . in St John's, Hurstpierpoint."[176] But the main accusation concerned the practice of confession. Woodard, of course, refused a categorical denial, and Golightly again jumped to the attack:

> Mr Woodard . . . admits the gist of my charge—viz., that confession is practised. He only denies that it is encouraged. But what greater

encouragement could be needed than is implied in this statement? e.g. a boy knows that he will find favour in the eyes of the masters if he goes to Confession.[177]

The charges themselves (except, perhaps, the one about confession) were ludicrous; but they caused considerable stir, and brought the College no small measure of notoriety. Both Dr Jeune and the Bishop of Rochester publicly withdrew their support from the schools.[178] Reaction to these defections was immediate and violent. The *Daily News*, referring to the way in which Golightly's charges had been dealt with at the Sheldonian meeting in November, observed that "the proceedings at Oxford show how easy it is for authority to trample down and triumph over inconvenient facts".[179] The *Record*, already ecstatic in its delight at Golightly's attack before the secessions of Jeune and Wigram, began after their defections, to take a new line:

> Why have Evangelical churchmen permitted the ground covered by these schools to be preoccupied? . . . it is quite a mistake to suppose that the farmers and tradesmen whose sons have crowded the schools . . . . send them there from any special sympathy with the semi-Romanism which leavens the religious teaching. . . . Let Evangelical Churchmen denounce, as they justly say, the system pursued at Shoreham, but they will find it difficult to parry the charge of inconsistency if their zeal ends there.[180]

A visitor to Hurst told Dr Lowe that "in trains and omnibuses and everywhere", people were discussing the Society.[181] A series of letters about the schools appeared in the *Daily News*.[182]

More significant perhaps than either the public discussion or the Protestant attack, was the appearance of a new sort of defence, not generated by Woodard or his colleagues but by outsiders. A High Church layman, W. H. Wilcockson, published a letter to the Bishop of Rochester on 8 February in which he defended the schools, not by denying the Golightly charges, but by pressing the legality of both confession and fasting in the Church of England.[183] In the *Guardian* of 12 February, a "north country vicar" publicly announced his sympathy for the schools. More important than such individual action was the support of the English Church Union, affirmed at a meeting on 10 March and expressed in a "Memorial" sent to Woodard.[184]

The Golightly charges were investigated by the Society's Visitor, Bishop Gilbert, who pronounced the schools free from any un-Anglican practices. But his judgment was not given until May 1863, over a year after the attack had reached its height.[185] In fact, the damage done to Woodard's non-party ambitions for the Society was accomplished during the first few months of 1862.

This damage was more serious that the Founder seemed to realize. The ultra-Protestants were henceforth not content merely to attack Woodard's scheme; they attempted to develop an opposition plan for middle-class education. These efforts resulted in Trent College, and in other similar foundations.[186] On the other hand, the English Church Union and independent High Churchmen began to defend Woodard and even to launch a counter-attack. Both these features of the Golightly episode and its aftermath pointed to the increasing strength of the "party" aspect of St Nicolas College, and to a corresponding decline in its "national" or "non-party" prospects.

In the South Protestant opposition did not seriously flare again, although it continued to appear from time to time.[187] But, from 1867, the chief focus of such attack was the new development in the Midlands counties. At about the time Sir Percival Heywood offered Woodard a site at Denstone, the Duke of Devonshire laid the foundation stone of Trent College, designed as an Evangelical middle-class public school for the Midlands.[188] There was no indication whatever that Woodard deliberately built Denstone in opposition to Trent; for although the Woodard school was not opened until 1873, five years later than Trent, Woodard had long considered the Midlands as his next objective.[189] Certainly it was not he, but the *Record* and supporters of Trent College, that drew attention to the two institutions as competitors and gave them distinct party labels.[190] Woodard himself resented such labelling. He wrote: "Confusion, quarrelling, and party spirit are obviously out of place in such a scheme as ours, and destructive of it. . . . Controversy is not to our mind."[191] But during its first years the new school had to weather a storm which undoubtedly gave publicity to its sectional character. A year after work on Denstone had begun Sir Percival Heywood informed Woodard that "the opposition to the schools is taking distinct form. . . . Contributions are undoubtedly affected and progress delayed."[192]

Protestant opposition of this sort continued in the 70s, although it never again found such violent expression as at Brighton in 1856,

Oxford in 1861, or even in Staffordshire during the first two years of the Society's work in that county. Later critics sometimes expressed themselves at meetings called to raise money for the schools;[193] on other occasions they vented their opposition through the ultra-Protestant Church press.[194] Even in the 80s the Church Association was still distributing literature condemning the Woodard scheme.[195] But during the last two decades of the Founder's life, Protestant opposition was conducted on a comparatively small scale. One reason for this mildness, no doubt, was the increasing realization, after 1865, that it was no longer possible to stop Woodard: his organization was clearly established on a permanent footing. Another was the gradual decline of party controversy in the Church, especially after 1880. A third, and perhaps more decisive reason, was that the Protestant controversialists had, by the end of the 60s, already achieved one great victory: they had successfully branded Woodard as a Tractarian and his schools as "party establishments".

There could be little doubt that St Nicolas College was an Anglo-Catholic institution; and it was the Society's Catholic features, notably the practice of sacramental confession, which called forth words of caution from Woodard's moderate supporters as well as fierce denunciation from more militant Protestants. But there is much evidence that Woodard was perfectly sincere in his desire to make the College acceptable to the whole Church. To this end he insisted upon certain limitation, not only on the hearing of confessions, but on the use of school chapels and ceremonial, as well as on the sort of external societies and guilds to which his masters might belong. These limitations caused Woodard to be chided, and even attacked, by extremists at the opposite pole to the readers of the *Record*.

His ultra-Catholic supporters and well-wishers normally confined their criticism to rather mild suggestions. Colonel Robert Moorsom, for many years chairman of Woodard's Brighton Committee and a staunch supporter of Radley as well as of S.N.C., admitted to Woodard in 1864 that his feeling "on hearing the answers to Golightly's questions was one of considerable disappointment that confession is practised to such a limited extent, and fenced with such unwarranted restrictions".[196]

Two years earlier, while the Golightly controversy was still in progress, Upton Richards, incumbent of All Saints, Margaret

Street, encouraged the Provost to stand fast on Confession;[197] and a clergyman named George Grundy wrote:

> I trust . . . that you will practice no reticence whatever from fear of public opinion, that you will fling open statements in the teeth of your accusers. . . . No clamour for a time can prevent the residuum of good sinking deep into the minds of men when the clamour dies away.[198]

But Woodard was subjected to at least one attack of some violence by "an English Catholic". In an anonymous pamphlet entitled *St Nicolas College and Compromise: A Letter of Remonstrance to the Reverend N. Woodard, B.A., Provost of St Nicolas*, written shortly after a meeting in Stafford in October 1867,[199] the author described the schools as "most injurious to the Catholic cause", and characterized by "the spirit of compromise, expediency, and inconsistency". He went on to describe the result of tension between Woodard's "party" and "national" aims in the following language:

> You have gained the support of anti-Tractarians on the understanding that the boys are not taught the doctrines of the Real Objective Presence, the Eucharistic Sacrifice, and the Adoration of Christ in the Sacrament, and that they are not accustomed to join in worship characterized by . . . "Ritualistic observance". . . . On the other hand you have had, for twenty years, the support of "Tractarians" in the belief that your whole scheme was a bona fide attempt to train up the youth of the middle classes in the knowledge of these truths, and accustom them to a Ritual Service. . . . You have . . . deceived both.

In particular, it went on, Woodard's system was lacking in four respects: (1) failure to observe fast days; (2) failure to require the use of full Eucharistic vestments; (3) failure to encourage non-communicants to remain for the whole Communion service; (4) failure to encourage boys to go to Confession. These omissions made the school unacceptable to true Catholics; yet such observances as *were* customary at S.N.C. "would, if publicly known, alienate nearly all . . . supporters who do not hold Sacramental Doctrine".

The author concluded with an appeal to correct the four faults mentioned, else the "Catholic clergy throughout England . . . [should] take steps for the establishment of a bona fide Church school, where the Church system may be as faithfully carried out as at St Alban's, Holborn, or at All Saints, Margaret Street". Woodard received a letter from one E. Soward, a member of the English Church Union, who made the same charges, and referred to a pamphlet in which he had originally stated his case;[200] it seems likely that Soward wrote *St Nicolas College and Compromise.*

There is no evidence of any other public attack of this nature, and there is no indication that this pamphlet aroused any positive response among Woodard's many Catholic supporters. Certainly it was the Protestant criticism and attack which affected the progress of the schools, and narrowed their appeal. To what extent the ultimate failure of Woodard's ambitious national scheme can be ascribed to this cause is very difficult to determine. The immensity of the task to which St Nicolas College was devoted, the changing educational outlook of churchmen, and the competition of the Endowed Schools Commissioners after 1869, were probably more formidable barriers to complete success than was anti-Tractarian feeling.[201]

Nevertheless there is evidence that some parents were reluctant to send their children to institutions suspected of Puseyism.[202] More important was the harm done by the Protestant attack in reducing support and contributions to the Society. This was particularly evident in Oxford after the Golightly attack of 1861–2,[203] but was also apparent early in the Midlands operation, and even in the last decade of Woodard's life.[204]

5

Nearly thirty years after Woodard began his work in Shoreham, the headmaster of Lancing assessed the part played by St Nicolas College in the Anglo-Catholic movement:

> In truth the Tractarian Movement has been too much confined to the educated and the learned. It had not reached the "people", who had learned from the Evangelicals to regard "Doctrine" as dry bones. Until your schools started no effort on any large scale was made to teach "The People" what the Church was.[205]

No doubt Dr Sanderson's statement was extreme. For by mid-century Ritualists had begun the work of popularizing Tractarianism in the slums, and the marriage of Anglo-Catholicism and the Gothic Revival, which did so much to interpret the Movement to the people, had already taken place. Under Tractarian influence priests all over the country were deepening and broadening the pastoral work of the Church. Even in the sphere of education, S. F. Wood and Manning, Sewell and Monro had each done something to inject Anglo-Catholic ideals.

But there can be no doubt that Woodard's work did constitute one of the great missionary efforts of Anglo-Catholicism. All Woodard's work was inspired by his religious belief. His particular gifts of social insight, imagination, and business acumen, together with the importance he attached to education and the approach he took to it, determined the particular form in which that inspiration issued. But the basis of his work was religious; and his religion was Anglican Christianity as interpreted by the Oxford Tractarians. For the sake of the social and educational aims of his Society, he took pains to discriminate between what he considered to be the essentials of Anglo-Catholicism and what he took to be its frills; he eliminated as many as he could of the latter. But he did not compromise fundamental religious principles, even for the sake of success. It is interesting that, in the mid-twentieth century, when the social purpose and the educational approach of the Woodard Schools have totally changed, their Anglo-Catholic religious tradition still distinguishes them from other public schools.

4

THE EDUCATIONAL APPROACH

1

Nathaniel Woodard's educational principles were quite opposed to what Matthew Arnold called "the movement of the modern spirit".[1] Indeed the Society in which those principles were embodied was a major element in the reaction against two developments in Victorian education: the growth of State intervention and responsibility, and the increasingly apparent divorce of sacred from secular learning.

Woodard was not a radical voluntaryist, and his objections to State interference in education were not based on the protection of individual rights and responsibilities, as, for example, were those of Edward Baines and the Congregational Union.[2] Woodard's view, like that of Archdeacon G. A. Denison and the generality of High Churchmen, was quite unlike that of the Nonconformist voluntaryists. In the strongest terms he and his associates asserted the historic responsibility of the Church for the education of the English people.

This tradition had a long and honourable history. In the tenth century English education was in the hands of the clergy; a canon of 1200 ordered that no man could keep a school without a licence from the Church. Following the Reformation the Church retained its power to license and examine schoolmasters; Canon LXXVII of 1604 provided that "no man shall teach, either in public school or private house, but such as shall be allowed by the bishop of the diocese or Ordinary of the place". At the Restoration the Act of Uniformity required of schoolmasters not only an episcopal licence but also conformity to the liturgy; in fact, wrote Montmorency, "by the end of the seventeenth century we find that the office of teacher was as much under the control of the Church as it was at the end of the eleventh century".[3]

After the Revolution of 1688 Dissenters were granted freedom of worship. But the Schism Act of 1714 was designed to eliminate Dissenters from the teaching profession by insisting on episcopal licence and conformity to the liturgy. It was repealed in 1718. But not until 1779 were conscientious Protestant Dissenters, who refused to subscribe to the Thirty-nine Articles, permitted to teach in their own schools.[4] An act of 1791 extended this freedom to Roman Catholics.[5] Despite these concessions Church control over education was still tacitly assumed to exist by the legislature into the nineteenth century,[6] and the responsibility of the Ordinary to license grammar schoolmasters was not finally abolished until the Endowed Schools Act of 1869.

In the nineteenth century the Church's right to occupy the position of national educator was directly and successfully challenged.

In the domain of primary education the battle was long and bitter and involved three groups: that consisting at first chiefly of Radicals, who supported and encouraged State action as the only effective means by which the enormous task of instructing every child could be accomplished; the voluntaryists, chiefly Dissenters, who feared for their independence and for their right to teach according to their distinctive traditions; and the majority of churchmen, some of whom were fortified by Tractarian principles, who insisted, in greater or less degree, on the historic rights of the Established Church.

In the early part of the century voluntaryists and Church monopolists generally united in opposition to the intrusion of the State. Later on all but the diehard element among Dissenters tended increasingly to support national State control against an alternative system dominated by inflexible Anglicans, who, like Archdeacon Denison, refused to allow exemption from instruction in the catechism to the children of Dissenters in Church schools.

As the great debate in elementary education developed, two things became clear: Parliament and the State began to play an increasing role in the support, control, management, and provision of primary schools; simultaneously the old Church dominance became less and less secure and found progressively fewer defenders.

Effective State intervention was blocked until 1833 by the combination of Dissenting and Anglican opposition; but in that year the first State grant was made towards the provision of elementary schools and distributed between the two dominant voluntary societies. This was followed in 1839 by the establishment of a Select Committee of the Privy Council to superintend the application of any sums voted by Parliament for the purpose of promoting public education. Under the able direction of its secretary, Dr Kay, Government contributions were followed by Government inspection and supervision and eventually, in 1846, by provision for teacher training and the actual maintenance of elementary schools. By the Act of 1870 school boards were set up in all parts of England empowered to establish schools financed by local rates wherever the provision of voluntary schools, Church or otherwise, was inadequate.

The Church monopoly was destroyed in principle in 1779. With the establishment of the British and Foreign School Society in 1808 and the subsequent foundation of denominational societies, that monopoly became, in fact, a thing of the past although the natural framework of the parish system and the greater affluence of its supporters gave the Church's National Society a permanent and significant lead in the provision of elementary schools.

The establishment of Government grants to the voluntary societies led to Government interference in the direction of schools. In the 1840s the State sought to enforce more representative management on Church primary schools; in particular it tried to wrench the oversight of parochial schools from the exclusive direction of the parish priest. The Government also sought to force Church schools to adopt a "conscience clause" stating that the children of Dissenters could attend the school without being subjected to distinctive Church teaching.

To those who still accepted the Church's responsibility for education, particularly to those like Archdeacon Denison, who interpreted that responsibility to include full Church teaching, these provisions seemed an intolerable interference by the State in the Church's sphere. Although the "High Church—Tractarian coalition"[7] prevented its adoption by the National Society in the 40s and 50s, the triumph of the conscience clause in the Education Act of 1870 was absolute.

At the opposite end of the educational scale the Church's exclusive control over university education also suffered during the nineteenth century at the hands of the State. At the beginning of the century Church control and Anglican membership of

Oxford and Cambridge, the only two universities in England, was virtually absolute.[8] Radical pressure, such as that exerted through the columns of the *Edinburgh Review*, led to increased Government pressure and, finally, legislation to defeat the monopoly. By Acts of 1854 and 1856 restrictions preventing Nonconformists from obtaining first degrees at Oxford and Cambridge were abolished; in 1871 another act eliminated religious tests for all degrees except those in divinity and for all "lay academical and collegiate offices".[9] These Parliamentary measures attacking Church privilege and monopoly were accompanied by other far-reaching reforms and were preceded by the foundation of a new university in London, which, from the beginning, was deliberately placed outside the jurisdiction of the Church.

In one sense Woodard's life-work was an effort to prevent the Church from being overshadowed in the realm of secondary education. It was a work which he shared with other Anglican educators, notably Edward Thring of Uppingham. Like Thring, Woodard knew that by statute, tradition, and custom the endowed schools were closely associated with the Church of England. But he was equally aware, not only of the inefficient state of many such schools, but of the fact that they did not provide for the great mass of the middle classes.[10] The failure of the Church to assume its responsibilities could only lead to the usurpation of those responsibilities either by dissenters and private individuals, or by the State.

Until the 60s Woodard was less disturbed about possible State interference than about the failure of the Church itself to realize its teaching function:

> My own observation has led me to conclude that the reason we have failed in our efforts to teach the people has been want of reverence for the work itself. We have never made it a religious duty: we have not come to the performance of it as part of our daily toil. . . . We of the Church of England appear to have failed in our confidence. . . . Let us then turn to the performance of the work of instruction as to any other undoubted duty, and let us do it with the reverence and consideration with which we perform the other parts of our Christian obligations.[11]

To promote a revival of the ministry of teaching, so that "the Church may take the education of the whole mass of the people into her hands"[12] was one of Woodard's principal objects. With

Dr Lowe, he asserted that school teaching was "decidedly an office in the Church of England", and he defined that office as "mainly concerned in seeing that all, from the highest to the lowest, are educated and trained in the revealed truths of our holy religion".[13] "If any one duty in particular", he wrote in 1881, "has been imposed upon the Church by the highest authority it is that of teaching."[14]

In view of the Government's activity in elementary education and of its interference in the ancient universities, it is not surprising that Woodard should early express apprehension of State intervention in the secondary realm. In the *Plea* he observed that "some look to the government for everything. For my part, in the present state of parties in this Kingdom, I heartily trust that Government will not interfere. It would be unjust."[15] Fourteen years later, at a time when interest in State intervention was perceptibly increasing, he made the following reply to a request for comment on a Russian Government plan for education: "We [in England] trust . . . to the patristic and religious zeal of our people to provide schools for the various classes of society, and we consider that it would be a very serious evil to hand over our schools to any government."[16]

While Woodard was busy re-creating the Church's image as the educator of the middle classes, the first real intimation of a direct challenge from the Civil Power came in the form of two Royal Commissions: the Clarendon Commission, appointed in 1861 to investigate the condition of nine great public schools, and the Taunton (or Schools Inquiry) Commission, appointed in 1864 to gather information and make recommendations about the state of education between the elementary schools and those institutions already examined by the Public Schools Commission. St Nicolas College came under the surveillance of Lord Taunton and his colleagues. But Woodard, suspicious of the Government's intention, rather coldly refused to give evidence before the commissioners, although he invited inspection of his schools.[17]

With the enactment of the Endowed Schools Bill in August 1869, Woodard's worst fears for the Church's position as national educator were realized. By that Act, the commissioners appointed by Parliament were empowered to reorganize and redirect the endowments of the ancient grammar schools with a view to rendering such endowments more "conducive to the advancement of the education of boys and girls". The constitutions of such schools and the make-up of their governing bodies could be adjusted by the Commissioners; indeed membership in the reorganized governing bodies was not to be affected by a man's "religious opinion . . . or his attendance or non-attendance at any particular form of religious worship". Clause twenty-one of the act reads as follows:

> In every scheme the Commissioners shall provide for the abolition of all jurisdiction of the Ordinary relating to the licensing of masters in any endowed school, or of any jurisdiction arising from such licensing.

A vital effect of interference by the State (and one which, as we have seen, was paralleled in the area of elementary education) was the introduction of a conscience clause:

> The Commissioners shall provide that the parent or guardian of . . . any scholar attending such a school . . . may claim . . . the exemption of such scholar from attending prayer or religious worship or from any lesson or series of lessons on a religious subject.[18]

Although Woodard's own Society was exempted from the effects of the Act,[19] the Provost's reaction to this legislation was swift and unmistakable. It was contained in his *Letter to Salisbury*, published in November 1869. He referred to the "present tendency of legislation" as directed at remodelling the ancient British constitution: "The Crown and the Church are both alike daily dropping out more and more from the essence of the British Constitution." Parliament, at a "time when commercial, social, and every other form of morality is giving way", was acting "so as to undermine the Institution, founded by Christ and indestructible". The Act was only "the thin edge of the wedge"; the actual end was a "State system of secular education", and the dissolution of "the union of Church and State", which, "in a moral point of view" had already taken place.[20]

Among the supporters of the "hard, commercial and un-English" schools to be set up by the new Commissioners were some former supporters of St Nicolas College: "Alas! How deeply do we regret the loss of some dear to us, associated in our mind with all that is good, who have been drawn aside to take part in this havoc." To such men Woodard imputed the basest motives:

> Politicians have seen in this neglect [of the middle classes by the Church] a great power for party purposes. . . . "Vote for me and I

will betray to you the interests of the Church and the religion of the country."[21]

One such supporter was Lord Lyttelton, formerly a member of the Schools Inquiry Commission and, at the time Woodard wrote, the chief Commissioner of Endowed Schools. A devout Anglican who had become a "reluctant secularist" in educational matters, Lyttelton was quick to reply to Woodard's pamphlet in a private letter in which he expressed his hurt and resentment at the Provost's tone.[22] Woodard responded in turn: "God is sifting us, and the results will cause pain to many and gloom where the brightness of hope once shone." He went on to express his belief in the tendency of governments to interfere in Education:

> It is not this Bill or that Bill that alarms us, but the rapidity and rashness with which the most sacred interests are attacked. The very Bill which you are now seeking to work, and which passed last August, is to be rendered far more offensive by a Supplemental Act next session. If the two are found to fail in subjecting the education of the country to the Government we may expect another and another . . . till the Church is . . . despoiled of what she has hitherto considered to be her own. . . . The Church is now reduced to the condition of a sect to the scandal of Christendom . . . [The State] openly professes that it cannot do its duty to the community and support the Church as a divine ordinance: that a separation must take place as soon as the people of England have been schooled to accept such an issue.[23]

Lord Lyttelton and his Commission had more than Woodard to contend with. Indeed the dispute with Woodard was dwarfed by one with Edward Thring, the headmaster of Uppingham. The Thring–Lyttelton disagreement also centred on the question of Church-versus-State control of endowed schools. Thring wrote to the secretary of the Commission, "I can testify most solemnly that my sole motive . . . was to do a work here for Christ, by which I am bigot enough to mean the Church of Christ as now existing in this Kingdom."[24] Unlike Woodard's Society, Thring's ancient foundation actually faced the possibility of active government interference. Should such interference result in the loss of Uppingham's Church character, Thring resolved "at once, as soon as that is clear, [to] place my resignation in the hands of the Commissioners".[25] It was under the shadow of the threat of Commission activity that Thring joined with other public school headmasters (including Sanderson of Lancing) to form the Headmasters' Conference.[26]

Unlike Uppingham, Woodard's institutions did not come within the scope of the Commissioners' endeavours. But from 1869 on Woodard never failed to voice his horror at the inroads continually made by the State and to express his conviction that such developments could only lead to the radical detriment of the Catholic Church in England. In 1872 he described Lancing Chapel as standing for "the old, liberal, refined, and Christian principles which used to be the glory of England", and against "the commercial element and the secular spirit now deluging the country".[27] A few years later he wrote to Lowe, pointing to the Church's poor past performance as the cause of her current disgrace:

> Had we properly attended to the parochial schools thirty years ago we would have had no Board Schools or Conscience Clause. Turn where you will, all seems to be going. As soon as we began, the College of Preceptors sprang up. Then Temple got out the University Examination scheme. Then the universities themselves went; and in one way or another neither the upper or middle classes have any religious training.[28]

Though discouraged, Woodard did not give up. The *Letter to Salisbury* was a challenge to churchmen as well as a rebuke to the State. From 1869 on he concentrated on building up an independent Society, which although it might be able to provide only a fragment of a national system of middle-class education, would be true to the "principles of the Church now established as the same is set forth in the Book of Common Prayer and Administration of the Sacraments and other rites and ceremonies of the said Church".[29]

2

When he asserted his opposition to State interference in education on the ground of the historic right and responsibility of the Church, Woodard was not arguing realistically.

The Church's responsibility for the education of the people was necessarily undermined as soon as elements of national society emerged which were hostile to the Church's teaching. If the Clarendon Code formally created Dissent, the Act of Toleration formally recognized it, and the legislation of 1779, which permitted Dissenters conscientiously to teach, recognized the educational results of Toleration. Repeal of the Test and Corporation Acts sealed the fate of the Establishment as a genuinely national Church; the subsequent educational activity of the State in primary, secondary, and university education served to complete the logic of Toleration in one important segment of national life.

But Woodard clung to the fiction of a national Church because he realized that one result of an indifferentist State acting in the realm of education was the separation of sacred from secular knowledge, and the removal of true religion as a vital and integral part of learning. Emotional attachment to the historic role of the national Church may have played some part in making Woodard such a stubborn defender of the rights of the Establishment. But there was a far more vital reason: as G. A. Denison fought for the integrity of knowledge by opposing government action in primary education, so Woodard carried the battle into the secondary field.

In the early part of the century the struggle to maintain the unity of education was by no means confined to High Churchmen or Tractarians. Thomas Arnold, in a sermon preached in Rugby chapel, expressed his entire opposition to the artificial separation of knowledge into secular and sacred compartments:

> I cannot reject from the range of religious education whatever ministers to the perfection of our bodies and our minds, so long as both in body and in mind, in soul and spirit, we ourselves may be taught to minister to the service of God.[30]

His failure to persuade his colleagues on the senate of London University of this principle led to his resignation from that body in 1838. F. D. Maurice too was convinced of the necessity for a unified curriculum in which all knowledge was seen to be religious.[31]

But as the century wore on State financial support, accompanied by official religious toleration or indifference, was generally accepted as inevitable, at least in the primary realm. Consequently opposition to State interference with the religious unity of the school curriculum grew feeble.

But to many of those steeped in the Catholic Revival no compromise was possible. Catholic sacramental doctrine, with its implication of the sanctity of the natural order, could allow of no restriction of religious teaching to the narrow realm of biblical or catechetical instruction. Newman expressed the Catholic position with great power in the first four of nine lectures "delivered to the Catholics of Dublin" in 1853:

> I lay it down that all knowledge forms one whole because its subject matter is one; for the universe in its length and breadth is so intimately knit together that we cannot separate off portion from portion and operation from operation except by a mental abstraction; and then again, as to its Creator, though He of course in his own Being is infinitely separate from it . . . yet He has so implicated Himself with it, so taken it into His very bosom, by His presence in it, His providence over it, His impressions upon it, and His influence through it, that we cannot truly or fully contemplate it without in some main aspects contemplating Him.[32]

To this view Woodard and his colleagues gave practical expression.

Religion was a subject among others at St Nicolas College. But it was much more. In 1852, the *Brighton Guardian* contained the following report of a speech by Dr Lowe:

> He was desirous that in designating theirs a religious school their meaning should be distinctly understood. Unfortunately the term suggested to many only the idea of a school in which boys were dragged to church, had certain texts of scripture and lessons of divinity driven into their heads, and so forth. That was not their notion of it [at Hurst]. They meant by it one in which the power and love of God entered into the performance of all the various duties and businesses of life.[33]

Dr Lowe pursued the theme of the unity of education in a sermon in 1856, when he said, "Our work . . . rests not with the soul; it is not alone religious discipline, strictly so-called, which is our work. It is the completion of the whole man; . . . the setting it in entire conformity to the Divine Image".[34]

Woodard himself was entirely opposed to education unpermeated by religion. In 1865 a clergyman named Rogers started a scheme for day schools in London which soon degenerated from an "unsectarian" to a "secular" basis.[35] Woodard expressed his disapproval of any such project.

> I am not objecting [he wrote to Lord Lyttelton] to Jews, Parsees (as Mr Rogers told us), Socinian, and other sectaries uniting to obtain a secular education for their children. With them it is consistent, as

> they do not recognize the sacredness of educating the mind of man. But the Church in her worst days has never fallen short on this head, but has consistently maintained that you may not teach secular learning in a secular spirit.[36]

In contrast to such a scheme as Rogers', Woodard and his supporters were "in favour of religion being made the foundation and starting-point, not only of [religious] education properly so-named, but indeed of every ordinary instruction".[37] The same feeling which caused Woodard to oppose Rogers' schools also led him, in 1877, to refuse his support to the secular Owen's College in Manchester.[38]

As we have seen, Government intervention in secondary education took the form of the Endowed Schools Act, and that Act included a conscience clause. Woodard's comment on that clause was concise: "It allows you to learn religion as part of the school course *if you do not object.*"[39] The act also forbade the interpenetration of religion and other subjects of instruction:

> If any teacher, in the course of other lessons at which any such scholar [i.e. one exempted from religious instruction on the grounds of conscience] is . . . present, teaches systematically and persistently any religious doctrine from the teaching of which exemption has been claimed . . . the governing body shall . . . make proper provisions for remedying the matter complained of.

In Woodard's view, the effect of the conscience clause was to destroy the unity of all knowledge in its religious basis. Such a clause was bad enough when imposed by the Government; it was far worse when it was voluntarily accepted by leading churchmen themselves.

This, in fact, is what happened when the Church Schools Company was formed in 1883, with the support of the Archbishop of Canterbury and twenty-one other bishops. The prospectus announced that "the schools will give definite Church teaching, the right of withdrawing a scholar . . . from religious instruction being reserved to the parent or guardian".[40]

Dean Plumtre of York, a supporter of the new company, noted

> the great change which has come over the minds of most reasonable churchmen . . . as to the principle of the Conscience Clause. In 1863 the defenders of that clause were few. . . . Now the principle which is asserted is accepted by Archbishops and bishops and by a majority of Convocation.[41]

So it was that churchmen as a whole finally abandoned the fiction that the Church and the State were coterminous bodies; by so doing they relinquished the unity of sacred and secular learning. Indeed many of Woodard's most prominent supporters—men like Beresford Hope and J. G. Hubbard—became supporters of the new company. But Woodard himself held fast. He opposed the new company as "a heretical scheme . . . inviting people to exercise a right which they do not possess, of choosing their own religion", and he sent Lowe to speak against it in the Lower House of Convocation.[42] Significant too was the alliance developed between Woodard and Archdeacon Denison, the veteran opponent of the conscience clause in primary schools. In 1883 at least thirty-four letters concerning the new Company were received by Woodard from Denison;[43] the archdeacon published a booklet praising Woodard at the expense of the Church Schools Company. He also led an unsuccessful attack in the Lower House of Convocation.[44] Woodard was suspicious of Denison's methods; nevertheless he was sure that "Denison is right in what he says and writes", and the two men recognized each other as allies.[45]

The conscience clause was evidently adopted by the Church Schools Company to ward off another danger to the primacy and pervasiveness of Church teaching: "undenominational" religious instruction.[46] The principle "that no religious catechism or religious formulary which is distinctive of any particular denomination shall be taught" had been adopted for rate-supported Board schools by the Elementary Education Act of 1870, and apparently formed the basis of such religious instruction as was allegedly given in Rogers' London schools.[47] It need hardly be said that Woodard, the Tractarian, had no sympathy with this alternative to the conscience clause. In 1866 Woodard wrote to a supporter of Rogers' scheme:

> You speak of the difference between my schools and yours to be that mine are sectarian, yours nonsectarian. . . . But can it be said fairly of my schools that they are sectarian when they keep strictly to the National Religion? Is the religion of a whole nation sectarian, and is the English Church, an integral part of the Constitution, only a sect?[48]

The trouble, of course, was that neither in 1866 nor for many years before had Anglicanism been "the religion of a whole nation". Yet this fictional assumption was basic to Woodard's whole educational approach; on it he founded his argument for the Church's right to educate the nation's youth. But Woodard was not a wanton reactionary. He realized that if he abandoned this fiction he must give up what he considered to be a vital principle: the unity of religious and secular learning and the penetration of all human knowledge by revealed truth. "Undenominational" teaching was no real alternative to Church instruction for it sacrificed the truth to public opinion. The conscience clause was no better, for it implicitly denied the relevance of religion to the whole of human life. The only choice left was to claim the Church's ancient privilege, albeit unrealistically, and to fight the intrusion of a religiously neutral State.

3

Woodard's principles of education were fundamentally conservative. So too was his chief instrument, the public school.

In the early part of the nineteenth century, according to E. C. Mack, the public schools appealed to the ruling orders of society because of the socially conservative influence they exercised upon their inmates: "The privileged orders needed boys trained to defend those orders against revolution at home and loss of prestige and power abroad, to fight the lower classes and the pestiferous French."[49]

When Woodard turned his attention from his first day school to establish a boarding school "conforming as far as may be to the rule of Winchester",[50] there can be no doubt that he too was persuaded of the desirable social conservatism of the public school.

Convinced that middle-class children must be removed from the "noxious influence of home",[51] after 1848 he concentrated nearly all his energies on the promotion of the public school ideal among "every shade of the middle classes, even down to mechanics and gentlemen's servants".[52] Woodard's ideal was "a large boarding school, in which from 300 to 400 boys live and work together". Through community life they would be "moulded into habits of self-control and moderation by the laws of the small world in which they live, and by the mutual wants of one another". Such a school, because of its endowments and government, was "removed from the evil influence of being a commercial speculation", and its work would be "guaranteed by examiners from the universities of Oxford and Cambridge, who do not test the proficiency of picked boys but the general work of all the upper forms".[53]

The community life and "lawful rivalry" engendered in such a school would train middle-class boys in the desirable aristocratic "habits of honour, integrity, and self-restraint".[54] In the words of the *Guardian*:

> Mr Woodard's idea has been to impart to middle-class education something of that element of loyal and loving respect which has belonged to the best of our great public schools under their best and most honoured chiefs.[55]

The public school was a profoundly English institution, and for that reason it was recognized as desirable by Woodard, and by his chief supporters, that as many Englishmen as possible should share in its benefits.[56] The prospect of an extension of the ideal roused sympathy in upper-class breasts and promoted contributions; after the 1861 public meeting in London to raise funds for building Ardingly, a "Public School Man" seriously proposed a scheme by which alumni of the great public schools would raise money for Woodard's projects.[57]

In fact Woodard's conception of the public school ideal differed markedly from the conventional idea in two respects. A public school, thought Woodard, should be available to all classes; and it must teach the "National Religion". The word "public", he felt, indicated "a school to which any boy might go who could pay a small fee"; thus "the old public schools were founded not for the rich *as such* but as a department of the public religion, and consequently for persons of every condition."[58] He went on to describe the object of those schools that were "founded by Kings and Bishops and by other religious and thoughtful persons":

> The object of these schools was a most Christian one, and well suited for those simple and painstaking days when no one could teach our youth without a licence from the Bishop of the Diocese to assure the faith and learning of the Master. It was then felt, as it should be now, that the greatest possible good that a nation can enjoy is *unity* among the several classes of society, and certain it is that nothing can promote this so effectually as that of all classes being *brought up together*, learning from their childhood the *same religion*, and the same rudiments of secular learning.[59]

Woodard's conception of the content of the "National Religion" and the steps he took to ensure its propagation in the schools were discussed in the previous chapter. The method he pursued to make the public school a unifying factor among various social classes, rather than the preserve of the rich, was somewhat paradoxical.

Woodard never expected to found one type of school to which all parents capable of paying fees for their children's education would send their sons. Indeed, he thought such a school impossible under Victorian social conditions. On the other hand he never for a moment considered reducing his aim by excluding the sons of any such parents. Woodard's solution was to found a series of schools of different types at different fees, yet all sharing in common the principal features of a public school, all united in a federal and fraternal relationship, and all subject to the same clerical direction and Church teaching. Thus Woodard sought to make three graded schools "in principle *one* school".[60] To the charge that the social and economic division of his Society's schools had the effect of hardening rather than softening class antagonisms, Woodard replied:

> In a scheme which included a course of education for the sons of the principal gentry, and the lowest sections of the middle classes; for those who seek a university degree, and for those whose future lot is cast in the workships of the artisans, it might be expected that class distinctions and prejudices may arise having a tendency to the disruption of social ties and setting class against class. . . . I am not an advocate for perfect systems, and do not expect that this will prove free from weak points, but, as it is impossible to educate on a large scale under the same roof boys paying £100 a year and boys paying £15 a year, the next best thing to do, as it appears to me, is to unite them by common bonds in some one particular system, which all through life, may tend to produce a harmony of ideas.[61]

Thus the group of public schools would provide the middle class with a vested interest in the *status quo*, a tendency to social conservatism, and an inclination to imitate the habits (political and social) of their betters.

4

Not surprisingly the practical operation of Woodard's schools was for the most part thoroughly conservative. Woodard was no

Thring; he made no radical contributions to the method of public school education. Indeed Woodard was quite explicit in his rejection of advanced methods:

> It falls to the lot of fewer persons than we suppose to be the originators of a set of ideas and regulations suitable to the requirements of human nature. Such a thing might, perhaps, not be impossible, but the times will not admit of experiments; all, therefore, that we can hope to do is to extend the provision which a past age provided.[62]

Among the contributions of the past was a predominantly classical curriculum and a definite resistance to science and other modern subjects.

The nineteenth century provided many critics of the grammar school curriculum; indeed, as E. C. Mack has shown, in the early part of the century Radical criticism of the old emphasis on Latin and Greek reached considerable proportions.[63] Jeremy Bentham proposed a curriculum based entirely on "utility": he emphasized the natural sciences to the exclusion of classics altogether. At University College School no subjects were compulsory, and chemistry, physics, botany, physical geography, and social science were taught.[64] In the lower school of the Liverpool Institute, founded in 1835, no classics were taught, and such subjects as chemistry, hydraulics, pneumatics, and astronomy were introduced; even in the Institute's High School classics formed only a small part of the course of studies.[65]

In 1865, "a Practical Man", in a pamphlet entitled *Public and Middle-Class School Education*, made a devastating attack on the classical basis of secondary education in the grammar schools, and recommended a heavily scientific curriculum. Three years later Robert Lowe described the futility of teaching Latin and Greek to the middle classes; he advocated instead that "the main study of the middle classes should be . . . some one or other of the physical sciences".[66]

Among such critics were to be numbered some churchmen. Canon Moseley of Bristol, for example, favoured replacing the traditional elements of the grammar school course with scientific subjects on these grounds:

> What is done with the head, with no relation to what is done with the hands, is the business of the universities and the public schools, and the occupation of the upper or non-working classes. Pure work is

> the occupation of the working classes. It seems the function of the middle classes to apply the thought of the educated classes to the work of the uneducated. Their schools should, therefore, be schools of application.[67]

Moseley's ideas were incorporated in the Bristol Diocesan Trade School, founded in 1851, at which the elementary subjects of reading, spelling, writing, and arithmetic were taught along with chemistry and "geometrical drawing"; not only the classics, but also geography and history, were eliminated.[68]

Canon Brereton's residential middle class "County School" in Devon opened in 1858 and included Latin only as an extra.[69] At the opening of Cranleigh in 1865, Charles Buxton, M.P., pointed to what he considered the good sense of restricting Latin to "seventh place in the curriculum . . . whilst the English language and literature, history and geography, stood in the forefront."[70] At Framlingham, founded in 1865, only the elements of Latin were taught, whilst natural science, agricultural chemistry, and "geometrical, engineering, model and architectural drawing" also formed parts of the curriculum.[71]

On the other hand such middle-class schools as that founded in 1839 by the Metropolitan Institution or those established by the Liverpool Collegiate Institution continued to give Latin a central place.[72] "A Head Master" wrote a letter to the *Guardian* in 1864 describing the "difficulty involved in the conflicting claims of two different systems of education—the classical and the commercial"; these claims were made respectively by "parents of the higher class, whether the country gentlemen or the professional men residing in the town" and by "the tradesmen who send their sons". His solution was to retain the classics as the basis of the curriculum, but to add modern subjects freely.[73]

No doubt some of the conservatism in the curricula of some grammar and proprietary and other Church-connected schools was a reaction to the superficiality of modern studies in the private schools. At such "academies" parental influence was strong; and middle-class parents generally requested only practical commercial subjects.[74] Mr Bryce of the Taunton Commission noted that

> the private schools pursue with very little energy any but the directly practical branches of knowledge. Arithmetic, penmanship, possibly

> also French are assiduously cultivated; Latin is languid; even mathematics is pushed on one side. . . . Nothing is easier than to make out a strong case against the tyranny of Greek and Latin, and the private schoolmasters do so to their own satisfaction. I do not find, however, that they have any other subject . . . which . . . can give tenacity and clearness to the scholar's mind.[75]

The Commissioners themselves were fairly conservative in their recommendations. First-grade schools, because they were chiefly preparatory to the universities, must continue to be rooted in the classics. Second-grade schools, although they should teach Greek only as an "extra", ought normally to retain Latin. Third-grade schools should teach either "the elements of Latin or some modern language". But the Commissioners were keen to emphasize the necessity of introducing modern subjects as important parts of the curricula in all schools, and they regarded the teaching of natural science as of particular importance at all three levels. In the second-level schools "it would often be worth while to lay great stress on practical mechanics and other branches of natural science"; and in the lowest schools "either botany or some branch of experimental physics or the rudiments of inorganic chemistry" was regarded as essential.[76]

The curriculum of Woodard's first day school at Shoreham was surprisingly non-classical; it comprised bookkeeping, navigation, land-surveying, mensuration, and added Latin and French only as optional "extras".[77] But in his first public school, the ancestor of Lancing, the curriculum was conservative, consisting of Greek and Latin, mathematics, history, and French.[78]

One of Woodard's first headmasters, C. E. Moberley, tried to prevent the Provost from establishing a traditional public school course of studies:

> We might make Latin and Greek one thing among several, adopting . . . some limit for classical study beyond which we would not profess to go. This would leave a margin for pure mathematics, for a thorough study of French, and above all for History and English literature.[79]

He received a rather cold reply:

> My view is not to introduce any new elements either into our religious or educational departments, but rather to try our strength on the present system which has stood the test of many generations.[80]

The first-grade school remained fully classical throughout the 50s.[81] Mr Giffard, examining Lancing for the Schools Inquiry Commission in the next decade, reported that

> the staple of education is Latin and Greek. The mathematics receive a moderate degree of attention; French scarcely any; no instruction is given in the physical science; instrumental music, German, and drawing are extras.[82]

Dr Sanderson, in a letter to the *Guardian* on 4 November 1868, pointed out that since the Assistant Commissioner's inspection more time had been allotted to mathematics and modern languages. In the following year he pressed Woodard on the subject of natural science; but it was not until 1872 that regular instruction under a qualified teacher was offered at Lancing.[83]

At the second-level school at Hurstpierpoint the curriculum was apparently more liberal; initially it included English, French, history, geography, writing and mathematics, navigation, surveying, and "the elements of natural philosophy" as well as Latin. Greek was an "extra".[84] Science was certainly taught at the school in the 50s;[85] but there is no doubt that Dr Lowe, the headmaster, gave the classics first consideration. He devoted a lengthy section of his book, *St Nicolas College and its Schools*, to a justification "of making classical learning an important part of the study of a commercial school".[86]

Parental complaints on the grounds of the predominance of classics at Hurst were heard as early as 1856 and were expressed in a letter to the *Daily News* in 1862.[87] Mr Giffard reported to the Taunton Commissioners that the predominance of Latin left inadequate time for English studies. Greek was at first excluded from the regular course, but it was subsequently incorporated into it; by 1886 it was again an extra.[88]

The lower middle-class school established at Shoreham in 1858 had a curriculum which, when compared with that at Canon Moseley's establishment at Bristol, appears very conservative. No natural science was taught at all from the inception of the school until the Founder's death; on the other hand Latin formed an important part of the curriculum.[89]

In general, the teaching of the Woodard schools was distinctly conservative; but there was one notable exception. The short-lived St George's Military and Engineering School was opened in 1851 to accommodate

> those who are candidates for commissions in the army under the new regulations, or have nominations to the Royal Military College, Sandhurst, the Royal Military Academy, Woolwich, or the Honourable East India Company's Seminary, Addiscombe, or for those who desire a sound Civil Engineering Education.[90]

At this institution the basic curriculum comprised English, French, German, Latin, history and geography, mathematics, surveying, levelling, hill drawing, fortification, landscape drawing, and the elements of natural philosophy. From the beginning Woodard planned to teach Hindustani at this school, a subject highly recommended a few years later by an authority on the needs of the East India service.[91] But very soon the school lost money heavily, probably due to the unpopular religious orientation of its parent body,[92] and it had to close down as a separate institution.

In one other respect Woodard demonstrated a capacity to adjust the content of education to the needs of the times. Despite his insistence on a literary curriculum at St Saviour's, he and his associates showed themselves very much aware of the pecuniary advantages of skilled labourers over inferior white-collar workers. In 1865 the headmaster of the lower middle school wrote: "The occupation of a stone mason or a carpenter or bricklayer is in these days more productive than that of the general run of clerks, is far more healthy, and is more open to advancement in life."[93]

In view of this the Society proposed to establish a system by which boys living at St Saviour's and receiving some instruction there could be made apprentices to the stone masons, carpenters, and bricklayers employed by the College.[94] The scheme was not intended to be a large one; and in 1871 there were only six such apprentices in residence at the new buildings at Ardingly.[95] This apprenticeship plan anticipated comments on the overcrowding of respectable middle-class occupations made many years later, and actually put into practice an idea about which churchmen twenty years later were talking and writing.[96]

5

Despite the conservatism of the Founder's educational theory and of the normal course of instruction at the schools, Woodard's

Society was not without certain liberal and even advanced educational features.

Perusal of the Woodard correspondence leaves the impression that E. C. Lowe, for many years the headmaster of Hurstpierpoint, and later Provost of the Midland Division, often encouraged the Provost to take a more radical and experimental line than he might otherwise have done. It was he who invited Mark Pattison to examine the school at Hurst in 1851.[97] In 1857 he established an annual examination of Hurst by Oxford dons, and apparently suggested making use of the newly-established Oxford Middle Class Examinations for testing picked pupils.[98] Although he forbade the latter, after the 1869 Act Woodard adopted the idea of regular inspection of all his schools by Oxford examiners with special vigour.[99]

We have already noticed that under Lowe's direction the Midland Division enthusiastically raised the matter of schooling for middle-class girls. Woodard himself was always suspicious of entering the field of female education, partly because he feared it would detract from his main work of educating middle-class boys,[100] but chiefly because he had grave doubts about the value of public school education for girls. As early as 1849 he wrote to Lowe's sister:

> It is a matter for consideration whether large schools are good for girls. A public school is the very thing for a boy because the world and public life is his destiny. But can this rule be applied to girls? . . . A large religious Sisterhood with small filiations about the country to teach girls of all ranks is the only thing that I can see likely to succeed on a large scale.[101]

Woodard himself was prevailed upon to take over the direction of St Michael's school by the foundress, Miss Mary Anne Rooper, to whom he had been devoted. As we have seen Woodard made a definite attempt to form this school along the lines of a religious community.[102] In 1866 the Lady Warden of St Michael's outlined the aim of the education provided:

> We all know how much the Church owes to godly women, and how much she has suffered from careless and irreligious ones. A pious mother is a tower of strength to any family, the absence of which can never be supplied. May God enable us . . . to train up the future mothers . . . in such sort that they may by their influence help to stem the torrent of ungodliness now overflowing our country.[103]

A contrast to this pious establishment was provided by Miss Beale's Ladies' College at Cheltenham, where in 1862 the girls were studying fossils in their own museum, and in the following year an annual examination by Oxford scholars was instituted.[104] Woodard's idea of female education contrasted too with that of Miss Isabella Tod writing under the auspices of the National Union for Improving the Education of Women. She pointed out that girls needed a real education and remarked on the silliness of parents looking forward to "all their daughters marrying, to all these marriages being satisfactory, and to the husbands being always able and willing to take the active management of everything".[105]

But Dr Lowe did not perpetuate Woodard's pious and conservative views in his Midlands schools. In his early appeal for funds to build "Middle Class Boarding Schools for Girls in the Midland Counties" he observed that

> in the cheaper of these schools it will be our aim to combine with sound general instruction training in practical and perhaps industrial matters, as will qualify girls leaving school for some of those various remunerative occupations which are daily being opened more and more to women. In the higher schools, the education given will prepare girls as governesses.[106]

In 1884 Woodard wrote:

> These fancy schools set up for girls are more fitted for show than solid and practical use. After all, we all know what women are for, and to draw them from these purposes and put them into conflict with men in universities, the Forum, and the public streets can only have an un-Christian ending.[107]

To this outburst Lowe, who approved of university education for women, simply replied, "I do not agree with you", although he admitted the Founder's right to restrict the Society's operations.[108]

To judge from the contents of the Society's Calendars, the contrast between the nature of girls' education in the South and in the Midlands was neither as sharp nor as permanent as these expressions of opinion might suggest. In 1871 only "thorough English instruction with French and music" was listed as taught at St Michael's; but by 1886 the curriculum had expanded to include not only mathematics and Latin but even physical science. In the same year it was stated that the work is periodically examined by independent and authorized examiners from one of the Universities. Candidates are prepared for the Cambridge Women's Examination, and special training is given to those intending to become teachers.[109]

6

From the very beginning it was Woodard's idea to have graduates in Holy Orders as the principal masters in all his boys' schools. Thus in the *Plea* he stated that "the responsible masters will all be in Holy Orders". In *Public Schools for the Middle Classes*, issued in 1852, he drew a parallel between the clerical agents of primary and secondary education.[110] The 1850 *Calendar* of the Society set out the ratio of clergymen to boys: "It is intended that in the First Class schools there shall be one clergyman to every twenty-five boys; in the lower class schools, one clergyman to every fifty boys." In 1859, when the Third School had been started, the *Calendar* prescribed one clergyman to every hundred boys in that class of school. In fact at Lancing in 1859 there was one clerical master to every fifteen boys; in 1871 the proportion decreased to one priest for every twenty boys; by 1884 there was one clergyman to every forty-three boys. At Hurst the assigned ratio was at first maintained; but by 1871 there were fifty-six boys to each clerical master, and by 1884 the proportion was fifty-eight to one. At St Saviour's school in 1864 the proportion was seventy to one. Although the proportion in 1871 was only one clergyman to one hundred and sixteen boys, the relative number of clergy had increased considerably by 1884.[111]

Expressions of the purpose of such arrangements were abundant. Most of them reflected Woodard's conviction that contact between the clergy and the middle classes had been dangerously small.[112] In all the *Calendars* of the 50s, immediately after the statement concerning the ratio of clergymen to boys, it is stated that "thus the middle classes will grow up in intimacy with their spiritual guides, and in a respect for and attachment to the clergy". In his *Letter to Salisbury*, in which the mature organization of the Society was described, Woodard gave, as the principal reason for the predominance of the clerical element in the Society, that "the more the clergy and people are brought together the better".[113]

It was through the clergy of his Society, and particularly

through the chaplains, one of whom was assigned to each of the schools, that Woodard hoped to bring the middle classes back to the Church and thus to strengthen the Establishment in English society. But there were other reasons for clericalism too. Dr Lowe reflected Woodard's convictions when he wrote that

> the clergy of the Established Church are instructors entirely relied on by the country; . . . if the opportunity were opened to them, the middle classes will as fully appreciate tuition at the hands of the clergy as do the upper class, who, with hardly an exception, place their sons under such charge, and as do the lower, who naturally look to the incumbent's superintendence of the National School.[114]

Not less important than parental confidence in the clerical order was the parson's moral stature: "The character of the clergyman is sacred: his moral life must be something near the mark. This is a guarantee to society, and is so generally regarded."[115] Not only were the senior instructors to be clergymen, but the juniors were often preparing for ordination, the proposed resident Seniority was to be predominantly clerical, and the Provost himself had to be a "graduate in Holy Orders".[116] In this way, Woodard sought to "complete the educational chain which passes between the Church of England and all orders of English Society".[117]

Woodard thought that qualified clergymen could be obtained without great trouble, and he fully expected that several of his masters would be "volunteers, fellows of colleges, etc." The prospect of tapping the resources of university fellowships fascinated Woodard:

> To draw forth . . . from the Universities . . . those who are paid to teach, and apply their exertions where they are needed for the good of the nation at large is our first object. . . . It is an opening for the zealous and conscientious Fellows of Colleges, who having endowments from our ancestors may come out into the country and give back in labour some return for the piety of past ages.[118]

His appeal to fellows of colleges did bring some results;[119] and in 1848 he proposed a system of "fellowships" by which the Society would assist qualified young men through university in return for a minimum of four years' teaching at the Society's schools.[120] But it would seem that most of the first graduate masters—men like Lowe and Field—accepted their positions without these advantages and lived happily on very low stipends. These early masters were young and inexperienced. A pupil who entered Lancing in 1852 later recalled: "At the time of my admission the oldest member of the teaching staff was, I think, just over thirty, the Provost himself being forty-one."[121]

When Woodard first outlined his scheme he expected that his graduate masters would receive an average of £100 per year and board.[122] When searching for a successor to the first headmaster of his first boarding school he offered £150 a year.[123] Sabine Baring-Gould, a graduate of Cambridge, earned £25 a year when he joined Woodard's Society in 1857.[124] In 1861, according to Dr Lowe, the minimum income for a teaching fellow was £75 together with room and board.[125] Two years earlier Woodard offered £400 together with a house for a headmaster of Lancing.[126]

When Dr Sanderson took over Lancing the cash income of the post was £200 together with fairly sizable, but largely theoretical, capitation fees.[127] He complained in 1869:

> The issue of my seven years here is that I am worse off pecuniarily than I was when I first came to Lancing. . . . When I . . . came you know that I only found one boarder in my house. By the end of my third year I had lost £600 by my office at Lancing.[128]

By way of comparison, in the early 60s the headmaster of Rugby received a net income of over £2,500; at the same school assistant masters earned between £440 and £950, together with profits from their boarding houses.[129]

No doubt religious enthusiasm drew a good many men to Woodard's project despite the low stipends; but in the 60s the Society certainly experienced difficulty in attracting graduates from the two ancient universities. In 1864 Sanderson went to Oxford, authorized to offer £200 for a master in Latin composition; after a fruitless search he informed the Provost that "unless we are prepared to give upwards of £400 a year we cannot hope for the services of a first-class Oxford man".[130]

The difficulty of acquiring masters was partly a financial one and partly a matter of the required religious views; it was enhanced by the inadequacy of Oxford and Cambridge as centres of modern studies. Sanderson experienced this problem in his search for a science master; in 1869 he reported having resorted to unproductive inquiries "in Berlin and Paris, and . . . through Matthew Arnold".[131] Seven years earlier Lowe solved a similar problem at

Hurst by resorting to a London University graduate. This radical step gave rise to discussion. "In my judgement", wrote Lowe, "London is quite as good as Dublin or any other place in the absence of residence."[132] The Provost was not wholly convinced:

> I will not say that I will in all cases admit the London University degree, but considering his [the new master's] qualifications . . . I will admit it in his case. I make this exception as we may get some queer characters from the London University; and it might happen that hereafter an M.A. of that university might be elected Provost—an event not to be desired.[133]

There can be little doubt that the difficulties experienced in acquiring suitable masters for the middle school at Hurst was the chief factor which led Woodard and his colleagues to embark on their own effort at teacher-training.

Public recognition of the need for adequately-trained teachers in middle or commercial schools was aroused in the early 60s and grew in intensity through the last decades of the century. In 1859 the anonymous author of *Notes on Middle Class Boarding Schools and Middle Class Education* complained that "any one, an unfrocked parson, an indolent beerhouse keeper, a plumber and glazier's apprentice, or an injured sailor or railway porter" could open a school without any test of their qualifications as teachers.[134] Two years later a writer in the *Museum* strongly urged "professional training for middle-class teachers" and recommended the establishment of "middle-class training colleges". "The first step", the author continued, ". . . is to confer some diploma or certificate which may serve as an unquestionable evidence of efficiency and attainment."[135] In 1868 the Taunton Commissioners pointed to the same need and recommended the public examination and certification of secondary school instructors. No action was taken on this recommendation and the need continued to exist.[136]

In fact Woodard recognized the problem and attempted a solution in the early 50s.[137] In 1854 a Training School for Commercial Schoolmasters was opened at Hurst and was listed in the *Calendar* as follows:

> Accommodation for thirty students is provided. . . . A residence of three years is required in order to qualify for a certificate as Associate of St Nicolas College. This certificate will enable the holder to take a class in any Middle or Lower school of the Society, or to open a

school of his own in connection with, and under the inspection of, St Nicolas College, enjoying the benefits common to the affiliated schools of the Society.

Candidates normally entered the Training School at the age of sixteen after having passed an entrance examination. If they were successful in a second examination at the age of seventeen candidates received the title of Probationer Associate and for two years were required to teach in one of the Society's schools as well as to be themselves instructed. At the end of this period Probationers would be examined again; if they passed and if they were able to "produce a testimonial from the headmaster in whose school they had been engaged, certifying their practical skill in teaching" they were granted the degree of Associate of St Nicolas College. Provision was made for adult candidates to take only the final examination without prior training in the Society's schools, although such candidates had to show evidence of previous successful teaching experience.[138] It seems that people drawn from outside the Society's schools were "often very poorly prepared".[139]

The original fee at the Training School was £25 per year, but there were exhibitions which could reduce this to about seventeen guineas.[140] No significant change was made in the charge for board and lodging at this Training School in the Founder's lifetime.[141] *The Regulations for the Admission and Examination of Probationer Associates*, drawn up in 1874, indicated that fee reductions were made after the student became a Probationer, and Dr Perry, the author of *Ardingly, 1858–1958*, notes that a stipend of from £10 to £15 was actually paid to Probationer Associates. The salary of a fully qualified Associate who taught in the Society's schools ranged between £20 and £50; those who achieved first class honours in the final examination received a premium of £15.[142] The degree of A.S.N.C. was regarded by the Bishop of Chichester as a title for Holy Orders; Associates who determined to enter the ministry took a prescribed course from the senior chaplain.[143]

In fact the Training School at Hurst was never large. The annual count in the Hurst school magazine (which does not distinguish between junior members of the Training School and Probationer Associates) shows that between 1859 and 1877 the school never contained more than thirteen or less than eight trainees. After 1877 it declined rapidly and, until the Founder's death, never had more than six students in any one year.[144] A second training school was established at Denstone which in this, as in other respects, was modelled on Hurst. In 1884 there were eleven Probationer Associates at Denstone; and, in 1888, the Midlands Division could boast of no less than twenty-three Probationer Associates teaching at Denstone and Ellesmere.[145]

The total number of teachers qualified in the two training schools is indicated by the number of Associates listed in the Calendars as "on the foundation". According to this information, in 1890 there were forty-seven Associates on the foundation of the Southern Division and twenty-six similarly connected with the Midlands Division. Excluding any Associates who might have died before Woodard, the two training schools had thus produced seventy-three fully qualified teachers at the time of the Founder's death.[146]

Many of the Associates remained as teachers in the Woodard schools. No doubt this accounts for the remarkable homogeneity of the teaching staff at S.N.C. In 1878 a contributor to the Ardingly school magazine could write:

> Twelve of the present masters were once boys at St Saviour's, and of the entire staff, with the exception of the head master and the chaplain, there is only one who is not an alumnus of St Nicolas College, and he is now an Associate and has been a master at the school for nearly twelve years.[147]

But the small salaries offered by S.N.C. and the need throughout the country meant that a good many went elsewhere at the end of their first required year of teaching. In the year 1884, for example, there were eight qualified Associates teaching in the schools of the Southern Division (including one at Taunton); but in the same year thirty-three Associates are listed as on the foundation of the Southern Division. Presumably the other twenty-five were scattered in other schools or teaching privately.[148] In 1864 Dr Lowe remarked on the difficulty of

> retaining valuable men on the small salaries we give, at a time when Middle Schools are spreading, and all managers will be glad to get one of our men before any other. Already H. J. Wilson, who was here, has issued a prospectus announcing himself as late Assistant Master here; and within the last day or two Swinnerton . . . has accepted an appointment of responsibility at £90 per annum . . . in the Diocesan

> College at Peterborough. *The Times* . . . has an advertisement for masters, plainly not graduates, at £75 with board and lodging for the Albert School in Suffolk. The Dean of Ely wrote me for a man, as Associate, offering £100 per annum for the Ely school.[149]

In 1869 one James Sunter, A.S.N.C. was Assistant Master at St Peter's College and Middle Class School at Rawdon.[150] Another Associate, J. H. Edmonds, wrote to the Provost in 1883:

> I have been appointed to the headmastership of the East Devon County School at Sampford Peverell, near Tiverton. . . . It will be my aim to reproduce . . . the aims and methods I have learned here and to carry further afield the good seed sown so liberally at Hurstpierpoint.[151]

The training scheme which Woodard founded was established years before the general public was aroused to the problem of training secondary school teachers.[152] As in the case of girls' schools, so in the matter of teacher training, Dr Lowe's liberal influence was considerable. He was a member of the Associate Educational Committee which worked out the scheme in 1852; as headmaster of Hurst, he presided over the experiment from its inception; he preached and wrote on the subject with enthusiasm.[153] It is not surprising that in 1869 Sir J. T. Coleridge, writing to Gladstone to recommend Lowe for preferment, remarked that "the success which has followed [Woodard's efforts] could not have been attained without Dr Lowe's zeal and good sense."[154]

7

Woodard's scheme not only included various grades of school designed for the different strata of the middle classes; it also provided, by means of scholarships from school to school, a "ladder" by which the son of a mechanic or small tradesman might achieve an education equal in quality (if not in attendant affluence) to that given the son of the noblest lord. Indeed Woodard did more than this, for he extended the "educational ladder" down below the humblest member of the middle class and upward to include the sons of gentlemen. In this way, although by far the greatest part of Woodard's time and energy was expended on his middle-class schools and the great majority of his pupils were of middle-class parentage, St Nicolas College could be described as a "national" scheme of education "for all classes".[155]

The lowest rung on the "educational ladder" was first represented by the Servitors' School at St John's College at Hurstpierpoint. It was described as follows in the 1854 *Calendar*:

> There is a foundation of eight servitors who are boys trained in household work, and regularly instructed in school for not less than three hours a day. These boys are intended to become either useful servants or they will be fitted to assist as teachers in the lower schools. . . . No boy is elected a servitor under twelve years of age.

After the establishment of the Lower Middle School in 1858, the *Calendar* contained the information that a scholarship was available from the Servitors' School at Hurst to the new cheap boarding school at Shoreham.[156] Subsequently Servitors' Schools were attached to the two lower middle class schools (Shoreham-Ardingly and Ellesmere) as well as to St Chad's, Denstone, the equivalent of Hurst in the Midlands Division. The fee at the Servitors' School was £5 a year,[157] and at Hurst the numbers soon increased above the limit of eight first imposed.[158]

Information about the servitors and about their progress is sparse.[159] I have not in fact been able to discover any record of a servitor who took advantage of the scholarship offered. But successful candidates at Shoreham, and later at Ardingly, there must have been; and the presence of a Servitors' Scholarship enabled the authorities of the College to boast of a "chain of institutions which link us, in one way or another, with every grade of society, and enable us . . . to put in the way of everyone an opening for advancement".[160] An imaginative writer in the Hurst school magazine noted that

> Adrian IV began life as Nicolas Breakspear, the kitchen boy of St Alban's Abbey. We hardly desire in our warmest aspirations for the success of an ambitious servitor that he should become Pope of Rome, but if in days to come a boy from the Servitors' School should rise to the Provost's stall it will be nothing more wonderful than has often happened in the Church.[161]

In the North another link was forged between St Nicolas College and the lower orders. At the opening of Denstone College in 1873, Dr Lowe announced the foundation of "a scholarship for . . . National schoolboys for each of the three counties making up the Diocese of Lichfield".[162] Subsequently the number of these scholarships were fixed at two, and they were transferred from

Denstone to Ellesmere when the latter was opened. The holder of one of these "Isaak Walton Scholarships" received board and education at Ellesmere for twelve guineas a year. Dr Lowe described them as affording "an opening through our various grades of schools to higher education and to the Universities themselves, and even to Holy Orders, if ability and means . . . are forthcoming to aid the aspirant".[163]

Of the three levels of public schools which Woodard established as links between the Servitors' Schools and the Universities, the highest was of comparatively small social significance. As the Servitors' School was a point of contact between Woodard's main work of middle-class education and the proper sphere of the National Society, so Lancing constituted a small intrusion into the well-filled arena of upper-class public schools.

The constitution and working of Lancing did not differ much, from a social point of view, from that of the many other new public and proprietary schools established between 1840 and 1880, although its charges remained comparatively moderate.[164] As we have seen, this school was originally designed to be of financial assistance to the lower schools; it was also thought that a first-grade school would attract masters to the Society's work generally.[165] But its significance in Woodard's social aim was twofold. It linked the middle and upper classes together in one Society, and so provided a microcosm of a desirable end for all national education. It also provided a means by which, through a scholarship from the middle school at Hurst, a middle-class boy could be adequately prepared to compete successfully for university scholarships. Thus, not only was the unity of national society emphasized, but the fluidity of the English "class" educational structure was, at least theoretically, maintained.

The two most important links in Woodard's scheme were the Middle Schools (Hurst, and the later Denstone) and the Lower Middle Schools (Ardingly and Ellesmere). These were the schools to which the Founder looked to recruit the middle classes themselves to his social and religious ideals. By means of scholarships which linked Ardingly with Hurst and Hurst with Lancing, as well as by the common brotherhood of the boys from all the schools in the Society itself, Woodard sought to integrate the middle classes into a settled social order.

St John's College, Hurstpierpoint, the first of Woodard's middle schools, was designed to accommodate the sons of the basic middle-class occupational trinity, "tradesmen, farmers, and clerks", as well as of "professional men of limited means".[166] A table of the parentage of the boys in the school (Appendix C) shows that, in the mid-sixties, this design had been adhered to, though there was a general reluctance on the part of farmers to pay even the comparatively modest fees Woodard required.[167] But the general success of the school was undoubted, and the University examiners remarked on "the sound and complete character of the education given" and the "accuracy and carefulness of the work".[168]

There is some indication that boys raised themselves socially by their attendance at Hurst; certainly a comparison of the parentage given in Appendix C with the rather scanty report in the Hurst *Register* of the subsequent vocations of students would suggest this. The future occupations of the early boys at the school were relatively humble. Those of nineteen out of the 109 boys registered in 1850 are given in the *Register* as follows: a builder; a patent agent; a farmer and miller; two farmers; "sea"; two in "business"; a brewer; a railway official; an "agent"; a schoolmaster; a Government clerk; a solicitor's clerk; an auctioneer; three Associates of S.N.C., of whom one went to university; a sculptor. In 1860 the occupations of twenty out of the 101 registered are listed: bank manager; solicitor; officer in the marines; two clergymen; officer in the army; four in "business"; auctioneer; schoolteacher; stock exchange, squire and patron of living; Bank of England; two surgeons; fuel manufacturer; carriage manufacturer; miner in Australia. One clergyman and the schoolteacher went to university. Of the 184 registrations in 1868, the occupations of eighteen are listed; of these four were clergymen, three were solicitors, and one became Minister of Agriculture in the Canadian Government. Despite the vagueness of some of these occupational descriptions, there is a clear progression to more exalted occupations over the years, and there is also a marked progression from the social position of the parents as this can be gleaned from Appendix C. Of course the very small number of parents listed, as well as the incompleteness of the *Register* records, reduce the value of this evidence.[169]

A hint of social-intellectual ambition is also reflected in Dr Lowe's anxiety to retain bright boys at Hurst and to prepare them directly for the University and for Civil Service examinations.[170]

In the Report of the Schools Inquiry Commission it was observed that from Hurst there were "three undergraduates now at Oxford holding exhibitions gained in that University at Exeter College, Magdalene Hall, and Christ Church".[171] Nevertheless Hurst remained a middle-class school, and a middle link in the Society's "educational ladder". Dr Lowe himself was determined that this should be so.[172]

St Saviour's School, established first at Shoreham in 1858 and moved in 1870 to Ardingly, was Woodard's first school for the lower middle class, the "sons of small shopkeepers, farmers, mechanics, clerks, and others of limited means".[173] As Hurst allowed for the attachment of the central part of the middle classes, so St Saviour's provided for that rather vague but undoubtedly large part of the population which could not afford the fees of a "commercial school" of the Hurst type, but yet was unwilling that its young should go to the parochial schools. To maintain the social position of this public school was one of Woodard's main concerns. He never permitted the minimum annual fee to rise above fifteen guineas a year,[174] and he applied a means test to all parents who sought to enrol their boys.[175]

Model family budgets of the period indicate that Woodard's charges were realistic.[176] But the best indication that Woodard actually did attract the classes he aimed at is provided by a table of the occupations of the St Saviour's boys' parents, printed in the Schools Inquiry Commission Report and reproduced in Appendix D.

From the beginning St Saviour's attracted large numbers. By the end of the 70s, "over three thousand five hundred boys" had passed through the school and "between a hundred and fifty and two hundred new boys" entered every year. The average stay of each student was only a little over two years;[177] but there is evidence that some of the boys took advantage of the opportunity provided by the Society for continued study. One George Stallard, we are told, "went up to Hurstpierpoint, gained a scholarship to Keble College, Oxford, took a First in Natural Science, and became a master at Rugby".[178] In 1881 the headmaster of Lancing (Sanderson) wrote to the Provost about the success of another alumnus of the Lower Middle School:

> You will glad to hear that Russell—our Captain—the old Ardingly boy who got an exhibition here in 1873, has been elected scholar of

> Trinity College, Oxford. . . . His conduct and bearing ever since he came to Lancing—a little lad of twelve years old—has been blameless. We have never had a more dignified, a more conscientious, or a more modest Captain of the School since I have had the charge of it.[179]

Thus the "educational ladder" did, in fact, provide a measure of fluidity between classes and sub-classes; because of this it may be described as a "liberal" element in Woodard's scheme, although in a sense the creation of the "ladder" itself strengthened and tightened class distinctions by giving them formal recognition.[180]

8

Closely connected with the Society's scheme for teacher training and with the idea of the educational ladder was the interest displayed by Woodard and Lowe in reducing the cost of residence for the poorer student at the ancient universities.

This interest was by no means an isolated phenomenon. By mid-century concern to make the universities available to poor scholars had resulted in at least three plans. The first, permission for non-collegiate students to fulfil the requirements for a degree, held no attraction for either Lowe or Woodard.[181] The second, the use of college facilities and endowments to enable frugal students to attend existing colleges and halls, was widely mooted. Finally, there were several efforts to establish new institutions at the universities at which poor scholars could enjoy the communal life of residence at a very inexpensive rate.

In 1848 the Reverend E. C. Woollcombe of Balliol suggested that each college should annex a separate building for poor scholars, in which, by the practice of the strictest economy costs could be reduced to £50 per year for each student. He estimated that "the vast majority of undergraduates are living . . . at the rate of full £200 a year".[182] In 1850 "A Member of the Oxford Convocation" deplored the suggestion of founding new institutions for poor scholars when "all the colleges in Oxford are, or ought to be, poor men's colleges"; instead he advocated reorganizing the ancient foundations so that the benefits of a university course would "cost the student no more than £70 or £80 per annum".[183]

In 1858 St Mary's Hall at Oxford actually offered twenty of its twenty-six available sets of rooms to "gentlemen willing to adopt a strictly frugal scale of expenses". Caution money was abolished, rooms were furnished by the Hall, and all meals were taken in common; as a result the total annual cost of tuition, room rent, battels, and wages for servants came to £80 annually, and a "fairly prudent student" could obtain a B.A. for £300 or less. A similar plan was adopted at St Alban's Hall.[184] At St Edmund's Hall, where twenty-five sets of rooms were available, the average annual bill for battels in the 60s was only £73 7*s* 4*d*, and the total cost of three years' residence was also under £300. The Principal showed that like economy could be encouraged by the larger societies.[185]

Dr Lowe also advocated opening existing colleges to poor students. Establishment of a Poor Man's College, he wrote, "suggests . . . little less than sacrilege to the pious memory of ancient founders". Instead he proposed that a careful distinction be made by each college between scholarships and exhibitions, and that the latter be awarded, not for academic excellence, but for need.[186]

Charles Marriott, although he approved Woollcombe's scheme for the expansion of existing institutions, thought it necessary to propose a completely new college for poor men.[187] Just before the onset of his final debilitating illness, he wrote to Woodard:

> I shall probably, after the long vacation, have a Private Hall at which I can receive men at £60 per annum, board and lodging and tuition, payable in advance by £20 per term. I believe this will be more comfortable for men with about £100 per annum than being at a College or Hall such as we have at present. . . . I shall have a printed or lithographed paper of rules for students, and I will send it to you as one of the likely people to know of the right students for me.[188]

A similar idea was in the minds of the founders of Keble and Selwyn Colleges. The proposed Keble College was described as "an institution . . . in which persons of narrow means may educate their sons for Holy Orders. . . . There appear grounds for hoping that the ordinary academical expenses of such a College may be reduced within very narrow limits." The establishment of a separate college for poor scholars seemed to the founders of Keble preferable to any alternative scheme "to engraft [on existing colleges] . . . a large, perhaps overwhelming body of students, taken from a different class . . . bound to an abstinence from the customary modes of social enjoyment".[189] Selwyn College, incorporated at Cambridge in 1882, was modelled on Keble.[190]

In 1870, the year in which Keble College opened, Lord Richard Cavendish, a trustee of the Keble Memorial, wrote to Woodard: "Keble College seems to be a necessary supplement . . . to your scheme, and I hope you will impress this on your friends if you also feel this to be the case, as I think you must."[191] In fact, although he evidently approved the scheme and Keble was popular with boys from S.N.C.,[192] Woodard never gave it any considerable backing.

An interesting, although ephemeral, effort to attract middle-class students to Cambridge resulted in the establishment of Cavendish College in 1876. Founded by Prebendary Brereton, an enthusiastic promoter of middle schools, it was designed to take younger undergraduates than the older colleges, to provide special training for middle-class schoolmasters, and to offer the advantages of a "wise economy".[193] It was recognized by the University as a "public hostel" in 1882; but despite a reorganization in 1888 it collapsed in 1892. A few boys from S.N.C. were resident at this institution.[194]

Woodard's interest in advancing the cause of cheap university education arose from his need for graduate clerical masters. In 1848 he tried to establish fellowships of eight years' duration, of which the first four would be spent at university and the second four teaching at one of the Society's schools.[195] Four years later he proposed eventually to establish a college of his own:

> If we succeed we shall require the labours of a very large body of clergymen—too many to be spared from the present insufficient number. To remedy this, it is our intention to apply, when our plans are more matured, to the universities for licence to open halls or colleges at Oxford and Cambridge where we may educate and board our candidates for degrees at half the present expense.[196]

Marriott's scheme was thwarted by his long illness ending in his death in 1858. Although Woodard was aware of the new system at St Mary's Hall and of Keble College,[197] for some unknown reason he did not wholeheartedly support either. In 1864 Lowe, who, as we have seen was opposed to the idea of a poor man's college, pressed for the adoption of a system of exhibitions to be granted to deserving probationer associates. He reported to Woodard

> what appears to me a new phase in the development of Hurst School. I mean the possibility of a steady supply, if not a numerous one, from the ranks of the probationary associates to the Universities. We have now three. Marc Thomson we help, but the other two, Burrow and Willis, receive nothing from us beyond permission to reside in the vacations. . . . These are indications enough to indicate a movement in this direction. . . . I am sure we ought to get some of our rich friends to found an exhibition or two.[198]

According to the Report of the Schools Inquiry Commission there were six undergraduates from Hurst at Oxford and Cambridge and three at London in 1867; but the Report does not state whether or not they were probationer associates.[199]

In the following decade a proposal was made by which qualified Associates might obtain a B.A. at Durham University after only three terms of residence.[200] But Woodard himself seems to have concentrated his efforts on establishing a cheap college of his own at the two ancient universities.

In a letter to Lowe Woodard hinted that Newman had offered him a site at Oxford.[201] But it was at Cambridge that he made his greatest effort to found a poor man's college in connection with S.N.C. In April 1879 he informed Lowe that he was negotiating for "the site of an old monastery in the Newmarket Road" with about twenty acres attached.

> My plan [he wrote] will be to open a College on a small scale at first only for those of our men . . . who are sure to take honours—with such to make special bargains as to mode of living, habits, and submission to social arrangements and refinements by which they may live there as cheaply as at Ardingly.[202]

The sale of the property took place by auction on 11 July 1879, and Woodard was unsuccessful in his bid.[203] He was not, however, immediately discouraged. Support was obtained from the Bishop of Ely,[204] and in August the Provost wrote of his plan to Lord Salisbury. A principal aim was to increase the ranks of the clergy by preparing boys of the middle and lower middle classes for Holy Orders.

> My plan [he wrote] would be to send up only youths of talent such as I had reason to think would distinguish themselves at the University, and so far lovers of learning as to be willing to live in the humblest possible way with the view of attaining it. They would have their rooms rent-free—tutorage the best possible at a very small

> charge. Their living need not exceed 10*s*. a week, so that with the present rates of University dues, they could get their degrees for a mere song.[205]

Despite an offer of £5,000 towards the project,[206] Woodard never went ahead with his Cambridge plan. Possibly the presence of Cavendish College, and the decision, taken in 1879, to build Selwyn College on the same plan as Keble, discouraged him.[207] In any case the cares and distractions of his expanding school system occupied his whole attention in the 80s, and nothing more was heard of his university scheme.

9

> The Reverend Nathaniel Woodard . . . though he has no claim to be reckoned among Quick's "Educational Reformers", will be remembered as the originator and organizer of a new class of schools which are one of the most marked educational features of this generation.[208]

So read the obituary in the *Athenaeum* on Woodard's death. Undoubtedly the writer was correct in his estimate of Woodard's capacity as a builder and organizer. Neither is there any doubt about the inherent conservatism of the public school ethos and curriculum in the Woodard schools. Furthermore Woodard's fundamental belief in the Church's responsibility for national education might well be regarded as reactionary.

But there were more liberal and inventive aspects of the educational approach of Woodard and his colleagues to which the obituary notice gave no attention. The curriculum of St George's School and of its successor, the Special Department at Hurst,[209] showed that Woodard was by no means tied to the tradition of classical dominance; the institution of the apprenticeship scheme at St Saviour's demonstrated Woodard's perception of occupational opportunities and needs. Dr Lowe's liberal concept of female education, upon which the Midlands girls' schools were founded, was in harmony with such famous developments as Miss Beale's Cheltenham Ladies' College and Miss Buss's Camden Collegiate Schools.[210] St Nicolas College provided an "educational ladder" by which a boy of humble birth might climb to the lofty heights of Oxford or Cambridge, and both Woodard and Lowe took an active interest in the plight of the poor student once he arrived at the universities. The teacher training scheme at Hurst was remarkably ahead of its time; a recent researcher has written that "Canon Woodard was a pioneer in the field of training commercial school masters".[211]

More prominent than any of these liberal practical features of Woodard's educational approach was his effort to preserve the unity of secular and religious teaching by warding off State interference and compromise on the conscience clause issue. The complexity of truth, thought Woodard, could hide the fact that it was one. The tendency of public opinion in Victorian England was towards the removal of definite religious instruction from the required curriculum; in Woodard's view, as in Newman's, this could only result in the disfigurement of truth. Woodard's unrealistic and reactionary view of the nature and function of the Established Church of England had its roots in this positive conviction.

5

THE POLITICAL BACKGROUND

1

It is commonplace that the strength of mid-Victorian Dissent lay in the middle classes. It is generally true that Dissenters expressed themselves politically through the Liberal party, especially through its Radical wing. This triple association of the middle classes, dissenting religion, and Liberal politics in the twenty years after the mid-century lay behind many of Woodard's political attitudes.[1] Especially was this true of his negative views. As in matters theological and pedagogical, so in politics, Woodard knew whom and what he was against and he expressed his antagonisms forcefully. In the summer of 1852 he wrote: "True religion and radicalism cannot at present exist together; an alternative is therefore offered. True religion or radicalism as it is must be sacrificed. Choose one or the other."[2]

This heretic radicalism was, in Woodard's view, a middle-class phenomenon; and until it was rooted out, it was dangerous to contemplate an extension of the franchise to encompass the lower regions of that class, or the class below it. "A new Reform Bill is asked for," wrote Woodard in 1852, "and another class is clamouring to have a voice in providing laws and religion for this great nation. At present the very idea is the height of absurdity. Have they either information or conscientiousness sufficient to guide them in their acts? . . ."

It is noteworthy that Woodard professed not to fear popular political power as such; his anxiety was about the results of an ill-prepared rush into democracy. The danger of a precipitate extension of the franchise was a moral one, and one which could be eliminated. "How large an amount of freedom", wrote Woodard, "may be granted to a people who fear God and who have, by the application of suitable means, had their consciences and judgements exercised to 'discern good from evil'." But the requisite godliness was not possessed by the lower middle classes: "If they are admitted in any large numbers, corruption and bribery or a far worse mischief must ensue. . . . [They] will have, through their representatives, a right to prescribe a religion for this great nation." Things might, of course, be different; for "if they [the middle classes] were educated and trained in religious and conscientious habits . . . no objection . . . could exist to the widest extension of political privileges which the most ultra-radical could desire".[3]

Whiggery, Radicalism, and Dissent comprised the political enemy. At first allied with the Whigs, many Nonconformists became increasingly Radical as Whig and Liberal governments proved reluctant to reduce the rights and privileges of the Established Church. Woodard, whose project depended squarely on the existence and on the vitality of the State Church, not unnaturally took an active and hostile interest in Liberal politics and politicians. No account of the Founder's political views would be complete without some attempt to understand this hostility.

The close alliance formed between the Whigs and Dissenters in the 1820s during the agitation for the Repeal of the Test and Corporation Acts persisted.[4] Civil liberty was associated with religious liberty, and the Whigs professed to be the proponents of both; consequently, after the victory of 1832, Dissenters confidently expected Whig attention to be directed towards removing their principal remaining grievances. In fact, neither the very few Dissenting M.P.s elected in 1833 nor the very large body of their co-religionists in the country could be satisfied with the Government's efforts.[5] Only relatively minor gains were made: in 1836 a national civil registration of births, marriages, and deaths was established, and a rather unsatisfactory amendment was made to the Marriage Act permitting matrimony according to Dissenter's rites. But the universities were not opened to Nonconformists and Church Rates were not abolished.[6]

During the 1830s division among the Whigs prevented successful Radical attack on the property of the Irish Establishment, and the initiative of Sir Robert Peel, together with Whig parliamentary votes, encouraged the English Church to self-reform and consequently to a position of greater strength. The effort to appropriate the Church of Ireland's surplus revenues for secular purposes had been made by both Radicals and Dissenters; the

Established Church Bill of 1836, which proposed the Ecclesiastical Commissioners, was opposed by Nonconformists as well as by extreme High Churchmen, and was passed by the combined efforts of Whigs and Peel's supporters.[7]

The fundamental issue which divided Whigs and Dissenters was the same one which united Radicals and many Dissenters and which eventually carried that alliance into the mature Liberal party. It was the issue of the Establishment.

Overt attacks by Dissenters on the Established Church began early in the 30s. In 1833 the Congregationalists declared against the principles of a State Church. From 1834 Voluntary Church Associations were formed and, in the words of an historian of the Free Churches, "it appeared that English Dissent was at last organized for the overthrow of the Establishment".[8] Although this agitation included by no means all Free Churchmen (the venerable Edward Baines, for example, held aloof), and the Dissenters were not a unified political group, the pressure did mount and the drift of many Dissenters towards Radicalism was accelerated.[9] In 1839 Radicals and Dissenters together formed the Religious Freedom Society; as early as 1837, writes Raymond Cowherd, "the union of Radicals and Dissenters on a platform of the ballot, triennial parliaments, and the exclusion of bishops, was strong enough to win several important constituencies".[10]

As Dissenters and Radicals came together in opposition to the National Church, so too they were often united in support of the Anti-Corn Law League, or, at a different level, of the Peoples' Charter.

The links between Nonconformity and the middle-class League were particularly strong. Cobden was anxious to present the campaign against the Corn Laws as a religious one, and many leaders of the Movement were themselves Nonconformists.[11] Its meetings were often held in chapel buildings, and the General Body of Protestant Dissenting Ministers of the Three Denominations gave its support to the cause.[12] In August 1841, 645 ministers (of whom only two were Anglican) met in support of the League at Manchester and announced that "on scriptural grounds we are called upon to denounce all human restriction upon the supply of food to the people".[13]

Less obtrusive, but very real, were the links between nonconformity and Chartism. Asa Briggs observed that one of three discernible groups within Chartism consisted of "a section of the superior craftsmen, including printers, cobblers, tailors, cabinet makers, booksellers, and small shopkeepers"; these men, often called, "a middle-class set of agitators", were frequently Nonconformists.[14] In Leicester, we are told, "many of the Chartists were active Nonconformists. . . . Chartist activities would sometimes assume a Nonconformist guise."[15] Not surprisingly, it was in moral force Chartism, and in the move to unite Leaguers and Chartists that the Nonconformist elements came to the fore. Joseph Sturge, a Quaker, and Edward Miall, the proprietor of the *Nonconformist*, founded the Complete Suffrage Union in 1841 to unite working-class and middle-class radicalism on a platform of complete manhood suffrage. Although the project ultimately failed, its brief history demonstrated a very considerable amount of Nonconformist ministerial backing.[16]

No doubt the Nonconformist Radicalism of the League alarmed some Anglican landlords, and the brief flight of Chartism terrified many Conservative churchmen;[17] but it was the apparently steady power of the forces ranged against the Established Church, and their gradual absorption into the Liberal Party which frightened Woodard.

The main Radical–Nonconformist campaign against the Establishment started in 1841 when Edward Miall, a Congregationalist minister, started publication of the *Nonconformist*. Although the militant political propaganda in which he engaged repelled some Dissenters, he soon succeeded in rallying a good deal of Nonconformist support for the disestablishment cause. In 1844 Miall promoted the British Anti-State Church Association, a society devoted to electing Dissenters to Parliament and to pledging other candidates against State Churches. In 1853 this organization changed its name to the Society for the Liberation of Religion from State Patronage and Control, and in the same year contributed largely to the election of forty Protestant Dissenters to Parliament.[18]

Miall himself, and the Society of which he was the principal spokesman, tirelessly spread the gospel of disestablishment and continually put pressure on Liberal politicians to adopt the Society's platform. Miall defined the State Church as

> the dispensation of the gospel of Jesus Christ . . . by worldly authority . . . Christianity taken under superintendence by men who, for the

> most part, neither bow to its claims nor appreciate its spirit, nor entertain even a passing care for its ends.

He described three-fourths of the clergy as "men anxious to undertake the duty of teaching divine truth simply that they might share the spoil".[19] For the Whigs' respect for the property of the Establishment such Nonconformist–Radicals had, in 1850, only sarcasm:

> The Whig premier has discovered a spiritual significance [in the Church Rate] that was not known formerly to belong to it. He views it in the light of a "tribute to Almighty God" and "an act of homage from a Christian state".[20]

The Liberation Society pressed its case throughout the 50s and 60s; by the time of the Second Reform Bill its activity had begun to bear fruit. Liberationist influence on Liberal candidates in the 1865 election was important, and it is clear that in the Parliament elected that year Liberationist policy was influential. Indeed the Society drew up a list of measures, passed between 1866 and 1868, for which it took credit. Probably the most important of these was the abolition of Church Rates.[21]

Nor, by 1868, was the Nonconformist-Radical alliance against the State Church channelled entirely through the Liberation Society. The comparatively staid Dissenting Deputies petitioned in favour of the Endowed Schools Bill in 1869 and they opposed later efforts to make it more favourable to the Church.[22] Far more important was the union of Dissenters and Radicals in the National Education League, founded at Birmingham in 1869.

Having discovered that voluntaryism in education played into the hands of the Established Church many Nonconformists were willing, by 1869, to join in the Radical campaign for "universal, compulsory, unsectarian, and free" education.[23] To promote this such Nonconformist-Radicals as Joseph Chamberlain and R. W. Dale founded the League; even before its first public meeting, 2,500 "influential persons" were enrolled as members, including forty M.P.s and between 300 and 400 ministers of religion.[24] Forster's Education Act, with its compromise between voluntary and Board schools and its offer to the Church and other voluntary societies of time to "fill the gaps" in the existing system, was deeply disappointing to the League's supporters. Indeed the Act of 1870, which to ardent churchmen like G. A. Denison seemed the abandonment of Church responsibility for education, failed signally to satisfy any but the most devoted Gladstonians among the Nonconformists.[25]

> In Chamberlain's sight and in the League's [wrote Garvin] and no less in the sight of the Free Churches as a whole and of their leading divines—whose ideal of disestablishment in Great Britain as in Ireland was inseparable from their hope of common schools—the Church of England was now to be doubly established and doubly endowed by the Liberal ministry whom with a boundless enthusiasm . . . they had helped to carry into office.[26]

The disillusioning effect of the Education Act ought not to obscure the continuing Liberalism of the Nonconformist-Radical constituency. The League, according to Herrick, was "frankly partisan politically. Only members of the Liberal party were enrolled; and no attempt was ever made to achieve its special ends through a Conservative Government."[27] The League continued as a nominally independent goad to the less advanced segments of Liberalism throughout the first Gladstone Government. But from 1874 a policy of infiltration was substituted for lobbying; in 1877 the League was dissolved and many of its members became prominent in the new National Liberal Federation.[28]

Neither was the Liberation Society less frankly and radically Liberal. Chamberlain took the chair at a meeting of the Society in 1871.[29] One speaker at the Society's tenth triennial conference in 1874 described the organization as a "wing of the party"; Goldwin Smith proclaimed that the Liberation and Liberal causes were bound together and that the "Tories would never pass disestablishment". It was the purpose of Liberationists not only to assist the Liberal cause, but to make certain of the candidates' satisfactory "views on the disestablishment question". The Reverend J. G. Rogers harangued the Conference:

> Liberals will be nowhere until they agree upon some distinct policy to put before the country, and it remains with the Nonconformists of England to say whether that policy shall be a distinct Nonconformist policy or not.[30]

It is clear that not all Nonconformists were radical Liberals of the League or Liberationist type. It is equally certain that the Nonconformist-Liberals did not control the Liberal party; the success of Forster's bill and the continuance of the English Established Church are enough to demonstrate that. But there is no doubt whatever that Nonconformist-Radicalism was steadily gaining ground in Liberal counsels. Establishment of the National Liberal Federation marked a signal advance; the Liberation Society actively helped right-thinking Liberal candidates in 1880, and by 1891 it had become an officially-recognized auxiliary of the party.[31]

The dangerous doctrine and noisy ways of Nonconformist-Radicals naturally attracted Woodard's attention and undoubtedly coloured his political outlook. Although always wary of Dissent and Radicalism, Woodard's antipathy to Liberal politics seems to have taken final shape only after the Reform Act of 1867.

We have already noticed Woodard's violent reaction to the Endowed Schools legislation;[32] he was terrified that the Act of 1869 would be followed by another enforcing government inspection and examination. To inquire about this he wrote to Forster directly.[33] A week or so before taking this step, he corresponded with J. G. Talbot:

> The question of inspection by Government involves the whole issue of religion or no religion in the schools. This may not appear as it is at present offered to us, but it is useless to blind our eyes to the object of the present ministry.[34]

Nothing came of this threat. But in 1871 the University Tests Act successfully and finally broke down the two most ancient centres of Church privilege. Woodard wrote encouragement to Salisbury as he opposed this legislation:

> This is the last chance. If these things go, all is gone and can never be recovered. It is as obscure as unjust to listen to a few Dissenters who will never form any important part of the Universities. . . . Men are treasuring up curses for their children. The next generation, if left alone, will be Communists.[35]

Woodard had no doubt concerning the root of Liberal sins. "Mr. Gladstone asserts", he wrote in 1879, "and it is admitted on all sides that Dissent is the mainstay of Radicalism. . . . From experience we apprehend it [Radicalism] to be a form of pure selfishness, tending to the disruption of settled government."[36] After the Liberal victory of 1880, he could write: "The country is now fairly in the hands of Dissenters and Sharpers, and with an ignorant population and household suffrage we have a pleasant prospect before us."[37]

Woodard's early comments on Radicalism and Whiggery did not apparently reflect any ill will towards Mr Gladstone, even after he joined Palmerston's government in 1859. We have seen that Woodard early solicited Gladstone's support.[38] In 1856 Gladstone was asked to move a resolution at the famous Brighton meeting;[39] in 1861 he delivered a gracious and much-appreciated speech at Woodard's great Oxford meeting.[40] As late as 1865, when Gladstone was defeated at Oxford, Woodard could write:

> At the termination of your connection with Oxford it is satisfactory to me to learn that on every occasion the whole staff of St Nicolas College have recorded their votes in your favour. And better still, as a pledge of the future, every boy educated by us who has reached the degree of M.A. has also given a like support. We have always felt that you specially represented the three leading ideas of Oxford—Religion, Learning, and Progress.[41]

This sanguine opinion did not survive the educational legislation of Gladstone's first year as Prime Minister. In fact, Woodard's change of heart dated from Gladstone's announcement, in March 1868, of his determination to disestablish the Irish Church. On 27 April of that year the Provost wrote to Lowe:

> If Mr Gladstone pleads conscience and duty it is to be hoped other people will do the same. . . . I shall in a quiet but constant and earnest way oppose all his doings. He will be backed by all the mob and ignorance of the town constituencies, but his old friends will now be obliged to work against him.[42]

As we have noticed, Woodard soon became convinced of the nefarious influence of Radicalism and Dissent in Liberal circles. As this conviction took hold upon him, he was quite unable to dissociate Gladstone from the party of which he was the leader and dominant personality. In 1869, Woodard's friend, T. A. Maberley, congratulated the Provost on breaking "altogether with Gladstone and his 'infidel' government".[43] In 1877 Woodard attributed "reckless daring" and "darkest wickedness" to the Liberal statesman.[44] A year before he rebuked Gladstone directly:

> When I read . . . your very able articles in the Contemporary Review, and consider the enormous circulation which they secure for that Review, with the flood of criminal errors with which the other articles in it, almost without exception, abound, I am led to inquire how a man of your reverent temper of mind . . . can fail to see that

> your . . . commanding influence [is] . . . made the instrument in spreading among the unlearned, as well as the more educated, blasphemies as bold and barefaced as any age has been a witness of.[45]

2

"The Christian religion in a Christian country," wrote the Earl of Selborne in 1866, ". . . is a Conservative principle." He went on to state the obverse truth:

> It follows that in a well-governed state the political leanings of the clergy of an ancient historical Church . . . may be expected to be generally towards that party which represents the principle of stability rather than change.[46]

That defence of the Establishment was a Conservative principle throughout the nineteenth century was undoubtedly true. That this support was reciprocated by the ordinary parochial clergy seems to be indicated by some recent research.[47] But the Evangelicals could not always be counted on, and "the rising Broad Church school, represented by Dean Stanley and Jowett, was naturally inclined to enlist under the banner of progress".[48] Furthermore, as we shall see, the Oxford reformers were far from dependable Tories. Nevertheless it is probably true to say that the mass of the clergy and prominent laity, particularly those to whom the epithet "High Church" (but not "Tractarian") could be applied, were solidly Tory. Thus Froude's father with his whiggishly Erastian view of the Church could be described as a High Churchman and a Tory "of the old school".[49] On the other hand such *bona fide* High Churchmen as the members of the Hackney Phalanx, who combined an exalted view of the Church with firm adherence to the principle of Establishment, were Tories also.[50]

On the face of it Woodard's anti-Radical, anti-Dissent, anti-Liberal opinions were but the negative side of this High Church Toryism, the main tenet of which was defence of the Establishment with its privileges. Certainly Woodard was not reluctant to express Tory opinions positively. He apparently hinted at the identity of Churchmanship and Conservatism when he impressed Salisbury with the political importance of gaining the middle classes to the Church. "Every Tory and every churchman", he wrote in 1880, "sees and confesses how much depends on the middle classes."[51] A year before he had pointed out: "It is . . . not too much to say that the Conservative weakness in the House of Commons is to be sought in its Scotch and Welsh members. Both these divisions of the country are lost to the Church of England."[52]

Very many of Woodard's chief supporters were prominent Tories and vigorous supporters of the Established Church. Earl Nelson, the Earl of Shrewsbury, Lord Redesdale, J. G. Hubbard, Beresford Hope, and the Marquess of Salisbury were all vice-presidents of the pro-Tory, anti-Liberationist Church Defence Institution;[53] and they were all keen Woodard partisans. Lord John Manners and the Earl of Carnarvon were staunch supporters of St Nicolas College. Less prominent but vitally important contributors like Sir Percival Heywood, Henry Meynell, and Walter Burrell were all Tories.[54] Lord Salisbury, at least, believed in the natural Toryism of churchmen. "It has been observed", he remarked in 1864, "that no one can be a good Conservative who is not also a good churchman. I beg to invert the proposition. Depend upon it, no churchman exists worthy of the name who is not also a good Conservative."[55] It is perhaps not surprising that Salisbury, the senior trustee of St Nicolas College, should find it necessary in 1872 "to deprecate the suspicion . . . of [S.N.C.] being a political, or, to speak frankly, a Tory organization".[56]

Even if the personal opinions of Woodard, the known political views of his supporters, and the anti-Church bias of Liberal Nonconformists and Radicals were to be put aside, there is still direct evidence, especially in Woodard's letters to Salisbury after 1880, of a Tory political purpose in St Nicolas College. In 1880 the Provost reminded Salisbury that though "these schools do not profess to deal with politics . . . naturally they influence a good many people".[57] In the following year he wrote:

> I was a Tory . . . before you were born, and my one remedy for all this shifting work has been and is to secure the "Lower Middle Class". . . . Had my advice been taken years ago, we might now have had hundreds of thousands of boys of that class in the way of forming habits of order.[58]

In 1882, he was willing to describe the purpose of S.N.C. as twofold: to "recover the body of the middle classes to the Church and to sound political sense".[59] On another occasion he was quite specific about the political effect of the schools in Sussex:

> I do not wish or even like to refer to my own work and its effects, but it is a notorious fact that whatever may be the cause, the political aspect of affairs in this county has changed *absolutely* since my work began. We have cleared out all the Radicals, and have now but *one* Whig M.P. in the county, and he holds his seat on sufferance. What share the thousands of young men who have gone through our schools have had in effecting this change here and the Home Counties generally I know not, but the change itself cannot be called in question.[60]

Whether or not Woodard was over-optimistic in his estimate of the influence of St Nicolas College (as he almost certainly was when he said in 1885 that "out of our very large and extended Society, not a single man would vote other than I do")[61] is not easy to determine. But that Woodard wished to convince Salisbury of the Society's political significance, and of the Tory nature of that significance, there can be no doubt.

Most of the evidence shows Woodard to have been a strong Tory; and such a conclusion is to be expected concerning one whose social and educational plans involved heavy dependence on an Established Church. But there is another strain in the evidence which casts some doubt on the orthodoxy of Woodard's High Church Toryism. This disturbing element makes it unlikely that Woodard could have agreed unconditionally to Salisbury's robust identification of churchman and Conservative.

In 1857 Woodard evidently joined Lowe in voting for the Liberal candidate, and in so doing, drew the wrath of a local Tory:

> I cannot see how we shall be able to resist or defend in future a charge of inconsistency among the High Church party in Sussex if we should find Mr A. Wagner, Mr Maberley and others voting one way, and you and Mr Lowe the other, and yet all professing the same political as well as religious principles.[62]

Undoubtedly the Provost's anti-Liberalism intensified in the 60s, and reached a pitch during Gladstone's first administration; and it is very unlikely that the episode of 1857 was ever repeated. But Woodard was not by any means happy about the alternative of Disraeli's Conservatism. Although, in 1874, he expressed perfect confidence in Salisbury, he was dubious about the rest of the government. "We can feel assured", he wrote to Salisbury, "that you and one or two of your colleagues are unlikely to be drawn aside by the Protestant rabies. . . . A few fanatics place their trust in Mr Disraeli, but confidence is assured by your name."[63]

The Public Worship Regulation Act, and the debates which preceded its passage, confirmed Woodard's fears. In 1878 he pointed out to Salisbury that "the High Church clergy no doubt have a grievance and look with a jealous eye on the acts of the government in Church matters".[64] Two years later, after the fall of the Beaconsfield administration, he remarked that "the late ministry was sadly deficient and unwisely narrow in dealing with Church matters".[65] Somewhat more explicit was his comment to Lowe a year later:

> The Tories at present are mere conjurors. They have no policy, and are too selfish to create one. The inertness of matter at the Creation was not more complete than is the hypostasis of selfishness in landowners.[66]

In 1884 Woodard's criticism of the Tory party drew Lord Beauchamp's wrath:

> To recommend the scheme you have at heart it is not necessary to attack the Conservative party. It may be true that they have not done enough for the Church or for dogmatic truth, but it must be remembered that for thirty years they have been held in check by the admiration entertained by yourself and others for Mr Gladstone.[67]

It is clear that some of Woodard's antipathy to Disraeli's government can be explained by the Prime Minister's avowed intention to "put down ritualism".[68] But at the root of the ambiguity in Woodard's Toryism was an uncertainty in his support of the principle of Establishment. On one hand, as we have noticed at some length, the existence of an Established Church was of basic importance to his educational approach. Indeed he clung tenaciously to the principle of a genuinely national Church long after it had ceased to be realistic.[69] But, as we have seen elsewhere, he was not willing to sacrifice the independent authority of a Catholic Church for the establishment of an Erastian but un-Catholic one.[70] This concern for the orthodoxy and independent authority of the Church is reflected in his scathing remarks on the bishops in 1875:

> The bishops are in terror lest they should be turned out of the House and the Church be disestablished, and they are at their wits' ends to know how to reconcile people of all creeds by a universal toleration.

It never enters their heads that they have the Gospel to uphold and the people to instruct in the *truth*. On the contrary, if they *allow* the truth to be taught, they bargain for liberty to teach error, and promise the people that if they will suffer a few maniacs to teach the doctrines of the sacraments and not cause a disturbance they will see that the true Protestant principles are taken care of.[71]

No such qualms bothered the Tory leaders. Tory policy demanded a defence of the Church Establishment pure and simple; it was not politically prudent to insist on a Catholic establishment, or even to defend the Church on theological grounds. Peel defended the Establishment (and perhaps saved it) not on theological but on utilitarian grounds. Disraeli's expressed reasons for supporting the Establishment were historical and cultural rather than theological:

Broadly and deeply planted in the land, mixed up with all our manners and customs, one of the main guarantees of our local government, and therefore one of the prime securities of our common liberties, the Church of England is part of our history, part of our life, part of England itself.[72]

He regarded an Established Church as a guarantee of toleration and an agency through which the State might influence the religious feeling of the country.[73] Even Salisbury, although no mean theologian and very much interested in making the Church into the embodiment of religious truth in the Tractarian sense, yet failed to resign from Disraeli's government despite its anti-Puseyite Endowed Schools policy and his leader's ultra-protestant view of the Public Regulation Bill. Salisbury was very urgent in his defence of Church endowment,[74] and in 1885 he devoted a good part of his election campaign to a defence of the principle of a State Church.[75]

Woodard's occasional lapses from wholehearted defence of the principle of Establishment, and hence from ardent political Conservatism, can be explained by his prime concern for religious truth. If Catholic truth and the principle of Establishment should conflict, it was the latter which must give way. It is hardly necessary to say that, however lightly Woodard may sometimes have taken his Conservatism, he was not tempted to adopt that Radical-Liberal policy which he so vigorously denounced. Except for the one early vote in 1857 there is no indication that his revulsion at the Conservatives had anything but a negative effect. That effect was a temptation to withdraw from political activity, and a growing feeling that such activity was futile. "The most that the best of governments can do in these days", he wrote to Salisbury in 1879, "is to dilute the poison administered to ancient principles."[76] A year later he wrote to Lowe in a moment of despair: "What you say about politics no longer interests me. Politics is no longer divine, nor is God's name or God's honour ever so much as referred to in it."[77]

3

Woodard's occasional lapses from habitual Tory conviction, no less than the normal strength of that conviction and the clear political aim of St Nicolas College, raise the question of the connection between politics and Anglo-Catholicism generally.

Historians have differed radically in their views of the relationship between the leaders of the Oxford Movement and the Tory party. G. Kitson Clark asserted that they "were not on the whole natural Conservatives", and R. B. McDowell takes the view that the Oxford Movement did nothing to strengthen the ties between Conservatives and the Church. More recently Eugene Fairweather has expressed the view that the chief Tractarians, though "conservative-minded", had "little feeling for political reform as such" and no interest "in the preservation of political monarchy or aristocracy". On the other hand, H. V. Faulkner characterized the politics of the Movement as "ultra-Tory", and John Tulloch described the Movement as a "new Toryism, or designed to be such, as well as a new Sacerdotalism". J. A. Froude portrayed Tractarianism as "Toryism in ecclesiastical costume". Newman and Keble, wrote Christopher Dawson, adhered to the classical High Church alliance with Conservatism, although Hurrell Froude reacted violently against it.[78]

Personally, wrote Tulloch, Keble was a "Tory of the old school to whom the Church of England was not only dear, but to whom there was no other Church".[79] He strongly supported the ultra-Tory Sir Robert Inglis against Peel in 1829 when Peel came out in favour of Catholic Emancipation.[80] Georgina Battiscombe, in her biography of Keble, demonstrates his confirmed Toryism and his absolute opposition to political reform.[81] Pusey was less firmly rooted. In 1865 he stated:

> I could have been a Tory; but 1830 ended Toryism. I could not be a mere Conservative, i.e. I could not bind myself or risk the future of the Church on the fidelity or wisdom of persons whose principle it is to keep what they think they can and part with the rest.[82]

Newman, though a firm anti-revolutionary and outspoken in opposition to the Whigs when they attacked the Church after 1832, evidently did not take much interest in politics as such. He certainly never aligned himself with the official Tory party and, in 1841, was capable of drastic criticism of Peel and his educational philosophy.[83]

Hurrell Froude was always an opponent of the traditional alliance between the Church and Conservatism. He composed a sonnet entitled "Farewell to Toryism", and he wrote against "Erastianism and Conservative compromise".[84]

But the contemporary attack on the Church made all the Tract writers anti-Liberal; and this, in itself, tended to propel them towards Conservatism. Thus, for example, Tract 83 is a negative expression of Toryism in 1838:

> Satan . . . promises you civil liberty, he promises you equality; he promises you trade and wealth; he promises you a remission of taxes; he promises you reform. . . . He tempts you to rail against your rulers and superiors. . . . He promises you illumination. . . . He scoffs at times gone by; he scoffs at every institution which reveres them.[85]

In fact, although the Tractarians were themselves anti-Liberal, and although the Movement "had its rise in the political shocks . . . by which the First Reformed Parliament curried popularity",[86] yet the Oxford Movement was not a political but an ecclestiastical stirring. It was primarily a theological and devotional movement; both its theology and its devotion centred on the Church.

It so happened that this Church was an Established one; and it is perfectly true that the Movement did make some effort to defend the principle of Establishment. Thus, in Tract 59, Newman stated that

> we are very naturally jealous of the attempts that are making to disunite, as it is called, Church and State; which in fact, means neither more nor less . . . than a general confiscation of Church property and a repeal of the few remaining laws which make the true Church the Church of England.

But preservation of the Establishment was not the primary aim of the Oxford Reformers; the purification and the maintenance of the Church of England as a true Church were their principal ambitions. Consequently even the author of Tract 59 could foresee a day when "state protection" might be replaced by "state interference" and when the Establishment would become a hindrance rather than an asset.[87]

Hurrell Froude early decided that "the country is too bad to deserve an Established Church".[88] Keble was "prepared to separate the two words 'Established Church' and to visualize the Church without the Establishment".[89] Newman came to the conclusion that disestablishment (or some approach to it) was imminent. He went on to comment:

> I confess I have before now had a great repugnance to the notion ... and if I have overcome it and turned from the Government to the People, it has been simply because I was forced to do so. It is not we who desert the Government, but the Government that has left us.[90]

Never was this stream of Tractarian thought better expressed than by Pusey in 1865:

> I believe that we are in the course of an inevitable Revolution; that the days of Establishments are numbered, and that the Church has to look to her purity, liberty, faithfulness to Catholicism, while I fear that the Conservatives would corrupt her in order to increase the numerical strength of the Establishment.[91]

Although it would be misleading to indicate a sharp and clear division, it is true that the post-Tractarian generation of Anglo-Catholics divided roughly into two categories. On one hand were those whose religious views sought embodiment in Conservative political activity, particularly in defence of the Established Church; on the other hand were those whose religious convictions demanded no such political defence of the Establishment and who viewed the State Church with varying degrees of distaste.

Into the first class naturally fell a group of politicians and Woodard supporters of whom Lord Salisbury, Lord Carnarvon, J. G. Hubbard, and (although to a less certain extent) Beresford Hope were leading figures. It is not always easy to distinguish such men from old High Churchmen of the Joshua Watson and William Cotton type. But at any rate by 1860 such distinctions were probably somewhat artificial; Hope himself remarked that year on "the extinction of those causes of difference, which, in earlier days, separated the 'new' from the 'old' school of High Churchmen".[92]

Of Salisbury's devotion to the Establishment and of his identification of Churchmanship and Conservatism it is not necessary to say more. On the other hand his religion was unquestionably influenced by the Oxford Revival. Lady Gwendolen Cecil noted that he subscribed to the "principles of the Church Revival, generally known as the Oxford Movement". He maintained a strict rule of weekly Communion and his close friend Carnarvon allowed that he had "the character of a ritualist".[93] This was a somewhat extreme statement, for there is no indication that Salisbury had any particular sympathy with advanced ceremonial;[94] neither was he in favour of the revival of regular and general auricular confession in the Church of England.[95] Yet neither of these was strictly necessary to the Anglo-Catholic position, and there can be little doubt that Salisbury's religion owed much to the Oxford Movement.

Carnarvon, whose opinions in matters political and religious were very close to Salisbury's,[96] was probably less personally associated with Anglo-Catholicism than was his friend. He was a vigorous defender of the Establishment and he was regarded as a "trusty champion" of the "clerical party".[97] Far from being a ceremonialist himself, and out of sympathy with the "highly emotional services of the extreme High Church party", he yet had great sympathy with the Ritualists, and he was not afraid to defend them against the attacks of such Protestant extremists as Lords Cairns and Shaftesbury.[98]

Associated by Archbishop Tait with Salisbury and Carnarvon as friends of the Ritualists were J. G. Hubbard and Beresford Hope, both Conservative Members of Parliament.[99] Hubbard, although not an extreme ritualist, built and endowed St Albans church, Holborn, and secured the famous ritualist, A. H. Mackonochie as incumbent.[100] Hope, though always a "churchman and a Conservative", was something of a political oddity. He followed Peel against protection in 1846, and his lasting dislike of Disraeli probably cost him ministerial office.[101] Furthermore he was quite adamant on the political neutrality of sound churchmanship, a view he found compatible with vigorous defence of the Establishment. He was, for example, opposed to making "Mr Gladstone's joining the Coalition cabinet [in 1852] a reason for withholding from him the confidence of any churchmen on the old-fashioned idea of churchman and Tory being correlative terms".[102] Like the members of Young England, Hope was early influenced by Frederick Faber and his religion was decidedly Anglo-Catholic.[103]

Associated with Hope in the Cambridge wing of Tractarianism were Lord John Manners and George Smythe,[104] the romantic Young Englanders who in the 1840s sought to infuse chivalry and Catholicism into the Tory party. Manners "believed . . . that the cause of the people was knit up inextricably with the cause of the Church. He took his stand upon the principles of Oxford. . . . To him . . . the religious aspect of the movement [Young England] was all-important." The Church, in Manner's view, "was a Church of the whole people, the centre of a revived religious life, a general and diffused worship".[105] Young England is remembered principally as a phase in Disraeli's rise to power; but Manners remained a High Churchman and a Conservative as well as a very vigorous supporter of the Woodard schools. He was Postmaster-General in Disraeli's cabinet of 1874, and in Salisbury's cabinet of 1885; with Salisbury and Carnarvon he was recognized as one of the few advanced churchmen in the Government of 1874.[106]

Politicians formed the most obvious group of Tory Anglo-Catholics, even if sometimes they were far from extreme in their churchmanship. More rigid in their theological views, if perhaps less consistent champions of the united cause of Established Church and Conservative Party, were the two great Anglo-Catholic leaders in education: Nathaniel Woodard and G. A. Denison.

Of Woodard's keen Conservatism and defence of the Establishment it is not necessary to write more. Denison, an equally devoted Anglo-Catholic, was no less a Tory. Unlike many others influenced by the Tractarians (e.g. W. F. Hook and Beresford Hope), Denison withdrew his support from Gladstone when the latter joined the Coalition government in 1852.[107] Many years later he described Gladstone as "identified with all the steps of the downward move in English politics which is steadily on its way to the ruin of the Constitution of England in Church and State".[108] Liberalism, thought Denison, was leading to democracy, a system which "deprecates what is high [and] . . . panders to what is low". Violently opposed to the "political heresy" of Erastianism he was yet (except for a brief period)[109] a vigorous supporter of the Establishment.

Some of those who were vigorous in their defence of the Church and not reluctant to employ political means to forward that end sought, at least occasionally, to work outside the existing party structure. In the summer of 1856, for example, Woodard envisaged a distinct Church party both in local constituencies and in Parliament itself. On 4 July he wrote to Gladstone:

> Your support may, in the hands of God, be the pivot on which success may turn. Sooner or later we must have a distinct Church party in the House of Commons, and whenever that is tried my conviction is that some of the best judges will find that they have miscalculated the strength of the Church party in the country.[110]

In the following month he wrote to his friend William Campion:

> I think thoughtful laymen must begin to see that if we are to be a Parliamentary Church a deep responsibility rests upon them to promote the election to Parliament of only such men as are consistent churchmen. . . . I am satisfied that a large Church party can be formed all over the kingdom and, if not at present the largest party, yet a party sufficiently strong to turn the elections.[111]

In fact a species of voluntary "Church Cabinet" was mooted in the 1840s, to consist of "a council of Churchmen, lay and clerical, of proved capacity, who should exercise a central influence in London on Church matters over a Church party which was willing to accord to it its confidence". At first called the "Watching Committee on Church Matters" this "cabinet" became the "Committee of the London Union on Church Matters" and remained very active until 1859, by which date, according to Beresford Hope, its activity declined as "churchmen could not be persuaded of the desirability of renewing and maintaining their organization as a party". In its last year of active work the committee had stirred up opposition to legalizing marriage with a deceased wife's sister, acted in the Church Rate question, and given encouragement to an Anglo-Catholic priest being attacked on the question of confession. Still to be attended to by a Church Party in 1860 wrote Hope, were "the maintenance of the residue of our marriage law, the defence of the prayer book, the foiling of the Liberation conspiracy".[112] The work of the English Church Union, and that of the Church Defence Institution (to which many politically-

Conservative Anglo-Catholics, such as Hubbard, Hope, and Salisbury belonged) undoubtedly continued the work of this rather vague body.

At the opposite end of the political spectrum of Anglo-Catholicism were those men, chiefly priests and ritualists, who not only refused to defend the Establishment, but who positively campaigned against it. Some such men were really disengaged from active political life and devoid of strong party conviction. Others, though equally reluctant to identify the Church with a political party, or even to see the Church itself as an active political issue, nevertheless found themselves compelled to assume a radical and even a socialist position because of their convictions.

The politically neutral ritualists are well typified by A. H. Mackonochie and W. J. E. Bennett, both prominent and controversial clerics. Mackonochie, from 1862 to 1882 pastor of St Alban's, Holborn, the church built by J. G. Hubbard, was an advanced ceremonialist and frequently prosecuted by the Church Association. All the traditions of his family were Conservative. But if he was formally a Tory, he was not an active one and was far from an orthodox dependable party man. Indeed he denied a principal tenet of Toryism: the perpetuation of the Church of England as an Establishment. He was described as a Liberationist[113] and he once remarked: "Let the State send forth the Church roofless and penniless, but free, and I will say 'Thank you'."[114]

Very similar were the views of W. J. E. Bennett, from 1840 to 1852 priest-in-charge of St Paul's, Knightsbridge, and thereafter Vicar of Frome in Somerset. Although described as "on the whole" a Conservative, he had no love for Disraeli[115] and he was outspoken in his desire for disestablishment. In 1862 he wrote:

> The question is—can we work our divine mission, can we go into the streets of our great towns as a Church? The answer is—not with the continuance of the junction of the Church with the State.[116]

The practical political neutrality which characterized these men and which they combined with definite views on the desirability of Church disestablishment bore a close resemblance to some of the opinions of the early Tractarian leaders. But there were others who not only rejected active Conservatism and refused to defend the Establishment, but who actually took up Radicalism. This they did primarily because they perceived in their parishes social problems which required Radical and even Socialist solutions. Unlike the Tory Anglo-Catholics, they were undaunted by the Liberationist cry and welcomed disestablishment pressure within the Liberal party.

A foreruuner of such men was W. F. Hook, the famous Vicar of Leeds and later Dean of Chichester. He differed from the later Radical and Socialist ritualists in not condemning the Establishment outright, although he "thought that many High Churchmen . . . dwelt too much on that aspect of the Church", and he was willing that the Church should abandon its ancient function as national educator.[117] Furthermore, although he was sympathetic to Tractarian doctrine and was regarded by the Tract writers as the principal instance "of one who worked out in a large parochial sphere fully and freely the principles which they taught";[118] yet Hook was no ritualist. Nevertheless, like the radical ritualists of the next generation his political views were turned leftward by his parochial experience: "I was . . . born and bred a Tory. When I devoted myself to the manufacturing districts, my sympathies being easily excited, I became heart and soul a Radical."[119] In 1851 he wrote to W. Page Wood, also a "strong High Churchman and advanced liberal": "Social reform is the grand point which must occupy the mind of the philanthropic politician for the next half-century. . . . We must have some working men in the House."[120] A. H. Stanton, who remained a priest at St Alban's, Holborn, for fifty years after 1862, adopted similar social and political views, and added to them extreme ritualism and cordial distaste for the Establishment. In 1871, according to his biographer, Stanton

> watched the course of events in France with eager interest; he "rejoiced" to see Liberty, Fraternity, Equality, on the walls of Paris; and he resolved to make those watchwords realities among the people whom he served.

He was a "Radical to the backbone", and entertained a very negative view of the principle of Establishment:

> "Mention Church and State to me," he once exclaimed, "and it is like shaking a red cloth before a mad bull. . . . For to me the whole thing seems like a religious get-up for the well-to-do."[121]

In 1877, another Anglo-Catholic priest, Stewart Headlam, founded the Guild of St Matthew, described by S. C. Carpenter as "the first English Socialist Society".[122] Among other Radical notions, Headlam disseminated his own "idea of Disestablishment", one which involved "doing away with patronage and patrons altogether . . . giving people the right to choose their own clergy".[123]

A few years later, in 1885, the Reverend Robert Dolling was put in charge of St Agatha's, Landport. He condemned the traditional "subservience of the Church of England . . . to the interests of political Conservatism", and "her timid hesitancy . . . or total apathy where social wrong ought to have been rebuked". He campaigned actively for the Radical candidate, and he leaned heavily towards Socialism.[124] As might be expected he was in favour of disestablishment:

> A free Church can reform herself, a fettered Church never. . . . If our Establishment forbids us to reform, let us burst our bonds and set ourselves free.[125]

As Tory Anglo-Catholics joined the Church Defence Institution, so many of those ritualists who adopted the radical policy of disestablishment in 1877 formed the Church League for the Separation of Church and State. Among others Mackonochie and another ritualist Bryan King contributed to the League's pamphlets.[126] Even G. A. Denison, in a brief period of disgust at the Establishment, joined the League and published a pamphlet under its auspices.[127] Encouraged, no doubt, by such accessions to the cause, the Liberation Society itself appealed to churchmen and published a pamphlet by a "High Church Rector" vigorously advocating disestablishment for the Church's own good.[128]

Mid-way between Catholic Conservatives and Catholic Radicals were those who, like Dr Lowe, formed Mr Gladstone's personal following.

Lowe's devotion to Gladstone is clear both in his letters to the Liberal leader[129] and in his correspondence with Woodard. Lowe, as we have seen, held certain relatively liberal educational views; but he was not an advanced political Liberal and was never, for example, in favour of either Welsh or English Church disestablishment.[130] He wrote to Gladstone in 1888 complaining of the difficulty which attached to his position as a Liberal in St Nicolas College:

> Experience and long deliberation convince me that my first duty is to the cause of Church education in which I have been working for

forty years. . . . Under the unfortunate prejudice, in matters political, that influences the large majority of my brother churchmen, lay as well as clerical, I should seriously shake confidence with them if I appeared as a public supporter of a political question at the present time, even when, like the Home Rule question, it appears to me to be based on the first principles of religion.[131]

Enough has been written about the political attitudes of the Tractarian leaders themselves to indicate that strain in their thought which resulted in the development of a radical disestablishment wing in Anglo-Catholicism. This development was bitterly resented by those Anglicans who remained politically active as Tories and friends of the Establishment. As early as 1868 the development of "High Church Radicalism" was condemned:

Forgetting the advantages of the ancient statutes, rights, and privileges of the Church of England [these men] appear willing not only to sacrifice many of them, but . . . to co-operate with Ultramontane Roman Catholics and political Dissenters in promoting the eventual disestablishment of that Church. . . . This policy . . . energizes and finds many defenders, and is seriously weakening the ancient alliance between the clergy and the Constitutional party. . . . This school of thought belongs to what is popularly known as the 'Tractarian' or 'High Church party'.[132]

During Disraeli's administration from 1874 to 1880 this Radical Anglo-Catholic feeling was exacerbated by the Prime Minister's stand on the Public Worship Regulation Bill, and by the persecution of Ritualists. By 1880 Salisbury could write:

I am very gloomy as to the future of the High Church party as conducted by the younger generation of High Churchmen. I fear they are likely to become an element in English society of a less and less Conservative character.[133]

Woodard agreed, and pointed to a specific example of the realization of such a fear:

The impression of the Highest Churchmen is that the Conservatives are their enemies, and in this way . . . the highest or ritualistic party carried the election in Brighton against their avowed principles. . . . I am surprised to find how many people there are, High Church or on the road that way, who complain of the Church policy of the late government.[134]

4

In the mind of Nathaniel Woodard the educational and social mission of St Nicolas College could be discharged only within the framework of an Established Church. But in the very years during which Woodard's organization was expanding and his plans were maturing, opposition to the principle of Establishment also grew apace. This opposition, which emanated largely from Nonconformist circles, increasingly assumed a Liberal aspect. Neither that party nor its leader was ever converted to disestablishment; yet the Nonconformist–Radical element in it became a very considerable power. At any rate, by the 70s and 80s Woodard clearly regarded Liberalism as dominated by its Nonconformist-Radical wing and consequently he viewed the Liberal party as the foe of the Church and of St Nicolas College.

Because the Tory party continued its traditional role as defender of the Church, Woodard was a strong Tory, and quite willing to see his own organization serve the Conservative party as well as the Church of England. In this sense, and to the extent that the majority of his supporters were Conservatives (some were prominent Conservatives), St Nicolas College was an active political force.

But despite Woodard's customary Tory enthusiasm there is puzzling evidence of his occasional detachment from active political encounter, from the Conservative party, and even from the principle of Establishment. The problem posed by this evidence is diminished when it is recalled that Woodard was a devoted Anglo-Catholic.

To the academic clergy of Oxford in the 30s and 40s the value of the connection between Church and State was not always clear. Despite their exaltation of sacramental doctrine (which itself would seem to break down the barrier between material and spiritual, between sacred and secular, between Nation and Church), the Tractarians possessed a strong conviction of the Church's proper freedom and independence. This conviction they passed on to the ritualist priests of the next and subsequent generations.

Persecuted by the judicial organs of Church and State these ritualist clergymen were insistent in their demands for freedom to pursue their priestly calling, often among the poor and neglected classes. Consequently they advocated disestablishment and they opposed traditional Church Conservatism. As they moved into the slums and came to grips with the evils of industrial society, such men as Stanton, Dolling, and Headlam sought to Christianize the nation not through Establishment, but in the activity of a free Church and through left-wing political action.

But Woodard, despite occasional outbursts of impatience and even disgust at the State Church, was an Anglo-Catholic who could find no substitute for the Establishment as an effective means of instilling Christianity into the general life of England. Nor, despite the vagaries of Church policy under Disraeli, could he abandon the Conservative party as the effective political agency of that Establishment. In these views he was united to G. A. Denison, the other great Anglo-Catholic educator, and to most of the important politicians who absorbed significant amounts of Tractarian influence.[135] Educators and politicians alike were in a position to see and value the ways in which the official recognition of religion promoted the penetration of Christianity into the secular life of England. And it was from these men that St Nicolas College received its most consistent and loyal support.

6

INFLUENCE AND COMPETITION

1

Concern about the educational needs of the middle classes was evident well before Woodard published his *Plea*. Churchmen shared this concern; and, as we have seen, not a few of the first practical efforts to meet these needs were undertaken by churchmen. Indeed it was a group of priests and laymen who, under the auspices of the National Society, first sought to provide a national system of middle-class schools.[1]

But the early efforts of the Church in this field, where they were successful, were fragmentary. It was not until Woodard began his work that the Established Church gained a really effective agency in the sphere of middle-class education. Recognized as the founder and manager of a growing Society, Woodard soon became the object of inquiries, requests, invitations, and offers from other men who had come to realize the vital importance of middle-class education. Indeed Woodard's influence spread far beyond the limits of the Established Church; as we shall see, he was consulted by Dissenters, by Government commissioners, by representatives of foreign states, and he was invited to extend his enterprise into the most remote colonies.

A great many people pressed Woodard for help of one kind or another; but many others wrote to him simply for information or advice and expressed no desire to be closely connected with the Society or to share its resources. Among these inquirers were agents of Government like John P. Fearon, who wrote in 1850 to ask about Woodard's financial arrangements at Hurst. The Charity Commissioners, of whom he was a representative, were about to convert an endowed school into a middle-class school and looked to St Nicolas College for a model.[2] Twenty-three years later Lord Lyttelton sought information to guide the work of the Endowed Schools Commissioners:

> The economical arrangement of your schools, particularly St John's and Ardingly, is a matter of great interest to us here, as we have in our schemes to fix the scale of payments of all kinds.[3]

The British Government was not alone in seeking information from Woodard. In 1861, Edward Fusco, who was about to "fill an office in the Ministry of Public Instruction in Italy", wrote requesting "the particulars, . . . constitution, regulations, and plan of instruction" in Woodard's schools.[4] In the next year William Ford of Gray's Inn introduced Woodard to a representative of the Russian government as "the chief authority in England for middle schools".[5] The Russian, Charles Warrand, wrote to Woodard:

> My mission in England . . . is to endeavour to obtain . . . opinions or remarks on projects for educational reform in Russia. I take the liberty of sending you a copy of a Project for the General Scholastic Establishment—i.e. for lower middle education, in the Empire. The favour I want to ask of you is to honour us with your opinion thereon . . . to present to my government on my return to St Petersburgh.[6]

Warrand was unable to accept an invitation to visit Shoreham, but Woodard did comment on the Russian plan.[7]

As his advice was sought by men outside the United Kingdom, so too his opinion was looked for by people outside the Established Church. In 1881 the head of the "Nonconformist Grammar School at Bishop's Stortford", a man "anxious to arouse the Congregational body to a sense of their responsibilities" in the field of middle-class education, asked Woodard for information about his schools. He was sent a pamphlet and an offer of further help if desired.[8] F. C. Pritchard in his book *Methodist Secondary Education* observed that Woodard's example "did much to influence those members of the Methodist connection whose thoughts were turning more and more towards higher education".[9]

Not surprisingly, most of those who sought advice from Woodard were churchmen. Occasionally requests came from well-known sources. The National Society, which was again making plans to take up the cause of middle schools, consulted Woodard in 1860.[10] On 8 December 1864, the Archbishop of York sought advice; he and others had "some thoughts of an experiment in Yorkshire of a . . . kind" similar to St Nicolas College.[11] A like request was made by the Bishop of Moray and Ross, the Primus of Scotland, in 1874.[12] Sometimes middle schools were the subject of conferences and meetings, and speakers asked Woodard for information about his organization.[13]

Very often letters of inquiry came from ordinary parish priests who saw the problems of the middle classes in their districts and who were attempting, or intended to attempt, to found small local middle schools. Typical of this class was a letter from the vicar of Holy Trinity, Portsea:

> We have a large number of skilled artisans who object very properly to send their children to a National School which they look upon as a charitable institution. . . . My desire is to see some school . . . set on foot for the artisans' boys, where, for a payment of 1*s*. weekly he [*sic*] would be taught properly. . . . If you can give me the benefit of your experience and advise me in the best way of proceeding in the matter I should be very grateful.[14]

From the earliest days at Shoreham Woodard was the object not only of inquiries, but also of frequent requests for the establishment of middle schools in different districts. One of the first to ask for help of this sort was Bishop Blomfield. In March 1850, Woodard wrote to Archdeacon Hare:

> A few days since, the Bishop of London sent for me, asked me to extend our schools and labours into London, and proposed to transfer to me the Diocesan Association of London, with its funds and offices. . . . I have determined nothing further than that I will make an effort to do *something* in London.[15]

Nothing, however, was done.

The pressure of such requests mounted. Archdeacon Hare wanted a school at Hurstmonceux.[16] Pleas for local schools in connection with St Nicolas College were received from Exeter, Salisbury, Folkestone, Hitchin, East London, and many other places.[17] Typical was a letter from the vicar of Stony Stratford, a village in the Diocese of Oxford:

> There is no school for the middle classes of a sound sort nearer than Bloxham or Cowley, 30 and 40 miles off. I have some hope that it might be possible for you to entertain the scheme of planning here an offshoot from your vigorous Sussex . . . College. I have no doubt but that such a scheme would be warmly fostered by our excellent bishop, and I hope that my own and my clerical neighbours' influence would not be unavailing.[18]

We have noticed that Woodard developed a rather Utopian idea of expansion into the colonies in 1859; although nothing ever came of this scheme, requests for new schools were received from British dependencies abroad. One communication came from Sydney, Australia. In 1875 a Royal Navy chaplain outlined a scheme for a branch of S.N.C. on Malta.[19] But the most importunate colonial pleas were received during the 1870s from the Bishop of Dunedin in New Zealand.

According to the bishop (S. T. Nevill), the province of Otago (which was coterminous with the Diocese of Dunedin) was largely under the control of a Presbyterian *élite*, which, by its political influence, prevented the clergy from visiting the state schools and gave the teaching of religious knowledge into the hands of Presbyterian teachers. Roman Catholics had begun a girls' school, run by the Dominican Sisters, to which a good many Anglican parents sent their daughters. But the Anglicans, who in Otago numbered 23,212 out of a total population of 85,082, had no secondary schools of their own.[20] To remedy this the bishop called on Woodard to extend his Society's operations into the South Pacific. In particular, he wrote,

> we might be thankful to receive from you the benefit of: your experience, a nominated head, [and] funds towards endowment. In return for which we would: raise additional funds, supply under-masters, give countenance and support, and, regarding you as our Founder, adopt all we could of your scheme.[21]

The extensive correspondence from the Bishop indicates that Woodard must have shown some real interest in this project. But it came to grief on the question of ultimate authority over the proposed schools. The Bishop wrote:

> The very compact condition of things in our infant Church makes our mutual relation more intimate than at home. . . . The visitorial office, which I should expect to be assigned to the Bishop of this diocese, would mean more than it is usually supposed to involve at home. . . . My idea is to institute Diocesan schools, not private schools within the Diocese.[22]

To this reduction of his supreme authority and of his Society's independence, the Founder could not agree, and the plans came to nothing.[23]

The pressure for new schools in new districts never let up. By the 80s, however, Woodard was becoming old and tired:

> The Duke of Newcastle has offered me 90 acres of land . . . [He will] make the roads, plant an avenue and give pecuniary aid for a school there. He is impatient for me to accept the conveyance of the property *at once*; but I cannot yet say what I can do. There is not a soul that makes themselves answerable for this now wide and costly scheme; and I am too ill to battle with the business it entails, not to say the demands of money. A lady in the Diocese of Ripon has also offered £4,000 down and an annual payment for a permanent endowment if I will build a L. Middle School in that diocese. I can give her no answer at present.[24]

Hardly less insistent than the demand for new schools was that for trained masters. We have noticed that Dr Lowe, when he was headmaster of Hurst, was under continual pressure to provide teachers from his training school for schools outside the Society. This demand was directed at Woodard also, and on one occasion the Provost was asked by Gladstone to recommend a Warden for Trinity College, Glenalmond.[25]

Woodard not only attracted invitations to expand his Society by starting new schools; he also received offers of actually-existing middle schools. Frequently such schools were small, local, and heavily dependent on the parish priest or individual founder. Such founders saw, in affiliation with or absorption into Woodard's corporation, the promise of permanency and continued usefulness. Such was the case of schools in Ulley, near Rotherham, Penmaenmawr, Teddington, Maidenhead, Southend, Wallasey, Torquay, Bristol, and Probus in Cornwall. One such proposal was that of the Rev. R. Linklater, who, in 1888, begged Woodard to take over some day schools in Portsmouth:

> I founded them for shopkeepers' children and the children of the dockyard officials some five or six years ago, and they answered admirably. I left 300 boys and girls in them when I gave up my work there three years ago. My successor would not carry them on, and I still manage them. . . . If you will undertake the schools I will present your Society with all the school fittings. . . . The cost of the beautiful new premises is only £100 a year for both [i.e. girls' and boys'] schools. . . . The fees of the boys and girls have been 1*s*. a week.[26]

In fact neither these nor any other small local schools were affiliated with the Society.

Larger and better-known establishments were also offered to Woodard from time to time. Such, for example, was the Oxford

Diocesan School at Cowley, founded in 1841 under the impetus of the National Society's first enthusiasm to provide an education "for the sons of tradesmen, farmers, and professional men of moderate means". In the spring of 1857 it was proposed that this school be turned over to St Nicolas College. Lowe was enthusiastic, and regarded it as "a good nucleus for the third school" (which had not yet started at Shoreham). For a year the proposal was debated by members of the Society. Finally Woodard's caution caused the offer to be rejected:

> Cowley school is worth having, but we must not have it at too dear a cost. There are many points to be considered, but one of the most consequence is our position in the diocese if we are only tenants of the Oxford Diocesan Board. Had we a place of our own, though it were only a cottage . . . we should possess a status from which . . . we could not be moved. But in a rented place we shall be on trial before the bishop [Wilberforce] and his friends and we know what he is capable of when pressed by the mob.[27]

Among the other established Church middle schools offered to Woodard (but not accepted) were St Mary's, Harlow, and, in 1882, the East Devon County School, an institution which had previously looked to Woodard's rivals for inspiration and direction.[28] In 1883, a rather different offer was received from the Diocese of Bath and Wells:

> Supposing we [i.e the Diocesan Board of Education] were to succeed in covering the diocese with a number of small middle class schools, day schools; in establishing a few, somewhat larger, boarding schools, and perhaps two or three large boarding schools for boys . . . we might also desire eventually to secure the great advantages . . . which are offered by your corporation. . . . Do you consider your Corporation to be capable of an enlargement of this kind?[29]

Two schools, mentioned earlier in another connection, both of which joined the Corporation after the Founder's death, were several times offered and rejected during his lifetime.

All Saints' School, Bloxham, opened by the Reverend J. W. Hewitt in 1855 was first offered to Woodard in 1857.[30] Two years later the property was bought by P. R. Egerton, who made a vigorous but unsuccessful effort to transfer it immediately to St Nicolas College. Egerton himself opened the school in 1860 "for the education of Tradesmen, Farmers, Clerks, and others of the

Middle Classes".[31] In 1880 he made another attempt to give the school to Woodard, and the Provost seriously considered making it the central school of the new Midlands Division. But Woodard's fear of over-expansion and his insistence on a sound financial policy led to its rejection a third time.[32] Nevertheless Egerton became a non-resident Fellow of the Midlands Division in 1882,[33] and in 1896 the school was taken over by the Corporation.

St Edward's School, Oxford, also a Tractarian foundation, was opened in 1863 "to place within the reach of parents of inadequate means a school where their children could be brought up in the true principles of the Church".[34] It was offered to Woodard in 1872, again in 1882, and was finally declined because of a heavy mortgage.[35] During the twentieth century it was actually incorporated into Woodard's Society for a few years.

A scheme almost exactly like Woodard's was outlined in a pamphlet published in 1870 by the Reverend Robert Howard, Vicar of Rawdon in Yorkshire.[36] In 1868 this gentleman, who styled himself "Provost of St Peter's Schools", had opened a small school for

> boys who are destined to occupy confidential posts in houses of business . . . or who are intended for the profession of a surgeon, a solicitor, or an architect . . . [or] sons of farmers, small shopkeepers, overlookers, master weavers, and others of the same social grade.[37]

The school had accommodation for only thirty boys, charged a fee of £30 10*s*, and included an Associate of St Nicolas College on its staff.[38] It was designed as the first unit in a series of schools, to be presided over by a Provost and Fellows, which would cover Yorkshire with middle schools under Church auspices and episcopal direction.[39]

Although Howard claimed that he had not modelled his scheme on that of Woodard, the similarities were striking. Indeed there are indications that Howard contemplated negotiation with Woodard's representative, Sir Percival Heywood, who hoped the two plans could be merged.[40] Nothing came of this, however, and I can find no evidence that Howard's plan found much support.

Few offers were accepted during the Founder's lifetime. Woodard did make vigorous efforts to acquire Taunton school, and he rather reluctantly took over Miss Rooper's girls' school at Bognor.[41] In 1863 Dr Lowe pressed for the affiliation of a preparatory school in connection with Hurst:

> We often have little boys sent to us who can read very imperfectly. . . . Boys from six and a half or seven up to nine years of age would advantageously be prepared for . . . Hurst. . . . A succession of such boys would soon raise the standard.[42]

Woodard was very cautious; but eventually a school called Little St John's was affiliated. Later on another school, preparatory to Lancing, was also attached to the Corporation.[43]

Invitations to start new schools and offers of already-existing schools were plentiful. The external pressure thus exerted on Woodard was augmented by pressure from within. Shortly after he became Provost of the Midlands Division, Lowe wrote: "I am anxious, where prudent, and where no burthens are thrown upon us, to extend the affiliations plan and so secure outposts, under cover of which to wait for opportunities of a general advance."[44]

In 1877 Lowe issued a paper in which he suggested a mode by which independent schools might be joined to the Society. According to this document, the Society would extend its aid to such schools

> by undertaking yearly examinations; by considering with the local managers how their operations might be enlarged or their organization improved; by endeavouring to supply them with trained masters; by admitting boys from them to compete for exhibitions in the Society's larger public boarding schools, and . . . in procuring freehold premises whereby the school may be permanently secured under a trust to the Church of England.[45]

Lowe actually entered into negotiation with at least two schools;[46] but he did so without much support from Woodard.

> One feature of the whole case [wrote the Founder] is the possibility of a large number of day schools being thrown into our hands, which we might not have funds to carry on with vigour and efficiency, and yet which, as a corporation, we could not abandon with honour.[47]

Certainly the large number of offers and invitations extended to Woodard, together with the many requests for advice and assistance he received, indicate a far wider renown than the very few institutions actually affiliated with the Society might suggest. Woodard's reluctance to incorporate the projects of other people into his scheme can best be explained by his extreme financial caution. Late in life the Founder wrote to Lowe:

Schools and property are offered to me continually, yet I have refused every offer, where, in cases of mishap, the Corporation could not sell it again at a great profit. . . . The success of my scheme does not depend so much on the rapid spread of our schools as it does on our making our way sure as we go by backing up our results from labour with marketable property to meet unexpected results.[48]

2

Woodard's project was the focal point of Church interest in middle-class education during the years after 1848; indeed, as we have seen, his project attracted respectful attention quite outside Church circles. But as interest in secondary education grew, the dominance of St Nicolas College did not prevent other churchmen, many of whom disagreed with one or other aspect of Woodard's approach, from starting their own independent schemes. There were several such centres of Church concern for middle-class education.

Undoubtedly the most prominent of Woodard's rivals was the Reverend J. L. Brereton, Rector of West Buckland in Devonshire. As early as 1853 Brereton aroused the interest of Lord Fortescue and of his son Lord Ebrington in the educational needs of the rural middle class in that county. Apparently ignorant of Woodard, Brereton later wrote of this period as "a time when no public attention had been called either to the importance or difficulty of middle-class education".[49]

He proceeded to plan a school at West Buckland to offset this neglect. Described as a "Farm and County School" this institution was to be modelled on the public school pattern with three notable variations: it was to combine study with practical apprenticeship on an attached school farm; its curriculum was to be basically non-classical; and the capital for its foundation was to be raised by selling shares upon which a dividend of 5 per cent was to be paid. The fees were expected to range from £10 to £45 per year for each boy, depending on how much time he devoted to farm work and study respectively.[50]

In 1858 the Devon County School opened with one master and three boys. By 1863 the numbers had increased to fifty-five boarders and fifteen day boys. A few years later, when the Schools Inquiry Commission investigated the school, the number of boarders had increased to ninety-four, the fees were set at twenty-five guineas, and all mention of the attached farm had disappeared.[51]

The boys were by no means all farmers' sons, but they did come from homes which corresponded generally to the central stratum of the middle class; socially, in other words, the school was parallel to that at Hurst.[52] By 1875 the fee at the Devon County School had increased to £35.[53]

In the minds of Brereton and his supporters this relatively small school was to form but a small part of a national scheme for middle-class education. The broad plan was outlined in 1861 and 1864;[54] in 1874 Brereton set forth his mature ideas, adjusted to take account of the Taunton Commissioners' work, in his book *County Education; A Contribution of Experiments, Estimates, and Suggestions.*[55]

Following the Schools Inquiry Commission's recommendations, he envisaged three levels of public secondary schools. Convinced that schools based on ecclesiastical traditions divided the middle classes, and equally certain that State action was "injurious . . . to education and perhaps also to the freedom and originality of the English character",[56] Brereton planned to root his schools firmly in the traditions of the counties and localities in which they were to be situated. Third grade boarding schools, for "smaller farmers, tradesmen, and artisans", at which the fee should be about fifteen guineas, were to be established in each small group of parishes;[57] a second grade school, such as that already functioning at West Buckland, was to be built in each county, in which farmers' sons could be educated at age sixteen for about thirty guineas a year;[58] finally, in each group of three or more associated counties there should be one first-grade school at which the annual charge would be £52.[59] The whole country was to be divided into four administrative "provinces", each with its centre at a university (Oxford, Cambridge, London, and one in the North), and each comprising a single educative unit.[60] At every one of these four university centres a "County College" was to be established with three principal purposes: to connect the University Local Examinations with university residence; to enable the graduates of county schools to obtain a cheap degree at a relatively early age; and to train a supply of masters for the local schools.[61]

Brereton's practical accomplishment was limited to the West Buckland school, to planning a first-grade school in Norfolk, and to establishing a County College at Cambridge named Cavendish College.[62] But his influence was greater than this modest achievement indicates. "Though West Buckland claims to be the first County School established", he wrote in 1875,

> it is by no means the only one, and . . . many others with equal success, and some with greater advantages to offer, are spread over the country, most of which in name, and all to a great degree in plan, acknowledge that they started from one source.[63]

All of Brereton's imitators seem to have aimed at the same general segment of society served by the West Buckland school and to have charged approximately similar fees. The East Devon County School was established in 1860, charged about £30 per annum, and served the farming community. In the Schools Inquiry Commission Report it was listed as having only thirty-five boarders and fifteen day scholars; it never grew large, and by 1882, just before it was offered to Woodard, the numbers had declined to thirty-two.[64] Another similar institution was the Dorset County School, founded in 1864 for the "sons of yeomen, tradesmen, merchants and professional men". In 1868 there were seventy-five boarders at this school paying between £30 and £34 each per year.[65]

The two best-known and most successful of the County School family were both established in 1865. The Suffolk County School at Framlingham, named Albert College after the Prince Consort, was founded "to provide for the middle classes, at a moderate cost, a practical training which shall prepare pupils for the active duties of agriculture, manufacturing, and commercial life".[66] Initially each boarder was charged £25; later this was raised to £30.[67] There were 270 students in residence in the first term of its existence; by the time the Taunton Commissioners made their report, this number had increased to 309.[68] The Surrey County School at Cranleigh, also founded in 1865 for the same class of parents, contained, in 1868, 177 boarders and charged a fee of £30 per year.[69]

The similarities between Brereton's plan and Woodard's scheme were striking. Both men aimed at the middle classes, although none of the County Schools, whether established on Brereton's direct initiative or independently of him, reached below the central or second level. Both Brereton and Woodard held firmly to the principle of the public boarding school. Both men were churchmen and clergymen. Both experienced difficulties in finding trained masters, and both sought to remedy this deficiency by training their own teachers: Woodard by establishing his training school at Hurst and Brereton by founding the County College at Cambridge.

Like Woodard, Brereton was fearful of State interference in middle-class education. He deplored the school of thought which

> substitutes the State for the parent. . . . I call it degradation in this country, when the independent classes look to government support . . . for the education of their children. And there is good authority for believing that this degradation is still so keenly felt by a large proportion of the farmers and tradesmen, that where no other schools exist, they prefer to keep their children at home to sending them to a Government-aided school.[70]

In his conviction that sacred and secular learning were inseparable Brereton was at one with Woodard:

> Hitherto it has been too much assumed that secular and religious must be hostile terms. But time and eternity blend in man, and whatever is for man's true welfare must have at once a temporal and eternal character. The power of reading and writing, and even of calculating, has this twofold direction. We can dissever them neither from moral nor from material effects.[71]

But if the similarities between Brereton's ideas and those of Woodard are striking, their differences are not less clear. Unlike Woodard, Brereton made full use of the universities' local examinations, established by both Oxford and Cambridge in the 1850s.[72] Indeed the aim of education at West Buckland was to prepare boys for the junior level of those examinations, and residence at Cavendish College served as a final preparation for the senior level.[73] Likewise Brereton deliberately adopted the proprietary principle for fund-raising, and he expected that shareholders in his scheme would be paid dividends at the rate of 5 per cent.[74] Woodard, on the other hand, regarded such a "commercial scheme" as "degrading to the Church".[75]

The features of Brereton's plan which most sharply contrasted with Woodard's scheme were connected with religion.

Brereton felt the need for a national system of education. For its organization he was unwilling, as was Woodard, to turn to the State. But, unlike Woodard, he was equally unwilling to let the matter rest with the Established Church. Brereton recognized the fact that Church and State were no longer coterminous as an insuperable stumbling-block in the way of a strictly Church-centred network of schools.

> If [he wrote] we could expect to make the whole a Church education, then the parish would supply the lowest, the Deanery or Archdeaconry the next, and the University the highest grade. . . . But, alas, this identity of Church and State, this common action of the Christian and civil body, so perfect in ideal, is esteemed by many impractical, and, therefore, delusive in fact.

Because it was practically impossible to take an "ecclesiastical basis" for national education "without giving or withholding a preference and thereby causing offence and sacrificing comprehension", Brereton took the county as his basic geographical unit and the universities as his "centres".[76]

Brereton was quite willing to recognize and to appreciate the influence of Dissent on the middle classes:

> We are bound to recognize the hold which the religion of Nonconformists has honourably taken of not the least religious portion of the Christian community. . . . The proposal to connect middle-class schools with the county rather than with the diocese was made very much with a view to find an honourable meeting-ground for the education of families . . . necessarily brought up in isolation and estrangement owing to religious differences.

He expected the new Cavendish College to be about one-third Nonconformist; the trustees of that body were to include professed Dissenters, "free" religious services were to be held in the Hall, and the vice-principal himself was to be especially acceptable to the Dissenting interest.[77]

This abandonment of the Church framework in deference to a realistic appraisal of the ecclesiastical and social situation was accompanied by a similar abandonment of Church teaching as Woodard understood that term. There is some doubt as to whether the religious instruction at West Buckland was "undenominational" or whether it included both catechism and conscience clause. Earl Fortescue suggested the latter in 1862; but Brereton's own views were rather in favour of a "secular basis" for the school, "with so much of religious teaching, e.g. scriptural knowledge, as would be undisputed, with school prayers for all and attendance at public worship, subject to the wish of parents." In addition, "a free opening . . . should be given to the special religious instruction of such public representatives of religious bodies as the directors of the school would sanction".[78]

Most County Schools which developed independently of Brereton adopted a liberal policy concerning religious instruction and worship. The East Devon School, for example, prescribed scripture for all and optional instruction in the Church catechism.[79] At Framlingham religious instruction was

> in accordance with the doctrines and practice of the Church of England. But special exemption from distinctive Church of England teaching and from Sunday attendance at the parish Church or College chapel is invariably granted to the sons of Dissenters.[80]

At Cranleigh, however, the situation was far different. Replying to a critic who attempted to distinguish between the "full Church system" of the Woodard schools and the "liberal" basis of Cranleigh, the headmaster wrote to the *Guardian*:

> The trustees are the Archbishop of the Province, the Bishop of the Diocese, and the rector of the parish in which the school is situated. The Visitor is the bishop of the diocese. All the members of the Council and all the masters of the school must be in communion with the Church of England. The Headmaster must be in Holy Orders. All the boys must be taught the Church catechism, and all attend the daily services in the school chapel, in which no prayers are used but those belonging to the liturgy of the Church of England.[81]

Despite the Anglican correctness of Cranleigh and the similarity of aim between the whole County School movement and Woodard's Society, it was not surprising that the two systems failed to draw closer together. The inculcation of religious truth, the preservation of Church dominance in secondary education, the maintenance of the unity of secular and sacred knowledge by resistance to the conscience clause principle: these were all fundamental to Woodard's purpose, and they all were denied by Brereton and by most of the other founders of County Schools.

But Woodard could not fail to notice the rival movement. There does not seem to have been any personal contact between Woodard and Brereton; but three years before Framlingham was opened, Woodard was warned about the "defects" of the proposed school.

> I must fear [wrote an early subscriber to Framlingham] that the result will not be satisfactory, especially as to the religious principle of Church Training to be maintained in the school. The first promoters began by inviting dissenters to join.[82]

Two years later, after the Framlingham promoters had investigated the domestic arrangements of Hurst with a view to emulation, they allegedly published a pamphlet in which they pointed out that the appeal of St Nicolas College was limited by the "peculiarities of its religious teaching".[83] Angered by this thrust Woodard wrote to Lowe: "I hope you have made those Suffolk impostors understand that you will give them no more information".[84]

As might be expected, the Society's attitude to Cranleigh, although aloof, was not so harsh. And we have already noticed that the promoters of the East Devon County School made a fruitless attempt to persuade Woodard to incorporate that failing school in his Society.[85]

The County School movement was an interesting effort by liberal-minded churchmen to enter the realm of secondary education. It was not a unified movement, although Brereton's plans provided an outline which was followed, more or less, by independent promoters. Nor did the County Schools include the lower portion of the middle classes. The attempt to introduce a middle-class education at the university level in Cambridge was not without interest of its own. But, on the whole, the practical results of the County School plan were small when compared with the success of St Nicolas College.

Mention was made in chapter 4 of yet another effort by a churchman to educate the middle classes in the 1860s. The Reverend William Rogers, who became rector of St Botolph's, Bishopsgate, in 1863, was a Broad Churchman and a friend of Jowett and Stanley.[86] Soon after his arrival in the City, he became convinced that for the children of "clerks . . . and tradesmen with moderate resources" in his neighbourhood no educational provision had been made. In the autumn of 1865 he proposed that the "city parishes should combine in the establishment of a day school for the children of parents who could not afford to pay more than . . . £1 per quarter for their education".[87]

A public meeting was duly held, subscriptions were raised, and by January 1866 the promoters (who included the Lord Mayor) were seeking no less than £100,000 for the establishment of a central school and smaller affiliated schools.[88]

A school opened in temporary buildings on Bath Street in October 1866, and by the end of the first quarter contained 518 pupils. A few months later this temporary accommodation was hopelessly overcrowded, and a total of £51,316 had been raised to start construction on a permanent structure. The foundation stone of the new school was laid in December 1868; from the time it opened the numbers "stood steadily at 1,000". By 1888, calculated Rogers, "not less than 10,000 boys [had] . . . passed through" the new school.[89] No affiliated schools were established.

This remarkably successful venture was distinguished from Woodard's scheme by several characteristics: it was a day school; it was concerned with a limited group within the middle class; it was designed to give secular instruction only.

Rogers' religious policy was not fully evident at first. Apparently under the impression that "undenominational" religious instruction would form part of the school curriculum, the Bishop of London (Tait) at first supported the scheme.[90] But by mid-1867 the purely secular nature of the school's instruction had been exposed and episcopal approval was withdrawn.[91] Rogers himself (who made the vigorous remark "hang economy, hang theology, let us begin" at the opening of the Bath Street School)[92] looked for donations from "Portuguese, Greeks, Parsees, and members of all denominations", and promised the Jewish Lord Mayor that the school would be "free, unfettered, and unsectarian". Unlike Woodard, Rogers was convinced that the families of clerks and shopkeepers comprised a "religious class" and that no definite religious instruction was necessary for them in a day school. He did not absolutely exclude the possibility that an individual master might introduce some sort of religious instruction; but such teaching could not take place in regular school hours. Rogers hoped that pupils would distil "a religion common to all citizens" from the regular secular classroom instruction.[93]

It was not surprising that Woodard and his supporters regarded Rogers without much positive enthusiasm. Amazed at the cash response to Rogers' appeal, Henry Tritton expressed his sorrow that so much money was "not going to our Lower Middle Boarding Fund"; but he was convinced that "people will not give such a sum for a Church scheme". Tritton unsuccessfully pressed

Woodard to start an opposition school scheme in London and promised his support for such a venture.[94]

Woodard drew his support principally, though not entirely, from High Churchmen. Both Brereton and Rogers were liberals and Broad Churchmen, willing and even eager to sacrifice "Church principles" for the sake of their educational aims. The Evangelicals also had representatives in middle-class education. We have noticed that Trent College was founded in direct opposition to Denstone.[95] It was opened in 1868 with fifty-three boys; by 1870 the number had risen to 225. The social aim and the general religious principles of the school were described by Lord Harrowby:

> I hope we are doing a good work here and are enduing the middle class with a sound religious education without any animosity towards our Nonconformist brethren and without enforcing our opinions upon those who object to the principles of the Church of England.[96]

In fact the fee of £45 a year charged at Trent in 1874 was very much higher than that exacted at the neighbouring Denstone,[97] and the two schools could hardly have attracted the same class of boy.

The next public school to be founded on Evangelical principles was the South Eastern College at Ramsgate, established by the South Eastern Clerical and Lay Alliance in 1879. But neither this school, nor the subsequent Dean Close Memorial School, founded in 1886 at Cheltenham, seem to have been opened explicitly for the middle classes.[98]

Early in Queen Victoria's reign the Committee of Correspondence and Inquiry of the National Society recommended that, in rural areas, parochial schools be organized so as to attract the children of farmers and tradesmen as well as those of labourers. Among others, Richard Dawes actually adopted this plan and, as we have seen, his "mixed schools" at King's Somborne were notably successful.[99] The Schools Inquiry Commissioners took note of several rural elementary schools with a deliberately mixed social clientele. At one of these, the National school in the small parish of Abbott's Ann, there were eighty-nine pupils who paid only twopence a week, two who paid threepence, twelve who paid fourpence, two who paid sixpence, six who paid eightpence, and twenty who paid one shilling; those who made the small payments were

M

children of labourers, but the others were the offspring of farmers and small shopkeepers.[100]

In the towns, where the pressure of numbers kept parochial schools well filled with the "poor", experiments in such mixed schools usually resulted in the addition of a higher and separate department in the National school. A pioneer in this development was the Reverend Robert Gregory, incumbent of St Mary's, Lambeth, for many years a close associate of Woodard and subsequently Dean of St Paul's.[101]

Convinced that the "sons of mechanics and small tradesmen" in Lambeth were badly served by the private schools and neglected by the Church, Gregory started a parochial school in 1854 specifically for that social group. Such was the success of his venture that in 1860 he erected new buildings which were divided into two parts: one for pupils paying sixpence a week, and the other for those whose parents could afford one shilling. In the higher division, boys remained until about the age of fourteen (about two years longer than in an ordinary parish school), and some were prepared for the Cambridge Local Examinations. Altogether in the two divisions there were about 200 pupils in 1866.[102] Despite the presence of a number of Dissenters' children, the compulsory religious instruction included the Church catechism and all children had to be baptized.[103]

An interesting feature of Gregory's work was his rather careful delineation of the social class for which these upper parochial schools provided. He was anxious to demonstrate that his students' parents were neither employers of labour nor payers of the income tax.[104] They were, in Gregory's definition, working men of a superior type, thrifty mechanics and skilled artisans, the "leaders of opinion" of the labouring class and the "natural guides" of the poor.[105] He estimated the average income of those who sent their children to his superior schools at two pounds per week, and the range of income from twenty-five to fifty shillings.[106] Clearly the class he had in mind corresponds fairly well to Mr E. J. Hobsbawm's aristocracy of labour, a class which possessed many middle-class characteristics. The list of parents in Gregory's superior schools (see Appendix E) shows the mixture of occupational groups which made up the lower middle class (or superior working class) in London during the mid-sixties.

Another important feature of Gregory's work was his success in obtaining a government grant for the maintenance of these "middle-class schools". Normally if a school charged more than ninepence per week for each child it was not considered a school for the "poor" and was refused government support. But by operating several different parochial schools, some of which charged only twopence or threepence a week, Gregory was able to persuade the inspectors that "the whole lot of children under his . . . tuition" paid, on an average, less than ninepence per week. On that ground he was permitted to accept public money even for the one shilling pupils.[107]

Although known to the public as "middle-class schools", both the shilling and the sixpenny divisions were officially described as National Schools. Gregory himself was anxious to promote the extension of such superior parochial schools in different parts of the country, and in 1865 he published a pamphlet with this object in view.[108] In fact other similar schools for the same social grade did develop. At Leeds, for example, where for many years the parish clergy had supervised large elementary schools, two parochial middle-class day schools were opened in 1870. Two years after they were started there were 150 boys and eighty girls under instruction, the fees ranged from fifteen to twenty-five shillings per quarter, and both schools were completely self-supporting. The National Society had provided a donation of £20 towards the capital cost of these schools.[109]

The National Society was the closest approximation to an "official" agency for Church education in the nineteenth century; as we have seen it early expressed concern about the problem of middle-class education. That concern resulted in comparatively little action between 1839 and 1860.[110] But by 1860 there were signs of a renewed interest. In that year plans were made for the Jubilee of the Society; among the projects to commemorate that event was a proposal to "introduce a Church leaven into middle-class education."[111]

Progress was slow. But by 1865 a committee had been formed "to report whether the Society can assist, and if so, how best, in promoting the education of the children of the class of poor just above those who usually attend National Schools".

In a circular these are referred to as the "Lower Middle and upper Artisan classes". Numbered among the members of the committee were several of Woodard's most prominent supporters:

Lord Cranborne (Salisbury); Lord Lyttelton, J. G. Hubbard, and, as might be expected, the Reverend Robert Gregory.[112]

By 1866 it was decided that grants would be made by the Society out of a special fund to be used for the construction of commercial schools the promoters of which guaranteed to provide education "on the principles of the Established Church". A good many such grants were made, and the committee evidently met regularly until 1879. But the sums of money involved were small and the passage of the Endowed Schools Act dampened the Committee's enthusiasm.[113]

Woodard was in touch with Robert Gregory about the National Society effort and he supported it.[114] Lowe, indeed, contemplated an alliance of some sort between St Nicolas College and the older Society. But this suggestion received a cool response from Woodard in 1880:

> When the National Society first attempted to extend its operations to middle schools some of its best supporters—e.g. Mr William Cotton, then its Treasurer—opposed it as attacking our Society. . . . Subsequently, through Gregory's exertions, it came to be. There was a possibility that it might succeed, but it never has, and I gathered from a conversation between Gregory and Cazenove at one of our late Committee meetings that they were in debt and had only £300 in hand.[115]

During the last decade of Woodard's life, the principal new development in Church middle-class education was the foundation of the Church Schools Company in 1883. The new Company, promoted by Canon Emery of Ely, Canon Francis Holland of Canterbury, Canon Robert Gregory of St Paul's, and others, was supported by a very large body of leading churchmen, both clerical and lay. Capital was to be raised by the sale of shares, and the Company's aim was "to establish, for boys and girls above the class attending elementary schools, schools of various grades, in which a general education shall be given in accordance with the principles of the Church of England".[116] It was first planned to concentrate on founding day schools, boarding houses and boarding schools would follow later. Fees at the day school were to range from £6 to £15 per year.

The *Guardian*, normally a supporter of Woodard, strongly backed the new scheme, including the conscience clause which so roused the ire of Woodard and Denison. That clause was introduced, it reported, "as a safeguard of even more importance to the definite character of the religious teaching given than to the religious liberty of the learners".[117]

Behind this reasoning, as we have noticed,[118] lay a fear of "undenominational" teaching: a fear intensified by the recent launching of two middle-class school companies in which the Church connection was very tenuous. The Girls' Public Day School Company originated in a meeting at Albert Hall in 1872; Sir James Kaye-Shuttleworth, the arch-fiend of government intervention in education, was the first chairman of the Council, and religious instruction was "undenominational". By 1900 this organization had established thirty-three schools and taught 47,000 pupils.[119] In 1882 a twin body, the Boys' Public Day School Company, was set up "for the promotion of middle class education, without aid from rates or taxes". Among the supporters of the Company was the "Principal of the Wesleyan Training College", and religious instruction was to be "conducted on the basis of biblical instruction as the best guarantee of moral influence and teaching".[120]

The Church Schools Company evidently set about its task in the hope of counteracting the influence of these two foundations of doubtful orthodoxy. Before the year 1883 had passed the committee had received forty-two applications for schools.[121] By February 1885 ten schools were actually established, although they were all small and the total number of students under instruction was only 378. By 1897 thirty-three schools had been founded; but only twenty-eight of these, containing 2,445 children, were still functioning. Of this twenty-eight none provided for boarders, and all but two were exclusively for girls. Indeed by 1892 the Company had decided that there was no demand for boys' schools.[122]

Throughout the period from 1850 to the 1890s Church interest in the education of middle-class girls lagged somewhat behind that in boys' schooling. Nevertheless there were some stirrings. As early as August 1850 a Church school for girls at Plymouth was advertised in a letter to the *Guardian*,[123] and in the next month another correspondent described a school for girls "of the trading part of the middle classes" at Hove.

> Its pupils [he wrote] consist of two classes—the superior one paying £15 per annum for board and education; and the lower £11 for board, clothing and education. The upper class are trained for

> governesses etc. and the lower for servants. . . . It is directed by a lady from pure love of the work, and from having been struck by the total want of Church instruction among the females of the trading part of the middle class.[124]

Concern about the lack of middle-class girls' schools showed itself from time to time during the 50s and 60s.[125] In the 60s the letter column of the *Guardian* contained several communications from Miss Elizabeth M. Sewell, who in 1865 started St Boniface's school in the Isle of Wight, at which she charged £6–£10 per year for day pupils.[126] The Bishop of Winchester was the Visitor, and the school was given the official designation of Diocesan School.[127] Some years later Miss Sewell attempted to arouse enthusiasm for the spread of "public day schools for girls on a Church foundation", and in 1881 she promoted "diocesan boarding-schools similar to that which has been recognized by the Bishop of Winchester . . . more generally known as St. Boniface School, Ventnor, I.W."[128]

Before the advent of the Church Schools Company other efforts besides those of Miss Sewell and Woodard were made to increase the number of Church-centred middle-class girls' schools. The Reverend Francis Holland, for example, established two schools in London in 1879 and 1881 in which instruction was strictly on Church principles and no conscience clause prevailed.[129]

The most important Church-based effort on behalf of middle-class girls was that begun in 1850 by Miss Frances Buss in North London. Known as the North London Collegiate School, this establishment attracted girls from "the upper division of the middle class" and charged nine guineas a year for day pupils. In 1865 there were 201 day scholars and eighteen boarders. Miss Buss was convinced that the education of a middle-class girl should not "differ essentially from the education of a boy in the same rank of life", and she provided a wide liberal curriculum and frequent examinations.[130] She also made extensive use of external examinations; in the year 1870–1, "one hundred and twelve pupils . . . passed the Cambridge, College of Preceptors, School of Art, and other examinations".[131]

In 1871 Miss Buss founded a second school, the Camden School "intended to fit girls of the lower middle class for business or domestic life, or to become the elementary teachers of their own children or of the children of others". The fees at this institution ranged from four to six guineas, and there were 220 pupils in the year of its opening.[132]

Miss Buss's schools were established as private institutions; but they were closely connected with the local parochial clergy. Under the "sanction and counsel" of the Reverend David Laing the first school "was opened and organized, and to the hour of his death he visited it regularly and exercised a general superintendence and management. Nothing was done without his knowledge."[133] In the 1860s two of the parish clergy visited the school weekly and taught scripture; the clergy also conducted examinations. Roman Catholics and Jewish children were not required to attend prayers and lessons in religious knowledge, but this dispensation was not apparently granted to the children of Protestant Dissenters.[134]

It is clear that Church interest and achievement in secondary education greatly increased between 1848 and the year of Woodard's death. At the same time as Brereton, Rogers, Gregory, Miss Buss, and the others were hard at work, small individual efforts were made here and there by churchmen throughout the country. Some of the promoters of these schools eventually offered the fruit of their efforts to Woodard.[135] Some small institutions, like the North London Collegiate School for Boys, developed into comparatively large and thriving schools.[136] Others, like Canon Henry Moseley's Bristol Diocesan Trade School, continued to be small but achieved some fame because of the distinctive methods used.[137] Yet others, like the Westminster and Pimlico Church of England Commercial School and the Burgh Middle School in Lincolnshire, evidently remained small, independent, and comparatively insignificant.[138]

All such efforts, whether large or small, successful or otherwise, witnessed to growing public awareness of middle-class educational needs. Despite the divisions of opinion among churchmen, despite the weakness and disunity which such divisions forced upon educational endeavour, the Established Church was in the forefront of the effort to educate the middle-class children of England. Of the agencies which competed for middle-class patronage, St Nicolas College was the most prominent; among individual churchmen who laboured for the educational, social, and religious welfare of that class, Woodard was pre-eminent.

3

Enthusiasm for the education of middle-class children extended far beyond individual school promoters and groups of educators. In the 1860s, when public concern for schooling generally was expressed in the Reports of three important royal commissions, one of those bodies, the Schools Inquiry Commission, and the greatest educational publicist of the day, Matthew Arnold, directed considered critical attention to Woodard's efforts.

Matthew Arnold's concern for middle-class education was first and most eloquently manifested in his book *A French Eton*, published in 1864, and was continued thereafter in a series of articles, reports, and books extending into the late 80s. Like Woodard, Arnold possessed an "over-riding sense of the importance of the middle classes and of the patent defects which they showed".[139] "The great work to be done in this country", he wrote, ". . . is not with the lower class, but with the middle".[140] Arnold was well aware of the influence exerted by the middle class on the working population. If the middle class could be changed, he wrote,

> this immense working class, now so without a practicable passage to all the joy and beauty of life . . . for whom in a middle class, narrow, ungenial, and unattractive, there is no adequate ideal, will have in a cultured, liberalized, ennobled, transformed middle class, a point towards which it may hopefully work, a goal towards which it may with joy direct its aspirations.[141]

Arnold, like Woodard, sought to achieve this transformation of the middle classes through education. Like Woodard, Arnold sought a national system of cheap public schools;[142] indeed he pointed explicitly to St Nicolas College as the only real effort currently being made to provide the sort of schooling the middle classes really required. He fully agreed with Woodard's remarks about the importance and neglect of the middle classes.[143] Like Woodard, he saw the need for schools which could provide the "salutary influences of greatness, honour and nationality", and inculcate "largeness of soul and personal dignity".[144]

Although he consciously agreed with Woodard in these respects, in other ways Arnold was no less conscious of disagreement. He was quite sure that Woodard's plan to create public schools by private subscription and to run them by private management was impracticable; only State support, in Arnold's view, would allow "sufficiency of provision of fit schools [and] sufficiency of securities for their fitness".[145]

Such an opinion indicated a basic disagreement about the role of the Church in the social order. For Arnold the State alone, and not the Church, was a national institution; and the State's true function was to "hold the balance perfectly fair between religious parties".[146] He was opposed to clericalism in education and opposed to Woodard's schools because of this feature:

> Their organization will be ecclesiastical. Mr Woodard tells us so himself; and indeed he (very naturally) makes a merit of it. This is not what the Dissenters want, neither is it what the movement of the modern spirit tends to.[147]

As Arnold disagreed with Woodard about the agency for middle-class education, so too he disagreed about the aim. Woodard aimed at drawing the middle classes into the Anglican fold and at attaching them to aristocratic ideals by means of an extension of the established public school system. Arnold was opposed both to the idea of the conversion of the middle classes to Anglicanism and to their imitation of aristocratic *mores*.[148] Instead, he proposed a "higher and more genial culture" as the proper middle-class ideal and hence the proper end of middle-class education.[149]

Matthew Arnold himself had a lot to do with the growing interest in secondary education in the 60s, and he played no small part in the establishment of the Schools Inquiry Commission.[150] The voluminous Report of that Commission contained a great deal about the condition and needs of the middle classes. Not surprisingly Woodard's view and accomplishments received considerable attention. Indeed the degree to which Woodard actually anticipated the recommendations of the Commissioners is astonishing.

Theoretically the Commissioners disavowed "class" distinctions when they recommended three levels of secondary schools; they based their classification on the "length of time during which they [parents] are willing to keep their children under instruction".[151] But, as we have already noticed, apart from the upper-class element in the first grade, the Commissioners equated these three classifications with three gradations in the middle-class social structure, based on the parental occupation criterion adopted by Woodard.[152] Furthermore, the occupational classifications used by the Commissioners in 1866 were remarkably similar to those already adopted by Woodard to differentiate the clientele of his three Sussex schools.[153] Indeed Woodard was recognized as providing for the different types of students which the Commissioners' three-fold plan intended to serve,[154] and his least expensive school (St Saviour's) was listed as "an almost solitary example" of a public boarding school of the third grade.[155]

The high value Woodard put on the lower middle class was shared by the Commissioners:

> The artisans, the small shopkeepers, the smaller farmers are in many places without any convenient means of educating their children. . . . The wealth and prosperity of the country depend to so great a degree on the industry, and that industry on the intelligence, of those who are left thus uneducated.[156]

In their Report the Commissioners recommended that exhibitions be established between schools of the different grades so that the exhibitioner may "prolong and complete his education". Particularly important was the proviso that "every school of the third grade ought to have the means of periodically sending up some of its boys to a more advanced school".[157] The similarity of this recommendation to the provision made by Woodard many years before is striking.

Despite this large measure of agreement with Woodard's view of the middle-class educational need, the Commissioners revealed their opinion that the State and not the Church was the keystone of the social structure.[158] Doubts about Woodard's understanding of the Church's function were made explicit by the Assistant Commissioner who examined the schools. The same gentleman, though he praised the schools, and especially St Saviour's, was highly critical of what he thought to be the reinforcement of class stratification by its recognition in the Woodard system. He recognized that scholarships from school to school could obviate this danger, but he felt that such provision at St Nicolas College was rather scanty.[159]

4

The Report of the Taunton Commissioners in 1868 and the resultant Endowed Schools Act of 1869 introduced a new era in secondary education. Not only did decisive State interference threaten the traditions of Church monopoly and private enterprise,[160] but the activity of the Government actually introduced a significant measure of practical competition to Woodard and to other churchmen labouring in the secondary field.

In their analysis of the condition of secondary education, the Commissioners pointed to the complete absence of effective State action up to that time:

> There is not . . . a single school in England above the class of paupers over which the State actually exercises full control. A few are under the control of the municipal authorities of a borough. The rest are under private individuals or private companies, or special ecclesiastical or eleemosynary corporations, or bodies of practically irresponsible trustees. There is no public inspector . . . No public board to give advice of educational difficulties, no public rewards given directly to promote educational progress, except those distributed by the Science and Art Department, hardly a single payment from the central government to the support of a secondary school, not a single certificate of capacity for teaching given by public authority professedly to teachers in schools above the primary schools.[161]

The Commissioners' review of the pressing need for increased and improved secondary instruction led them to make recommendations which, if implemented, would have altered the situation radically. The endowed schools were to be remodelled and their endowments put to the best possible use, through two public agencies: provincial authorities and a central authority.[162] The former, one to be established in each of the "eleven divisions made by the Registrar-General for the purposes of the census",[163] were to be responsible for adjusting the endowments of grammar schools in their localities according to the needs of the local population, and in conformity with the three grades recommended by the Commissioners. These local bodies were also responsible for providing exhibitions by which bright pupils might rise through the system from elementary schools to the universities.[164] The central authority (either a strengthened Charity Commission or an entirely new commission) would submit the particular recommendations of the provincial bodies to Parliament, and provide for the inspection of every endowed school in each division.[165]

In fact this machinery, which was designed to provide an adequate system of national secondary education under parliamentary direction, was only very partially realized. No provincial authorities were ever set up, and the careful adjustment of grades of school to the needs of particular districts was not properly undertaken. Nor was the "ladder which should lead from the gutter to the universities" ever effectively established.[166]

But the Commissioners' recommendations did result in the Endowed Schools Act of 1869, which, in turn, established the Endowed Schools Commission. This body set to work immediately to reorganize endowments and to reform defective local schools. By 1873 the Commissioners had published 317 schemes of which eighty-nine had passed into law.[167] Although, in 1875, the functions of the Endowed Schools Commissioners were transferred to the Charity Commissioners, the work continued as before. By 1886 no less than 764 schemes had been published and received the Royal Assent.[168]

The effect of this work can be illustrated from a table included in the Report of the Select Committee on the Endowed Schools Act in 1886.[169] A group of 189 schools investigated by the Schools Inquiry Commission were remodelled during the fifteen years following 1868 in accordance with the principle enunciated by the Commission. The endowments from these schools, together with some new capital, provided for 265 schools in 1883. Whereas the schools of 1868 had 13,851 pupils under instruction, those of 1883 contained 27,912 children. In accordance with the Taunton Commissioners' recommendations, the schools were divided into three classes, according to the age at which pupils left school. The number in the first grade in 1883 was considerably less than double that in 1868; that in the second grade just less than double, and that in the third grade was nearly two and a half times greater than it was in 1868.[170] Just why this particular group of 189 schools was chosen for this table is not explained in the text of the Report.[171] But whatever may have been the principles of selection, the figures were certainly published to show that the educational effectiveness of the income from a large number of grammar school endowments was much enhanced by the Commissioners' activities. Indeed the operations of the Commission between 1869 and 1886 constituted a very considerable degree of State activity in middle-class education. According to Mr Brian Simon, "by the 1890s, the middle classes enjoyed a subsidized system of secondary education".[172]

By their numbers, their wealth, and their newly-found efficiency and modernity, the schools reorganized or refounded by the Endowed Schools Commissioners and by the Charity Commissioners provided Woodard with serious competition. No longer could the middle classes regard the grammar school curriculum as irrelevant and antiquated. In Queen Elizabeth's Grammar School at Barnet, reorganized as a second-grade grammar school under a Charity Commission scheme in 1876, the course of studies included English, arithmetic and mathematics, geography and history, Latin, French, and German, drawing, vocal music, and natural science.[173] This school, which was socially comparable to Hurstpierpoint, had no difficulty in attracting the sons of the central part of the middle class; although on the one hand there were a few children of clergy and professional men, and on the other a few whose parents were "artisans and labourers", over half the parents of boys taught between 1876 and 1885 were engaged in trade of some sort.[174]

Even before schools such as that at Barnet were reorganized and functioning effectively, the Endowed Schools Act had proved an obstacle to Woodard's national scheme. In September 1870, Lord Wharncliffe, one of Woodard's supporters in Yorkshire, indicated the effect of the Act in that county:

> When I had a meeting at my house in London to which the Bishop of Ripon and the Dean of York came, besides other clergymen, it was unanimously agreed to be useless to try to raise money for the erection of a middle-class school in the West Riding whilst there were so many endowments extant doing no good and which might be directed by the endowed schools commissioners to the same objects you now have in view.[175]

A month later a county meeting was called in York for the purpose of co-operation with the Commissioners. Attended by the High Sheriff, the Archbishop of York, and many distinguished county residents, it was addressed by Canon Robinson, one of the Endowed Schools Commissioners. The York Education Society was formed "to improve and extend middle-class education and to co-operate with the Commissioners in reorganizing the endowed schools of this county".[176] Lord Wharncliffe was a member of the Society's organizing committee, as were also the Archbishop and Dean of York and the Bishop of Ripon. The new Society was charged with raising money to supplement the existing endowments, as well as with offering advice.[177]

This pattern of organized co-operation with the Endowed Schools Commissioners was evidently repeated in other counties. County meetings were held in Devonshire (where it was organized by the Earl of Devon, the Bishop of Exeter and Sir Stafford Northcote) and in Westmorland.[178] The Bishop of Lincoln wrote to a promoter of Woodard's plan:

> I have not given any definite reply to your enquiries concerning Mr Woodard's scheme because a sub-committee has been appointed in Lincolnshire to consider the measures that might be adopted under the . . . Endowed Schools Act for the improvement of Grammar schools and Middle schools in the County; and I much desire to see a similar committee appointed for Nottinghamshire. . . . I do not wish to commit myself to a new design before I am enabled to understand fully what may be done with the old.[179]

There was one other way in which, after 1870, the State contributed substantially to secondary education. We have noticed that Robert Gregory and others succeeded in attaching upper divisions to parochial schools in which more extended schooling was provided for the children of lower middle-class parents.[180] Gregory succeeded in maintaining a grant from the Education Department for this school. So too did those in charge of a similar parochial school at Bunbury in Cheshire. But at the Cheshire school additional public money was obtained by submitting large numbers of pupils to the examinations of the Department of Science and Art.[181]

After 1870 these two sources of income (grants from the Education Department and "South Kensington grants") were both used, not only to finance relatively advanced education in voluntary schools such as that at Bunbury, but also to provide for similar instruction in certain Board schools. Such establishments, known as "higher-grade" schools, kept their pupils to an older age than did the ordinary elementary schools, charged higher fees, and were in fact "what the Schools Inquiry Commission had wished to term 'third-grade secondary' schools".[182] In January 1890 there were fifty-three such higher-grade Board schools,[183] in each of which, presumably, were numbers of lower middle- or upper-working-class children.

5

When Woodard died his Society was vigorous and strong. It was still educating that class of society for which it had been designed, and it still professed to be a national, rather than merely a local organization, charged with a national and not just a sectional mission.

As the Society expanded after 1848 its fame grew and its influence spread not only within the Church, but throughout the nation and indeed, far outside the British Isles. It became the principal focus of interest in English middle-class education, and it attracted the attention of many whose aspirations and efforts in the same field were smaller and less self-sufficient.

But the sphere of influence surrounding Woodard by no means included all those churchmen who devoted themselves to middle-class schooling. Differences of situation, of churchmanship, of educational theory, and of social outlook prompted other clergymen and laymen to adopt their own independent schemes. Some of these—notably that originated by J. L. Brereton—were ambitious and themselves constituted centres of educational effort and influence in some sense competitive with Woodard's own. Others were small and localized.

As the interest of churchmen bore fruit in various ways, the State entered the field through the Taunton Commission and the Endowed Schools Act. Incomplete as its intervention was, the Government did begin to organize English secondary education; in so doing it diverted support, attention, and prospective pupils from independent schemes such as Woodard's. Combined with the growth of "higher-grade" Board schools, the activity of the Commissioners foreshadowed a time when private Church efforts, no matter how grand and ambitious, would be pronounced inadequate.

Woodard never lived to see that day. But only four years after his death the Bryce Commission concluded that "an adequate supply of inexpensive secondary schools could only be secured by State intervention".[184] The Commission's report was followed, in 1899, by an Act establishing a central government authority to supervise both primary and secondary education. Three years later the Education Act of 1902 created local education authorities empowered to co-ordinate elementary and higher education.

7

THE ACHIEVEMENT

> Mr Woodard is, and is not, a remarkable man. He is neither a very learned nor a very eloquent person. He is absolutely deficient in all popular arts. He is uncompromising, stiff, resolute—some people might say obstinate. . . . He is a man of one idea, but he pursues that one idea, not only with unflagging energy, but . . . with considerable *savoir faire*. . . . He persuades men, he attracts, he talks, he wins over, he brings people round—not by graces of manner, but by sincerity and a good cause, by rough common sense and by a determination to succeed. *The Saturday Review*, 16 July 1864.

The Victorian mind, wrote Walter Houghton, "tended to follow one line of thought, to look at objects from a single point of view, to shut out wide interests".[1] If Houghton is correct then Nathaniel Woodard was a model of Victorian rigidity, narrowness, and dogmatism. In vain does the student search his correspondence for some hint of a hobby, some hoped-for picture of Woodard the gardener, or Woodard the reader of light fiction; much less does one discover any evidence of serious independent interest in cultural or literary matters. Nor, as his views of F. D. Maurice, James Fraser, and the founders of other schools amply illustrate,[2] is there any indication of a capacity to sympathize with good men of other persuasions. Woodard's single-mindedness was also narrow-mindedness.

A single interest and a narrow point of view may well reduce a man's attractiveness in liberal eyes. But they do not necessarily diminish his importance. That depends on the significance of the single concern, on the truth of the subject's view, and on the magnitude of his accomplishment.

Measured according to these criteria Nathaniel Woodard was a notable man. He was important as a prophet, as a pioneer, and as a reactionary.

Insight, not foresight, is the chief quality of a prophet. As he applied himself to the rescue of the middle classes from educational starvation, Woodard exhibited insight in abundance. English education in the nineteenth century, wrote R. L. Archer, radiated from two sources: the monitorial schools and the universities. With the universities can be coupled the great public schools and the superior grammar schools, whose own reform followed closely on the reawakening of Oxford and Cambridge.[3] The monitorial schools were professedly for the poor; the public schools and universities were for the nobility and gentry, together with increasing numbers of the offspring of wealthy business and professional men. Neglected both by the public schools and by the monitorial schools was a great and growing element in society which Woodard and his contemporaries knew as the middle classes. Too proud to send their children to the parochial schools, too poor to send them to the public schools, farmers, tradesmen, and clerks, superior skilled workmen, small businessmen, and manufacturers could only resort to the inefficient private academies or the unsuitable instruction of inadequate and corrupt smaller grammar schools.

Woodard was not the first to notice that a whole class was suffering from educational neglect. But he was the chief and most forceful commentator on that neglect. The *Plea For the Middle Classes* reads like a prophetic oracle. The challenge which it contained was taken up in the years after 1848 not only by many other individuals, but by the State itself. The threefold social pattern adopted by its author in his middle-class schools was accepted two decades later by a Royal Commission and incorporated in an act of Parliament.

The prophetic office is critical; that of the pioneer is creative. There was much of construction in Woodard's work; indeed it was his constructiveness that lent weight to his prophetic utterance. For Woodard not only pointed to a need; he set about filling it.

Perhaps the most striking feature of Woodard's life was its productiveness in terms of stone and bricks and mortar. No sooner had the *Plea* been issued than capital funds started to accumulate in his hands. Meetings, letters, circulars, luncheons, committees: the whole machinery of a modern campaign appeared. All this effort was made not for one school, nor for one diocese or county or region, but for the whole country. His was the first serious effort to provide secondary education systematically on a national scale.

The physical achievement of building, staffing and running Lancing, Hurstpierpoint, Ardingly, Denstone, Ellesmere, and Taunton, to say nothing of the girls' schools, the preparatory schools and unsuccessful ventures like the military and engineering school at Leyton and the day school at Dewsbury, was great enough to assure Woodard of some place in educational history. None of his competitors or successors, except the State itself, achieved such an extensive organization.

Many pioneers have been radicals; but Woodard was not. His method was to adapt tried institutions to new purposes. Hence the public school structure, the predominantly classical curriculum, and the traditional clerical masterships were all pressed into middle-class service.

But there were some educational problems which could not be solved by adaptation. Chief among these was the provision of masters: to staff his schools Woodard was obliged to establish a unique system of teacher training for secondary schoolmasters. Equally unusual was Woodard's provision for an "educational ladder": a system of scholarships by which boys might pass from the lowest grade school to the universities. We have seen that a not dissimilar proposal was made many years later by the Schools Inquiry Commission.

Woodard's creativity was evident in his buildings and in the education he provided. It was even more obvious in his religious activity. For Woodard was a pioneer of Anglo-Catholicism. It was he, more than any other, who introduced the Oxford Movement into secondary education. Thousands of children were subjected to his system of spiritual discipline, to rigorous religious teaching and practice, and to the ecclesiastical atmosphere induced by gothic architecture, plainsong, and Anglo-Catholic clerical masters. The influence of the confessional alone, slight compared to that of chapel and classroom, must have been considerable. Certainly Woodard was the chief apostle of Anglo-Catholicism to middle-class England; and there is much evidence to show that he was recognized as such by anti-Puseyites.

If Woodard was important as a prophet and as a pioneer, he had some significance too as a reactionary, as a man who refused to admit change and who tried to preserve a condition long since swept away.

Like most Tractarians he was contemptuous of an Establishment in which the Church was dominated by the State. But he was acutely aware of the danger, and even of the absurdity, of the Christian religion divorced from ordinary life, of sacred truth separated from secular knowledge. It was to prevent these developments that he clung, in a manner not altogether typical of Anglo-Catholics, to a Tory view of the union of Church and State, to the Church's vocation as national educator, and consequently to a wholly unrealistic view of the position and prospects of the Established Church. However absurd such reaction may be *per se*, it is difficult not to sympathize with Woodard in his recourse to it. At the heart of his reactionary educational scheme lay a truth very imperfectly grasped by many advanced educators: that Christians must recognize God as the source of all truth, whether scientific, historical, or religious, and that their children must be educated accordingly.

Woodard was a successful as well as a significant figure. Yet when his accomplishment is measured against his ambition, his success is seen as fragmentary and partial. Woodard set out to re-establish the Church as the national educator, and especially to make St Nicolas College the national agency of middle-class education. Certainly his Society was designed as the Church's instrument in secondary education. Yet he never succeeded in acquiring the support of more than a minority of churchmen; and his few schools, however large and impressive, hardly constituted a national system of education.

The reasons for his failure are not hard to find. The Religious Census of 1851 demonstrated the substantial strength of Dissent. Indeed the total number of attendances on the census Sunday was greater at Nonconformist than at Anglican places of worship.[4] Even more alarming was the estimate that only 21 per cent of the population bothered to attend Anglican worship at all on the day of the census.[5] Under such circumstances Woodard's conception of the Established Church as the educator of the nation is seen to be quite unrealistic. Particularly is this evident when we discover that he insisted that all children under his care be confirmed. The Anglicanism of the Woodard schools was no mere formality; and it is impossible to imagine a genuinely national system of secondary education in the mid-nineteenth century which did not allow for Dissenters', if not secularists', consciences.

If the national ambitions of Woodard were unrealistic, what

about his vision of St Nicolas College as the instrument of *Church* secondary education? Even this much less exacting ambition was thwarted. For Woodard was an Anglo-Catholic; and Anglo-Catholicism was the party of a minority, probably a very small minority, of churchmen.[6] Indeed, as we have seen, large numbers of churchmen were hostile, and some very actively hostile, to the elements of Catholic worship and teaching which formed a regular part of life at St Nicolas College. Under these circumstances it is hardly surprising that Woodard's Society failed to become the Church's instrument in middle-class education. Its base was too narrow even for that.

Religious narrowness was perhaps the clearest reason for Woodard's ultimate failure. But no less formidable an obstacle to success was the sheer magnitude of the task. As we have discovered, it is impossible to find, or to make an accurate accounting of the middle class. But we do know that the number in that category was very great indeed.[7] As early as 1832, Thomas Arnold recognized that nothing short of State action could provide adequate schooling for such a vast body of children:

> The interference of Government seems to me indispensable, in order to create a national and systematic course of proceeding, instead of the mere feeble efforts of individuals; to provide for the middling classes something analogous to the advantages afforded to the richer classes by our great public schools and universities.[8]

Twenty-two years later Matthew Arnold echoed his father's opinion.[9] But Woodard acted upon the conviction that the Church, through the agency of St Nicolas College, and by means of private subscription and endowment, could do the job. When the task is measured against this agency the ultimate failure of Woodard's largest ambitions is hardly astonishing.

It is clear that Woodard was intensely conservative in most educational matters. Certainly by the 50s and 60s the curricula and structure of his institutions were far less advanced than that of other middle schools, including some of those run by churchmen.[10] R. H. Quick was of the opinion that "for education *per se* he [Woodard] cared nothing, and he did not think people were the better for secular instruction".[11] This was a far too extreme statement. But there can be little doubt that Woodard's conservatism and his preoccupation with a fundamentally religious aim detracted from his schools' educational effectiveness.

There is one more contributory reason for the failure of Woodard's national aims. His division of the middle class into three groups, each with a level of schools assigned to it, was, in the 1840s and 1850s, an acute piece of social analysis and planning. Indeed it is evident that in the 60s the Schools Inquiry Commission adopted his analysis almost precisely. But it is also evident that the Commissioners preferred the term "secondary" to "middle class", and that they sought to disguise the class basis of their three levels of schools by listing them according to the age at which the students left. No doubt this reluctance to distinguish types of education explicitly on a class basis reflected a gradual breakdown of the mid-Victorian class structure which, as we have seen, changed noticeably in the decades after the 1867 Reform Act.[12] The tendency away from education by class culminated in its official abandonment in the 1902 Act when elementary and higher education were considered parts of a single whole.[13] But the explicit restriction of schools to certain income and occupational groups was continued in the Woodard schools into the 90s. Although there is no positive evidence that such class restrictions reduced the schools' popularity during the Founder's lifetime, it is doubtful if a national system of secondary education could have been set up on such a basis in 1890.

St Nicolas College failed to become the national system of secondary education; neither did it succeed in becoming the Church's instrument in middle-class schooling. Yet it is only when measured against such vast ambitions that Woodard can be said to have failed. Where he failed he failed grandly, and in so doing bore witness to a forgotten ideal: the Church as the educator of the nation.

NOTES

INTRODUCTION

1. Below, p. 249.
2. See Sir John Otter, *Nathaniel Woodard, A Memoir of his Life* (John Lane The Bodley Head, 1925), Chapters 1 and 2.
3. See Asa Briggs, "Language of 'Class' in Early Nineteenth-Century England", *Essays in Labour History* (ed. Asa Briggs and John Saville), (Macmillan, 1960).
4. Ibid., p. 59.
5. H. J. Burgess, *Enterprise in Education* (National Society, S.P.C.K., 1958), p. 208.
6. Cheltenham College, 1841; Marlborough College, 1843; Rossall School, 1844, and others.
7. London: Printed by Joseph Masters, 1848. Cited hereafter as *Plea*.
8. Below, pp. 14ff.

CHAPTER 1

SCHOOLS FOR THE MIDDLE CLASSES

1. Asa Briggs, op. cit., and Asa Briggs, "Middle-Class Consciousness in English Politics, 1780–1846", *Past and Present*, April 1956.
2. W. L. Burn, *The Age of Equipoise* (George Allen and Unwin, 1964); Briggs, *Essays in Labour History*, p. 70.
3. Although this definition was challenged in the 90s it persisted throughout the century. See Olive Banks, *Parity and Prestige in English Education* (Routledge and Kegan Paul, 1955), pp. 16–18.
4. F. Musgrove, "Middle Class Families and Schools", *The Sociological Review*, Vol. VII, New Series (1959), pp. 174–5. See also G. D. H. Cole, *Studies in Class Structure* (Routledge and Kegan Paul, 1955), p. 64.
5. Hence Woodard provided for the "sons of poor gentlemen, tradesmen and small farmers, mechanics and others of small means" in one establishment, his lower middle school at Ardingly (*Calendar*, 1886).
6. J. A. Banks, *Prosperity and Parenthood* (Routledge and Kegan Paul, 1954), p. 105; and *Education: England and Wales: Census of Great Britain, 1851* (Parliamentary Papers, 1852–3, Vol. XC), cxl–cxli.
7. L. Levi, *Wages and Earnings of the Working Classes* (1867), quoted in E. J. Hobsbawm, "The Labour Aristocracy in Nineteenth Century Britain",

Democracy and the Labour Movement, ed. John Saville (Lawrence and Wishart, 1954), p. 210. Cole, op. cit., p. 55.

8. Hobsbawm, op. cit., p. 202.
9. *Calendar*, 1859, p. 23.
10. 15 November, 1865.
11. See T. E. Kebble, "The Middle Classes", *The National Review*, Vol. I, 1883, p. 688.
12. *Blackwood's Edinburgh Magazine*, August 1885, p. 177.
13. For Dudley Baxter's attempt see R. Dudley Baxter, *National Income: The United Kingdom* (Macmillan, 1868), p. 15.
14. London: Edward Stanford, 1886.
15. He included dealers in "Raw Materials", "Clothing Material and Dress", "Food, Drink and Smoking", "Lodging and Coffee Houses", "Furniture, Utensils and Stationery", "General Dealers and Unspecified". He estimated the number of people in this class as 351,000 in 1841 and 924,200 in 1881. (Ibid., p. 16.)
16. D. C. Marsh, *The Changing Social Structure of England and Wales, 1871–1951* (Routledge and Kegan Paul, 1958), p. 133. See also, A. L. Bowley, *Wages and Income in the United Kingdom since 1860* (Cambridge University Press, 1937), p. 128.
17. *Plea*, 4. The description of this school changed somewhat as it became more expensive and took its place with the other new public schools. In the *Calendars* from 1850 to 1859, it was described as for the "sons of clergymen and gentlemen of limited means"; in 1873 it was for the "sons of noblemen, clergymen, professional men and others". (Woodard Papers, Pamphlets, 1873.)
18. *Calendars*, 1850–9. Later on it was called simply a "Commercial School", and, later still, included "professional men of limited means" among its intended patrons.
19. *Calendar*, 1859.
20. Below, pp. 9 and 176.
21. S.I.C., I, Appendix II, p. 12. Note that labourers' children were not thought to stay at school beyond the age of 12 or 13.
22. S.I.C., VII, p. 237. (Italics mine.)
23. Robert Lowe, *Middle Class and Primary Education. Two Speeches . . . Delivered at the Annual Dinner of the Liverpool Philomathic Society, and at the Conference on Education at the Town Hall* (Adam Holden, Liverpool, 1868), p. 3. Also see, F. V. Thornton, *The Education of the Middle Classes in England* (Smith, Elder and Co., 1862), p. 6.
24. See, *The Guardian*, 13 December, 1865; Leading Article.
25. S.I.C., I, pp. 106ff. and pp. 138f.
26. *The Saturday Review*, 16 July, 1864.
27. S.I.C., I, p. 102. The private schools are not considered in this statement.
28. "Schools Cheap and Nasty", *Chambers's Journal of Popular Literature, Science and Arts*, 1857, p. 374.
29. *Plea*, 3. Woodard's view was substantiated by the S.I.C. twenty years later (S.I.C., I, p. 285). The inadequacy of the private schools was particularly

evident in the lowest or third of the S.I.C. categories, in which the parents were totally incompetent judges of an adequate and suitable education (S.I.C., I, pp. 308–9). See also, Matthew Arnold, *A French Eton* (Macmillan, 1892), pp. 41ff.

30. S.I.C., I, p. 285.
31. *The English Journal of Education*, Vol. VI, (1852), pp. 202–3.
32. In the Report it was stated that "the elements of Latin or some modern language" should be taught in schools of the Third grade; in nearly all schools of the Second grade Latin "would be a necessity" (S.I.C., I, pp. 80 and 84).
33. Below, pp. 104ff.
34. Of a boarding school of the Third grade, "the Shoreham school established by Mr Woodard is an almost solitary example". (S.I.C., I, p. 101. Also see, S.I.C., I, pp. 184–5 and 311–12.)
35. Brian Simon, *Studies in the History of Education, 1780–1870* (Lawrence and Wishart, 1960), p. 72.
36. "We are all aware of the growing power of the middling classes of society, and we know that the Reform Bill will at once increase this power and consolidate it. . . . It seems to me, then, that the education of the middling classes at this time is a question of the greatest national importance." J. J. Findlay (ed.), *Arnold of Rugby: His School Life and Contributions to Education* (Cambridge University Press, 1914), pp. 198–9.
37. *The Times*, 1 July 1861.
38. *The Nottingham Daily Guardian*, 29 November, 1869.
39. *A French Eton*, pp. 115, 63, 66.
40. Ibid., p. 90.
41. Robert Hussey, *A Letter to Thomas Dyke Acland, Esq., M.P. on the System of Education to be Established in the Diocesan Schools for the Middle Classes* (Rivington, 1839), p. 31.
42. H. E. Manning, *A Charge Delivered at the Ordinary Visitation of the Archdeaconry of Chichester in July* 1846 (John Murray, 1846), pp. 37–9.
43. C. F. Secretan, *Middle Schools, the Want of the People and the Duty of the Church* (W. Blanchard, 1857), pp. 3–7.
44. Letter from "N", *The English Journal of Education*, Vol. I, New Series (1847), p. 251.
45. H. J. Tiffen, *A History of the Liverpool Institute Schools, 1825–1935* (Liverpool Institute Old Boys' Association, 1935), pp. 62–74.
46. Simon, op. cit., pp. 175. Proprietary schools for boys, opened by Dissenters, included: Mill Hill School (1807); Friends' School in Wigton (1815); the Friends' Proprietary School in York (1829); the Northern Congregationalists' School at Wakefield (1831); the Wesleyan Proprietary Grammar School at Sheffield (1838), and the Wesleyan Collegiate Institution at Taunton (1843). These institutions charged various (mostly rather high) fees. Most took boarders.
47. Burgess, *Enterprise in Education*, p. 68. Manning's biographer included Thomas Acland and G. P. Mathison: E. S. Purcell, *Life of Cardinal Manning* (Macmillan and Co., 1896), I, p. 147.

48. National Society, Minute Book of the Committee of Inquiry and Correspondence, p. 13. (Hereafter cited as I. C. Minute Book.)

49. Members of the Committee were listed in the entry of the I. C. Minute Book for 16 May, 1838 (pp. 1 and 2) as follows:
T. D. Acland, Esq., M.P.
Lord Ashley, M.P.
*The Dean of Chichester (Chandler)
H. M. Coleridge, Esq.
*William Cotton, Esq.
The Rev. Dr Dealtry
Sir W. R. Farquhar, Bt.
*W. E. Gladstone, Esq., M.P.
The Rev. J. Jennings
The Rev. H. H. Milman
W. M. Praed, Esq., M.P.
Lord Sandon, M.P.
The Rev. Dr Spry
The Rev. J. C. Wigram
S. F. Wood, Esq.
R. W. S. Lutwidge, Esq.
Added on 19 May, 1838:
(I. C. Minute Book, pp. 7 and 8)
Rev. R. W. Browne
*Hon. Richard Cavendish
James R. Hope, Esq.
Thomas Tancred, Esq.
Added on 4 May, 1839:
(I. C. Minute Book, p. 111)
G. F. Mathison, Esq.
(Starred names subsequently became important Woodard supporters)

50. See, A Member of the National Society [G. F. Mathison], *How Can the Church Educate the People? The Question Considered with Reference to the Incorporation and Endowment of Colleges for the Middle and Lower Classes of Society in a Letter Addressed to the Lord Archbishop of Canterbury* (Francis and John Rivington, 1844), p. 36.
Also see, I. C. Minute Book, entry for 14 February, 1839; and Burgess, op. cit., p. 68.

51. I. C. Minute Book, 16 May, 1838, p. 4.

52. Ibid., p. 60.

53. The suggested curriculum was divided into two parts, General and Special. The General part, which was recommended for all middle schools, included: Scripture; English grammar and literature; spelling, writing, dictation, and composition; arithmetic and book-keeping; history and geography; astronomy; music. The Special curriculum would vary from school to school, depending on whether it was in an agricultural, manufacturing, commercial, or maritime district. But included in it would be some of the following subjects: languages (ancient and modern); mathematics (pure and applied); drawing (including mechanical, architectural, perspective and ornamental); modelling; surveying and engineering; chemistry; physics; natural history; agriculture and commerce. A chemical laboratory and museum for specimens were to be provided where required (I. C. Minute Book, pp. 44 and 45).

54. H. J. Burgess, "The Work of the Established Church in the Education of the People, 1833–1870" (unpublished Ph.D. thesis, University of London, 1954), p. 115. Hereafter referred to as Burgess, Thesis.

55. George Chandler, *An Address Delivered at the Opening of the Church of England Metropolitan Commercial School, Rose Street, Soho Square, January 28, 1839* (London: John M. Parker, 1839), pp. 10 and 14.

56. Burgess, Thesis, pp. 115f.

57. Chandler, op. cit., pp. 16 and 11.

58. Ibid., p. 10.

59. I. C. Minute Book, 16 May, 1838, p. 4.

60. Burgess, *Enterprise in Education*, pp. 71–2.

61. I. C. Minute Book, p. 36.

62. Purcell, op. cit., I, p. 147.

63. Burgess, *Enterprise in Education*, p. 134.

64. Mathison, op. cit., p. 15.

65. *Annual Report of the Oxford Diocesan Board*, 1841, pp. 8–9 (Pusey House Pamphlets, No. 70447).

66. *Annual Report of the Oxford Diocesan Board*, 1842, p. 9. (Pusey House Pamphlets, No. 70538). It was still in operation in 1860 (see, Pusey House Pamphlets, No. 692).

67. *The English Journal of Education*, Vol. I (1843), p. 294.

68. T. D. Acland, Jun., Esq., *A Letter to William Henry Powell Gore Langton, Esq., on the Subject of the Proposed Church of England School at Taunton* (printed for Private Circulation, 16 October, 1847), p. 15. This is available in the Woodard Papers, Non-Woodard Middle Class Education Envelope.

69. Burgess, *Enterprise in Education*, p. 134.

70. The cathedral schools of the Committee of Inquiry and Correspondence were to be "open at all times to the reception of such pupils from the National Schools as from their aptness to learn and to teach might be considered as proper persons to be admitted to the higher advantages it would offer". (I. C. Minute Book, p. 35.) Below, pp. 115ff.

71. Above, note 53, and below, p. 105.

72. S.I.C., I, p. 49.

73. S.I.C., I, p. 305.

74. The Committee proposed to offer the master of any existing private school "such terms as should, on the one hand, induce him to desire a recognized connection with the Church, and on the other, afford to the public a guarantee for the sufficiency of the attainments of the master and for the soundness of the religious principles inculcated in the school". (I. C. Minute Book, p. 45.)

75. *The English Journal of Education*, Vol. I (1843), p. 39.

76. Simon, op. cit., p. 116.

77. Howard Staunton, *The Great Schools of England* (Strahan and Co., 1869), p. 577.

78.

DATE	SCHOOL	RANGE OF FEES PER ANNUM (1869)
1841	Cheltenham	£ . . . . . .
1843	Marlborough	£52.10 to £70
1844	Rossall	£42 to £65
1847	Radley	£105

(Staunton, op. cit., pp. 399, 403, 511)

79. The Girls' school charged a fee of £1 per quarter for day pupils and £5 a quarter for boarders; the boys' school charged £1 per quarter for day pupils and took no boarders. For the curricula, see *The English Journal of Education*, Vol. III (1845), p. 36.

80. *The English Journal of Education*, Vol. II, New Series (1848), p. 429. Children of labourers paid 1*d* or 2*d* a week.

81. Ibid., p. 427

82. Ibid., p. 430.

83. Ibid., pp. 461–4.

84. *The English Journal of Education*, Vol. VI, New Series (1852), p. 201. See also, S.I.C., I, pp. 195 and 196 for later examples of this sort.

85. Above, pp. 6 and 7. See also, *The Guardian*, 26 September, 1849. Letter from "Mesites"; in this the "smaller tradesmen and higher artisans" are mentioned as an important part of the middle class.

86. Burn, op. cit., p. 22.

87. For example, King's Somborne at the "lower" end, and Marlborough at the "higher".

88. James Cornford, "The Transformation of Conservatism in the Late Nineteenth Century", *Victorian Studies*, VII (September 1963), pp. 64–5.

89. G. D. H. Cole, "The Conception of the Middle Classes", *British Journal of Sociology*, I (1950), p. 280.

90. Cornford, op. cit., *passim*. See also, E. J. Feuchtwanger, "The Conservative Party under the Impact of the Second Reform Act", *Victorian Studies*, II (June 1959), pp. 289ff.

91. H. C. Barnard, *A History of English Education from 1760* (University of London Press, 1961), p. 204.

The adequacy or inadequacy, abundance or dearth, of middle-class schools in the period after 1868 has been the subject of a controversy in the *Economic History Review*. F. Musgrove wrote "Middle-Class Education and Employment in the Nineteenth Century" (Vol. XII, Second Series [August 1959], p. 100); H. J. Perkin replied in "Middle-Class Education and Employment in the Nineteenth Century: A Critical Note" (Vol. XIV, Second Series [1961–2], p. 122); Musgrove answered this in "Middle-Class Education and Employment in the Nineteenth Century: A Rejoinder" (Vol. XIV, Second Series [1961–2], p. 320).

92. Olive Banks, op. cit., pp. 3 and 17.

CHAPTER 2

PLANNING AND BUILDING

1. *The Morning Chronicle*, 24 June, 1853, Leading Article.

2. N. Woodard to W. E. Gladstone, 2 December, 1846, British Museum, Gladstone Papers, Vol. CCLXXX, Additional MSS, 44,365, fol. 76.

3. N. Woodard to J. B. Mozley, undated, Woodard Papers, 1846 envelope, "Organization of schools". This letter was written after the letter to Gladstone quoted above but before the school opened.
4. Prospectus, New Shoreham Grammar School. Woodard Papers, Pamphlets, 1847; N. Woodard, printed letter, February 1847, Woodard Papers, Pamphlets 1847. Below, p. 24.
5. Prospectus. Pamphlets, 1847. Below, p. 115ff.
6. Ibid. Below, p. 62.
7. N. Woodard to W. E. Gladstone, 2 December, 1846, British Museum, Glad. Papers, Vol. CCLXXX, Add. MSS, 44,365, fol. 76.
8. This Fund was, in fact, collected and administered as Woodard anticipated in this early letter, although the inscription of names was neglected. It became a permanent feature of the mature society.
9. *Preamble*, undated, Woodard Papers, Statutes Envelope, undated. Cited hereafter as *Preamble*. The three long sheets of print are not dated. But in the text Archdeacon Hare's death is mentioned; so also is the fact that William Wheeler is Vicar of Shoreham. Hare died on 23 January, 1855; Wheeler resigned the Shoreham living on 4 January, 1856. Hence this document must be dated in 1855 or the first four days of 1856.
10. N. Woodard, *The Scheme of Education of St Nicolas College with Suggestions for the Permanent Constitution of that Society in a Letter to the Most Noble Marquis of Salisbury, D.C.L., Chancellor of the University of Oxford* (Oxford and London: James Parker & Co., 1869). Cited hereafter as the *Letter to Salisbury*.
11. N. Woodard, *Draft of Statutes for the Corporation of SS. Mary and Nicolas College*, undated and unpublished, Woodard Papers, Statutes Envelope. Cited hereafter as *Draft Statutes*. The date 12 January, 1874 is referred to in the document, a number of copies of which are preserved in the Woodard Papers. But on 5 May, 1873 Woodard wrote to Lowe that he had just sent off "copies of the first . . . of the statutes to the Bishop of Lichfield" (Lancing Archives, Letters to Lowe). This must have been an earlier recension of the same document. Evidently copies of this Draft were sent "to some, if not all, of the members of the Corporation but for many years until 1880 were not signed". (Charles R. Freeman to Sir John Otter, 13 June, 1922, Woodard Papers, Statutes Envelope.)
12. *Plea*, p. 15. This term is not used again in later writings; it seems to correspond to the later "Provost".
13. In these, wrote Woodard, "boys may gain a sound and Christian education at about four or five pounds per annum". (*Plea*, p. 13.)
14. Ibid., pp. 13–15.
15. Ibid., p. 15.
16. The Rev. Edward C. Lowe was Headmaster of Woodard's second school from 1849 to 1872; from 1873 to 1891 he was Provost of the Midlands Division of the Society. On the Founder's death, he became Provost of the Southern Division.
17. N. Woodard to E. C. Lowe, 16 October, 1848, Lancing Archives, Letters to Lowe.
18. *Preamble*, p. 3.
19. N. Woodard, *A Brief Report on the State of the Buildings, Labours, and Finances*

of St Nicolas College (printed by J. Masters & Co., 1858), pp. 4 and 5. Referred to hereafter as *A Brief Report.*

20. N. Woodard, printed letter, 9 July, 1849, Woodard Papers, Pamphlets, 1849.
21. N. Woodard, printed letter, August 1849, Woodard Papers, Pamphlets, 1849.
22. N. Woodard, *Public Schools for the Middle Classes. A Letter to the Clergy of the Diocese of Chichester* (printed by Joseph Masters, 1851), p. 16. Cited hereafter as *Public Schools for the Middle Classes* (1851).
23. N. Woodard to Julius Hare, 6 December, 1848, Lancing Archives, Letters to Hare. Below, pp. 34 and 115.
24. *Preamble*, p. 2. (Italics mine.)
25. *Plea*, p. 6.
26. Ibid., p. 5.
27. *Public Schools for the Middle Classes* (1851), pp. 7 and 9. But a contemporary of Woodard, H. W. Cole, described the Church of England as "emphatically the Church of the middle classes" (*The Middle Classes and the Borough Franchise* [Longmans, Green, 1866], p. 83). Evidently opinion on this matter was not unanimous.
28. H. E. Manning, *A Charge Delivered at the Ordinary Visitation of the Archdeaconry of Chichester in July, 1843* (John Murray, 1843), pp. 43–4.
29. S.F.W. [S. F. Wood], "On Attaching the Middle and Lower Orders to the Church", *The English Journal of Education*, Vol. I (1843), p. 44.
30. See, *Plea*, p. 5. See also, N. Woodard to the Marquess of Salisbury, 22 August, 1879, Christ Church, Salisbury Papers, Letters from Woodard.
31. *The Guardian*, 7 December 1864.
32. Quoted in E. R. Wickham, *Church and People in an Industrial City* (Lutterworth Press, 1957), p. 116.
33. *Religious Census*, clviii.
34. H. Dunckley, *The Glory and the Shame of Britain* (Religious Tract Society, 1851), p. 74.
35. *The Guardian*, 2 November, 1850. Letter from "W.H.L.".
36. *Preamble*, p. 2.
37. *Plea*, p. 13.
38. Woodard encouraged affiliation. See N. Woodard to the Rev. D. Trinder, 20 May, 1854, Woodard Papers, 1854 Envelope: "We are willing to accept alliances . . . either generally upon very easy terms leaving the schools to act for themselves, or, particularly by making ourselves responsible for the success and proper working of the schools."
39. Woodard, *Public Schools for the Middle Classes* (1851), p. 17.
40. N. Woodard, Printed Letter, Advent 1853, Woodard Papers, Pamphlets, 1853.
41. N. Woodard, Printed Letter, July 1859, Woodard Papers, Pamphlets, 1859.
42. Below, p. 154.

43. See Edward C. Lowe, *St Nicolas College and its Schools. A Letter to the Rt. Hon. Sir J. T. Coleridge* (Oxford and London: J. H. & J. Parker, 1861), p. 7.
44. Woodard, *Letter to Salisbury*, p. 16.
45. *Draft Statutes*, p. 5.
46. Ibid., pp. 15 and 16.
47. Ibid., p. 3. The Corporation never met during Woodard's lifetime. After his election to be Woodard's successor as Provost of Lancing, Dr Lowe wrote: "My position will be difficult by reason of many complications arising out of the infirmities of his [Woodard's] later years. . . . The pressing need of our position is to put in action the *Corporation* (so-called) of St Nicolas College, as distinct from the several societies which compose it. Canon Woodard could not be induced to summon the Corporation to meet tho' his statutes provided its constitution." (E. C. Lowe to W. E. Gladstone, 9 September, 1891, British Museum, Gladstone Papers, Vol. CCCCXXVIII, Add. MSS. 44,513, fol. 153.)
48. Woodard, *Letter to Salisbury*, p. 18.
49. *Draft Statutes*, p. 14.
50. Ibid., p. 17. Below, p. 62.
51. Woodard, *Letter to Salisbury*, p. 25.
52. In view of the development of the Society it may seem strange that Girls' schools had no place in the Founder's vision. His views on the nature of female education, and the almost accidental nature of his first venture into it, do much to explain this omission. Below, p. 107.
53. Woodard, *Letter to Salisbury*, p. 15.
54. N. Woodard, Pamphlet, January 1888, Woodard Papers, Pamphlets, 1888.
55. N. Woodard, Speech at the opening of the crypt of Lancing Chapel, quoted by W. B. Woodard, Pamphlet, 1890, Woodard Papers, Pamphlets 1890.
56. N. Woodard, Printed circular entitled *St Nicolas College Library*, March 1875, Woodard Papers, Pamphlets, 1875.
57. W. Awdry, *An Opening Address to the Senior Members of the College of St Mary and St Nicolas, Lancing, at their Octave Meeting for "Purposes of Devotion, Business, and the Exercise of a More Extended Hospitality"* (printed by Charles Cull & Son, London, 1875), title page.
58. E. Field to Woodard, 17 October, 1877, Woodard Papers, 1877 Packet, School Religion. See also, K. E. Kirk, *The Story of the Woodard Schools* (Hodder and Stoughton, 1937), pp. 101 and 102.
59. N. Woodard, Pamphlet, 1848, Woodard Papers, Pamphlets, 1848. It remained possible to receive full board and education at this fee until 1857, when the minimum was raised to 50 gns; it was later increased to 55 gns, at which figure it remained until the Founder's death. (*Calendars*, 1850–9; 1871; 1886; 1890.)
60. No such description appears in the 1849 Prospectus. (Woodard Papers Pamphlets, 1849.)
61. The initial expenditure was estimated by Woodard at £30,000 (Printed Letter, Michaelmas, 1855, Woodard Papers, Pamphlets, 1855); by 1890

nearly £70,000 had been spent on the Chapel (W. B. Woodard, Pamphlet, 1890, Woodard Papers, Pamphlets, 1890); in addition many thousands of pounds were spent on completing and finishing the school buildings; one alumnus paid fully for the completion of the upper quadrangle. (See H. M. Gibbs to Woodard, 7 August, 1875, Woodard Papers, 1875 packet.)

In 1849 there were "upwards of 40 boys" (Prospectus, December 1849, Woodard Papers, Pamphlets 1849); in 1850, 70; in 1851, 79; in 1852, 66; 1857 (before the move to Lancing), 77; 1858 (after the move to Lancing), 97; 1859, 76. (*Calendars*, 1850–9.)

62. Sanderson was headmaster from 1861 until 1889.
63. Below, p. 111. See Musgrove, *Economic History Review*, 2nd Series, XII (1959–60), p. 102.
64. R. E. Sanderson to N. Woodard, 31 March, 1871, Woodard Papers, 1871 Packet, School Life.
65. In 1871, there were 121 resident pupils; by 1886 this number had risen to 215. (*Calendars* 1871 and 1886.)
66. At the beginning of 1849, his staff consisted of three clergymen, all graduates. (N. Woodard to Julius Hare, 10 January, 1849, Lancing Archives, Letters to Hare.)
67. N. Woodard to Julius Hare, 13 February, 1849, Lancing Archives, Letters to Hare. It seems, however, that the school did not open until August. (N. Woodard, Printed Letter, August 1849, Woodard Papers, Pamphlets 1849, p. 3.)
68. N. Woodard, Printed Letter, 1 June, 1853, Woodard Papers, Pamphlets 1853.
69. N. Woodard to his Aunts, 4 January 1850, Woodard Papers, Packet C.; E. C. Lowe, *St Nicolas College and its Schools. A Record of Thirty Years Work in the Effort to Endow the Church of England with a System of Self-supporting Public Boarding-Schools for the Upper, Middle, and Lower Middle Classes* (James Parker & Co., Oxford and London, 1878), p. 21.
70. Lowe, *St Nicolas College and its Schools. A Record* . . ., p. 21.
71. *Calendars*, 1850, 1851, 1859, 1871. After Lowe's departure, the numbers declined rapidly due to the inefficiency of his successor, William Awdry. (See, N. Woodard to the Marquess of Salisbury, 29 October 1877, Christ Church, Salisbury Papers, Letters from Woodard.)
72. *Calendars*, 1862, 1864, 1876, 1886, 1890.
73. Above, p. 28; and below, pp. 112f.
74. Lowe, *St Nicolas College and Its Schools. A Letter* . . ., p. 5. *The Guardian*, 5 November 1856, Leading Article, p. 849.
75. *Calendars*, 1854 and 1871. Below, p. 116.
76. N. Woodard, *A Brief Report* . . ., p. 13. *The Calendar* (1859) listed "mechanics" as the humblest element acceptable at St Saviour's; in a pamphlet written the previous year, but published in 1859, the word "artisan" is used in place of "mechanic" (N. Woodard, *St Saviour's Lower Middle School*, Woodard Papers, Pamphlets 1859). The designation "mechanic" appears also in 1871, 1886, and 1890 (*Calendars*). Clearly these terms refer to that aristocracy of labour which could afford to pay Woodard's fees.

77. Printed notice of the Ardingly stone-laying, Woodard Papers, Pamphlets, 1864.
78. Richard Cavendish and John G. Talbot, Printed announcement of Ardingly Opening, March 1870, Woodard Papers, Pamphlets, 1870. It is clear that much by way of "fitting-up" would have to be done in order actually to accommodate this number. It remained an impossible potential for some years.
79. N. Woodard, Printed Letter, May 1869, Woodard Papers, Pamphlets 1869.
80. *Calendar*, 1859. This number is extraordinary when it is considered that on opening, the year before, there was accommodation for only forty boys; the remainder were put in private houses, "the rent of which the parents divided amongst themselves". (N. Woodard, *St Saviour's Lower Middle School for the Sons of Small Shopkeepers, Artizans, Clerks, and Others of Limited Means* [printed by J. F. Eyles, Brighton, 1859], p. 6.)
81. *Calendar*, 1871.
82. *Calendar*, 1886. Evidently this was very minimal, and a few extra pounds were usually necessary. (J. G. Talbot to the Bishop of Moray and Ross [Robert Eden], 22 July 1875, Woodard Papers, 1875 Packet, School Life.)
83. In 1886 this group numbered twenty-one (*Calendar*, 1886).
84. Printed Announcement, 30 August 1850, Woodard Papers, Pamphlets 1850.
85. Below, pp. 105f. The fees rose from £60 to £80.
86. In 1854 it reached a peak of twenty pupils; by 1857, it was down to seven (*Calendars*, 1854 and 1857.)
87. £36 in 1856; £80 in 1871 (*Calendars*, 1856 and 1871).
88. *Calendar*, 1871. There were two pupils in 1856; five in 1859; nineteen in 1871. By 1876 it seems to have disappeared altogether (*Calendar*, 1876); at Denstone it was not dropped. (*Calendars*, 1876 and 1880.)
89. Below, pp. 107ff.
90. N. Woodard, Pamphlet entitled *St Michael's Schools*, Lent 1856, Woodard Papers, Pamphlets, 1856.
91. *The Guardian*, 3 October 1866, p. 1012.
92. The upper school was "exclusively for the daughters of gentlemen"; the middle school for "children of professional men of moderate means, farmers and tradesmen"; and the lower school was for "the training of domestic servants" (*Calendar*, 1871).
93. *Calendar*, 1886.
94. In 1890, there were forty-six pupils (*Calendar*, 1890).
95. N. Woodard to Julius Hare, 9 December 1851, Lancing Archives, Letters to Hare.
96. N. Woodard to Lord Cranborne, 21 November 1866. Christ Church, Salisbury Papers, Letters from N. Woodard.
97. E. C. Lowe, Printed Letter entitled *Middle-Class Public Boarding Schools in the Midland Counties*, Michaelmas Day, 1872, Woodard Papers, Pamphlets 1872.

98. There was, however, some early talk of an upper school and Centre. In 1867 Woodard wrote that "the Denstone school must, ere long, be subordinate to some greater establishment like Lancing". (N. Woodard, *Denstone Public School, in Union with St Nicolas College. A Letter to Sir T. Percival Heywood, Bart.* [Joseph Masters, London, 1867], p. 9.) In 1873, Lowe was still looking for a suitable site for a Centre. (E. C. Lowe to N. Woodard, 19 December 1873, Woodard Papers, 1873 Packet, Other Schools.)
99. *The Guardian*, 13 August 1873.
100. E. C. Lowe, Printed Letter entitled *Middle-Class Public Boarding Schools in the Midland Counties*, Michaelmas Day, 1872, Woodard Papers, Pamphlets 1872. *The Manchester Guardian*, 1 August 1888.
101. The fee remained at 34 gns until the Founder's death.
102. H. Meynell, Printed Letter, 20 May 1874, Woodard Papers, Pamphlets 1874 (*Calendar*, 1890). Lowe, *St Nicolas College and its Schools. A Record*, p. 42.
103. N. Woodard, Pamphlet entitled *Midland Counties and Manchester Public School for the Sons of Persons of Small Means*, September 1871, Woodard Papers, Pamphlets 1871.
104. N. Woodard, Printed Letter, December 1877, Woodard Papers, Pamphlets 1877.
105. N. Woodard to E. C. Lowe, 26 March 1878, Lancing Archives, Letters to Lowe.
106. E. C. Lowe, Printed Letter, 5 August 1882, Woodard Papers, Pamphlets 1882. Also Printed Invitation To the Opening of Ellesmere, Midsummer 1884, Woodard Papers, Pamphlets 1884.
107. E. C. Lowe to N. Woodard, 16 September 1884, Woodard Papers, 1884 Packet, School Life. E. C. Lowe to N. Woodard, 18 August 1885, Woodard Papers, 1885 Packet, School Life. The school opened with only 160 places for pupils, although 500 was the ultimate aim.
108. E. C. Lowe to N. Woodard, 9 February 1886, Woodard Papers, 1886 Packet, School Life.
109. *Calendars*, 1886 and 1890.
110. Duke of Newcastle to N. Woodard, 26 February 1887, Woodard Papers, 1887 Packet, Midlands.
111. E. C. Lowe, Pamphlet entitled *Middle Class Boarding Schools for Girls in the Midland Counties.*
112. George Mackarness to N. Woodard, 30 March 1867, Woodard Papers, 1867 Envelope, Midlands.
113. E. C. Lowe, Pamphlet, Woodard Papers, Pamphlets 1875.
114. E. C. Lowe, Pamphlet, Woodard Papers, Pamphlets 1882.
115. *Calendars*, 1886 and 1890.
116. *Calendar*, 1890.
117. Below, pp. 170ff.
118. Prospectus, Lady Day 1884, Woodard Papers, Pamphlets 1884.
119. E. C. Lowe to N. Woodard, 25 December 1885, Woodard Papers, 1885 Packet, Midlands.

120. E. C. Lowe to N. Woodard, Whit Tuesday 1885, Woodard Papers, 1885 Packet, Organization. E. C. Lowe to N. Woodard, 19 June 1885, Woodard Papers, 1885 Packet, Organization. For definition of "Conscience clause", see below, p. 92.

121. Kirk, op. cit., p. 129.

122. N. Woodard to The Marquess of Salisbury, 5 November 1879, Christ Church, Salisbury Papers, Letters from Woodard.

123. N. Woodard, Printed invitation to the opening. 8 October 1880, Woodard Papers, Pamphlets 1880. Lowe, who conducted a survey of the property before Woodard bought it, considered it too small for either a First or Third school, and suggested either a revival of the long-defunct "Military and Engineering" type or a "superior modern school". (E. C. Lowe to N. Woodard, 28 September 1879, Woodard Papers.)

124. R. E. Sanderson to N. Woodard, 14 June 1887, Woodard Papers, 1887 Packet, School Life.

125. G. O. L. Thomson to N. Woodard, 26 October 1881, Woodard Papers, 1881 Packet, School Life. Thomson was the headmaster at Taunton (*Calendars*, 1886 and 1890).

126. In 1897 it became the headquarters of the Western Division. See, Kirk, op. cit., p. 133.

127. *Calendar*, 1890. Of this number about 250 were at Lancing, St Anne's and St Michael's; the remainder—i.e. about 1,100—were (with the exception of the few servitors) according to the Society's definition, middle class. There was, in fact, some fall in numbers in the South during the last few years of the Founder's life. That this was probably due to the age of the Provost (he was eighty when he died), and to his preoccupation with Lancing Chapel, is indicated by the fact that the schools of the Midland Division continued to attract an increasing number of pupils (*Calendars*, 1886 and 1890).

128. He was always quite clear that no donations or subscriptions would be used to subsidize school operations. In the *Plea* he spoke of the schools helping each other financially; but the unit as a whole was to be self-supporting. Later on each school was advertised as self-supporting. (E.g. N. Woodard, *St Saviour's Lower Middle School for the Sons of Small Shopkeepers . . .*, p. 6.)

129. There is no really accurate account of the total amount of money that was raised. In the *Letter to Salisbury* (1869) he wrote of having spent about £250,000 by the year after the foundation stone of Lancing Chapel was laid, on which "little short of £70,000" had been spent by 1890. (W. B. Woodard, Pamphlet, 1890, Woodard Papers, Pamphlets, 1890.) Between 1868 and 1884, £90,000 had been spent on the schools of the Midland Division alone. (Printed Letter, Michaelmas 1884, Woodard Papers, Pamphlets 1884.) Woodard gave £8,000 for Taunton in 1879. These figures total over £400,000; yet this does not include expensive additions and improvements (e.g. Ardingly and Denstone chapels and the Lancing Upper Quad), or the sum raised to build Worksop.

130. R. C. Carpenter to N. Woodard, 6 October 1840, Woodard Papers, Pre-1846 Envelope.

131. Woodard Papers, 1847 Envelope.

132. Several letters, dated in 1841 and 1842, have to do with Church building in Bethnal Green. (Woodard Papers, Packet B.)

133. Sir John Otter (the Founder's grandson) includes Sir John Patteson, Henry Tritton, and Baron Alderson among Bethnal Green acquaintances (Otter, op. cit., pp. 32 and 33). See also, B. W. T. Handford, *Lancing: A History of SS. Mary and Nicholas College, Lancing, 1848–1930* (Basil Blackwell, 1933), pp. 18 and 19. Handford writes of a group of friends, including Hope, Tritton, and George Talbot, who met in Woodard's vicarage during 1847.

134. Henry Tritton, partner of Barclay, Bevan, Tritton and Company, was treasurer of the Society from its inception and a Trustee from 1855 until his death in 1877. According to Woodard he gave £5,000 a year. (N. Woodard to the Marquess of Salisbury, 24 May 1886, Christ Church, Salisbury Papers, Letters from Woodard.) Cecil (in 1866, Lord Cranborne, and in 1868, Marquess of Salisbury), also a trustee, and for some years chairman of the London Central Committee, was a lifelong adviser and major contributor.

135. "We are thinking how it would be best to approach such men as Lords Derby, Westminster, Egerton, and others. . . . O that we had you amongst us. . . . But I suppose we may not ask for it." (The Reverend Henry Meynell to N. Woodard, 11 August 1868, Woodard Papers, 1868 Envelope, Midlands.)

136. E.g. to Gladstone. Above, note 2.

137. Many letters in response to the *Plea* are preserved. Those from William Jacobson, Philip Cazenove, E. B. Pusey, Charles Marriott, Bishop Gilbert of Chichester, George Moberly, C. J. Abraham, Dean Chandler and some others, are especially interesting as they indicate real interest which lasted and increased. (See Woodard Papers, 1848 Envelope.)

138. Over 230 such printed papers (exclusive of school prospectuses), dated between 1848 and 1891, are preserved amongst the Founder's private papers.

139. E.g., printed invitations and programmes were issued for the laying of the first stone of Lancing Chapel in June 1868 (Woodard Papers, Pamphlets 1868); on the appointed day 3,000 spectators, including a bevy of noblemen turned up and 300 clergy took part in the ceremonies (*The Guardian*, 5 August 1868). It is not recorded how much money was collected at this gathering. But at the very much smaller event centring about the laying of the foundation stone at Denstone in the same year, £313 were contributed. (*The Guardian*, 28 October 1868.)

140. Often by a distinguished clergyman. Preachers included Bp Thirlwall, Bp Wilberforce, Bp Selwyn, Archbp Benson, Dr Mozely, Archdeacon Hare.

141. There were, for example, five or six hundred at the opening of Hurstpierpoint, 21 June 1853 (*The Guardian*, 22 June 1853); 450 sat down to lunch at the opening of Denstone (*The Guardian*, 13 August, 1873); 600 had lunch before the Alton Towers "Demonstration" (*The Staffordshire Advertiser*, 10 August 1872).

142. *The Staffordshire Advertiser*, 10 August, 1872.

143. Woodard always, for example, listed the times of trains to and from London, and provided transport from the local station to the site of the

festivities. We have already seen how many people often attended (note 139 above). As for collections, £500 was taken in at the Ardingly stone-laying (London Committee Minute Book, 1864, Woodard Papers); £400 at the Hurst opening (*The Guardian*, 22 June 1863); the offering alone (exclusive of new subscriptions) at the service forming a part of a "demonstration" at Denstone amounted to £650 (*The Staffordshire Advertiser*, 10 August 1872).

144. H. Tritton to N. Woodard, 10 June 1861, Woodard Papers, 1861 Envelope, London Meeting.

145. *The Guardian*, 12 June 1861.

146. Below, p. 80.

147. *The Guardian*, 27 November 1861.

148. London Committee Minute Book, 1865, Woodard Papers.

149. N. Woodard, Pamphlet, February 1872, Woodard Papers, Pamphlets 1872.

150. Pamphlet, Advent 1855, Woodard Papers, Pamphlets 1855.

151. Lord Robert Cecil, Printed Letter, 15 March 1855, Woodard Papers, Pamphlets 1855.

152. Lord Robert Cecil to N. Woodard, 4 November, 1856, Woodard Papers, London Committee packet.

153. Robert Gregory to N. Woodard, 22 March 1858, Woodard Papers, London Committee packet.

154. London Committee Minute Book, 4 May 1864, Woodard Papers.

155. In 1864, Gregory founded a South London committee; in 1865 a City Committee was organized. Others in Highgate, Shoreditch and the south-west part of London were formed in 1866. (London Committee Minute Book, 1866, Woodard Papers.)

156. London Committee Minute Book, 7 February 1877, Woodard Papers.

157. N. Woodard, *The Society and Schools of St Mary and St Nicolas College*, 1878, Woodard Papers, Pamphlets 1878.

158. N. Woodard, Pamphlet, 1871, Pamphlets 1871.

159. Bp Fraser to N. Woodard, 7 November 1870, Woodard Papers, 1870 Packet, Midlands. Above, p. 44.

160. E. C. Lowe to N. Woodard, 22 September 1884, Woodard Papers, 1884 Packet, Midlands.

161. E. C. Lowe, Paper Printed for Private Circulation, Michaelmas, 1884, Woodard Papers, Pamphlets 1884.

162. Printed Paper, Advent 1885, Woodard Papers, Pamphlets 1885. Extension Fund Subscription List, 1885, Woodard Papers, Pamphlets 1885.

163. H. Meynell, *Canon Woodard's Scheme for the Education of the Middle Classes and its Claims on the Confidence of Churchmen*, July 1881, Woodard Papers, Pamphlets 1881, pp. 8 and 9.

164. E. Blackmore to N. Woodard, 23 October 1874, Woodard Papers, 1874 Packet, Organization. Blackmore was the Bursar of the Southern Division.

165. See, Correspondence between N. Woodard and H. M. Gibbs, 1875, Woodard Papers, 1875 Packet, Gibbs.

166. H. M. Gibbs to N. Woodard, 13 June 1885, Woodard Papers, 1885 Packet. H. M. Gibbs to N. Woodard, 22 July 1886, Woodard Papers, 1886 Packet. The Association never raised enough for a new school; the total amount raised by 1891 was £1,000, and was devoted to improvements at Ardingly (R. Perry, *Ardingly, 1858–1946, A History of the School* [London, Old Ardinians Society, 1951], p. 23).

167. Woodard accepted the Canonry at Manchester chiefly as a device to gain a firm foothold in the Midlands. (See, Otter, op. cit., p. 229.) His own personal finances were largely devoted to the scheme. Indeed, his family seem to have been forced into a rather Spartan existence; on a visit to Beresford Hope in 1860, he wrote to Lowe that his "wife would not come after all. We can't afford it. She has hardly had a new gown since the College was first begun." (N. Woodard to E. C. Lowe, 7 January 1860, Lancing Archives, Letters to Lowe.)

168. *Draft Statutes*, 1873. He signed and delivered a copy of this draft in 1880. (C. R. Freeman to Sir John Otter, 13 June 1922, Woodard Papers, Statutes Envelope.)

169. Lord Robert Cecil to N. Woodard, 1856 (no other date), Woodard Papers, London Committee Envelope.

170. *The Derbyshire Advertiser*, 1 February 1867.

171. George Mackarness to N. Woodard, 19 November 1870; H. Meynell to N. Woodard, 18 November 1870; N. Woodard to Lowe, 29 November 1870; N. Woodard to the Bishop of Lichfield (Selwyn), 9 February 1871, Woodard Papers, 1870 and 1871 Packets, Organization.

172. Alfred Plummer to N. Woodard, 23 March 1871, Woodard Papers, 1871 Packet, School Life.

173. R. E. Sanderson to N. Woodard, 24 August 1868, Woodard Papers, 1868 Envelope, School Life.

174. N. Woodard to E. Field, 21 June 1877, Woodard Papers, School Religion. Field was Senior Chaplain of the Society, and had been a Fellow for twenty-three years. He had written to the Bishop of Chichester about his membership in the Holy Cross Society to which the Bishop objected. Subsequently Woodard wrote to Field: "If you have been drawn into this abominable affair and have been in correspondence with the Bishop, without consulting me, I must decline to read your letter to the Bishop or to myself. . . . I have no intention to be mixed up with this wicked folly of playing at being priests."

CHAPTER 3

PUBLIC SCHOOL CATHOLICISM

1. See, Brian Heeney, "Tractarian Pastor: Edward Monro of Harrow Weald", *Canadian Journal of Theology*, Vol. XIII (1967), pp. 241–53, and Vol. XIV (1968), pp. 13–27. Also see, Dieter Voll, *Catholic Evangelicalism* (Faith Press, 1963).

2. After Newman's secession, Charles Marriott took a great interest in the question of opening the ancient universities to poor scholars; in 1849 he wrote a pamphlet on the admission of Dissenters to Church schools. See, C. Marriott, *University Extension and the Poor Scholar Question* (Alexander

Ambrose Masson, Oxford, 1848) and C. Marriott, *A Letter to the Reverend H. W. Bellairs, M.A. One of Her Majesty's Inspectors of Schools. On the Admission of the Children of Dissenters to Church Schools* (Alexander Ambrose Masson, Littlemore, 1849).

3. H. J. Burgess, *Enterprise in Education*, p. 150.
4. G. A. Denison to N. Woodard, 21 October 1879, Woodard Papers, 1879 Pack, Supporters.
5. Above, pp. 13ff.
6. A. K. Boyd, *The History of Radley College, 1847–1947* (Blackwell, 1948), pp. 4, 7 and 32.
7. A. F. Leach, *A History of Bradfield College* (Henry Frowde, 1900), pp. 42 and 43.
8. James Skinner, *The Church in the Public School. A Sermon Preached at the Annual Commemoration Festival at St Mary's College, Harlow, Essex, with a Letter to the Rev. the President of the College* (J. H. and Jas. Parker, London 1861), p. 13.
9. *History of All Saints' School, Bloxham, 1860–1910, with Supplement, 1910–1925* (Published at the School, 1925), p. 49. Below, p. 156.
10. Ibid., p. 36.
11. C. P. S. Clarke, *The Oxford Movement and After* (A. R. Mowbray, 1932), p. 296. Below, p. 157.
12. William Butler to N. Woodard, 26 May 1848, Woodard Papers, 1848 Envelope, Enquiries, etc. Doubtless there were other such schools. A writer in *The Guardian* of 14 December 1870, advertising the Stoke Newington Middle Class School perhaps hinted at Anglo-Catholic inspiration when he remarked that the school was "intended for a neighbourhood overriden with Dissent and secularism", and referred to Canons Gregory and Woodard as "patrons" (*The Guardian*, 14 December 1870). Marcus Donovan, in his book *After the Tractarians*, referred to a Mr Brooke, who became Assistant-Missioner at St John's, Kennington in 1871, and who extended Anglo-Catholic influence into a large middle school which he established in that parish (Marcus Donovan, *After the Tractarians* [Philip Allan, 1933], p. 87).
13. T. Mozley, *Reminiscences Chiefly of Oriel College and the Oxford Movement* (Longmans, Green, 1882), II, p. 22.
14. John Keble, *Sermons Academical and Occasional* (J. H. Parker, Oxford, 1847), p. 321. *The Guardian*, 7 July 1847.
15. Keble, *Sermons*, p. 338.
16. *The Guardian*, 5 November 1851, Leading Article.
17. The official National Society Committee (the Committee of Inquiry and Correspondence), formed as the result of the agitation of Wood, Manning, and others, had Lord Ashley as one of its members (see above, Chapter I, Note 49). Diocesan Boards also included men of various views.
18. Boyd, *History of Radley*, p. 99.
19. Leach, *History of Bradfield*, p. 134.
20. Below, p. 84.
21. N. Woodard to R. E. Sanderson, 7 December 1861, Woodard Papers, 1861 Envelope, Religion.

22. The Covenant of Works, 20 November 1830, Woodard Papers, Packet A.
23. See, H. L. Mencken to N. Woodard, 30 April 1832, Woodard Papers, Packet A; and Thomas Mortimer to N. Woodard, 17 November 1834, Woodard Papers, Packet A.
   Rowland Hill to N. Woodard, 12 January 1832, Woodard Papers, Packet A. Hill (1744–1833) was an eccentric Evangelical (the term Dissenter is perhaps not technically accurate), who had a chequered but successful preaching career. He early took to field evangelism, and although he obtained deacon's orders in 1773, he was refused advancement to the priesthood because of his irregular preaching activities. But "he continued to preach wherever he could find an audience, in churches, chapels, tabernacles, and the open air, often to immense congregations and sometimes amid great interruption and violence". (Thomas Hamilton, D.N.B., XXVI, p. 411.) From 1783 he occupied the pulpit of Surrey Chapel. He was prominent in the Religious Tract Society, the British and Foreign Bible Society, and the London Missionary Society. Also see, George Flint to N. Woodard, 31 August 1831, Woodard Papers, Packet A.
24. N. Woodard to the Bishop of London (Blomfield), 15 June 1843. Quoted in Otter, op. cit., p. 12.
25. Thomas Mortimer to N. Woodard, 14 August 1841, Woodard Papers, Packet B.
26. Frederick Oakley to N. Woodard, 29 July 1845, Woodard Papers, Packet B.
27. N. Woodard to Frederick Oakley, 8 November 1845, Woodard Papers. Packet B.
28. Edward Heap (?) to N. Woodard, 31 July 1846, Woodard Papers, 1846 Envelope, Religion.
29. N. Woodard to Lady Shrewsbury, 14 December 1868, Woodard Papers, 1868 Envelope, Religion.
30. "I shall not hold my tongue if I hear people calumniate the Church of England, but will without breach of charity or unkind intentions place things in their true light so far as I know how." (N. Woodard to W. Wheeler, 16 January 1856, Woodard Papers, 1856 Envelope, Personal.)
31. *Preamble*, p. 1.
32. The Bishop of London (Blomfield) to N. Woodard, 6 July 1843. Quoted in Otter, op. cit., p. 14.
33. N. Woodard to the Bishop of London (Blomfield), 17 August 1843. Quoted in Otter, op. cit., p. 17.
34. N. Woodard to the Bishop of London (Blomfield), 7 December 1843. Quoted in Otter, op. cit., p. 28.
35. The Bishop of London (Blomfield) to N. Woodard, 6 July 1843. Quoted in Otter, op. cit., p. 13. The Bishop of London (Blomfield) to N. Woodard, 26 December 1843. Quoted in Otter, op. cit., p. 29.
36. C. Marriott to N. Woodard, 28 January 1848, Woodard Papers, 1848 Envelope, Religion. J. Keble to N. Woodard, 21 July 1851, Woodard Papers, 1851 Envelope, Religion.
37. Edmund Field to N. Woodard, 18 April 1864, Woodard Papers, 1864 Envelope, Masters; J. Braithwaite to N. Woodard, 28 July 1853, Woodard

Papers, 1852–3 Envelope, Masters. Josiah Allen to N. Woodard, undated, Woodard Papers, 1849 Envelope, Parents and Boys; Jackson Taylor to N. Woodard, 16 July 1849, Woodard Papers, 1849 Envelope, Parents and Boys.

38. N. Woodard to Lady Shrewsbury, 14 December 1868, Woodard Papers, 1868 Envelope, Religion.

39. N. Woodard to Christopher Wordsworth, 11 December 1846, Woodard Papers, 1846 Envelope, Contributions and support.

40. Fragment of a letter from Woodard to an unknown bishop, undated, Woodard Papers, "Undated" Envelope, Religion.

41. N. Woodard to E. C. Lowe, 15 March 1875, Lancing Archives, Letters to Lowe.

42. N. Woodard to E. C. Lowe, 12 June 1880, Lancing Archives, Letters to Lowe.

43. S. L. Ollard, *A Short History of the Oxford Movement* (A. R. Mowbray, 1933), p. 8.

44. N. Woodard to Christopher Wordsworth, 11 December 1846, Woodard Papers, 1846 Envelope, Contributions and Support.

45. N. Woodard to Julius Hare, 19 April 1850, Lancing Archives, Letters to Hare.

46. N. Woodard to the Bishop of Lichfield (G. A. Selwyn), 9 February 1871, Woodard Papers, 1871 Packet, School Life.

47. Above, p. 46, and below, p. 154.

48. N. Woodard to the Marquess of Salisbury, 18 March 1872, Woodard Papers, 1872 Packet, Religion.

49. N. Woodard to E. C. Lowe, 26 June 1885, Lancing Archives, Letters to Lowe.

50. The Bishop of London (Blomfield) to C. Miller, 5 September 1843. Quoted in Otter, op. cit., p. 23. N. Woodard to E. C. Lowe, 28 May 1854, Lancing Archives, Letters to Lowe.

51. Sarah Neale to N. Woodard, 14 July 1856, Woodard Papers, 1856 Envelope, Personal.

52. J. M. Neale to N. Woodard, 24 July 1856, Woodard Papers, 1856 Envelope, Personal.

53. S. F. Green to N. Woodard, 12 December 1881, Woodard Papers, 1881 Packet, Religion; S. F. Green to N. Woodard, 18 February 1882, 21 February 1882, 18 August 1882, 23 February 1882 ("Eve of St Matthias"), 10 November 1882, Woodard Papers, 1882 Packet, Religion. Each of these letters is written in reply to one from Woodard.

54. N. Woodard to E. C. Lowe, 1 December 1881, Lancing Archives, Letters to Lowe.

55. Archdeacon Denison, in reply to a letter from Woodard, wrote: "I am much of your mind about Ritualists and generally young Church People. They are more than half hankering after medievalism, and but very cranky servants of the Church of England." (G. A. Denison to N. Woodard, 31 August 1883, Woodard Papers, 1883 Packet, Church Schools Co.) Pusey, also replying to a letter from Woodard, wrote:

"There are indeed rocks ahead, and people on both sides (especially the ultra-Ritualists) are steering the vessel straight against them." (E. B. Pusey to N. Woodard, 10 November 1872, Woodard Papers, 1872 Packet, Supporters.)

56. N. Woodard to Upton Richards, 28 June 1865, Woodard Papers, 1865 Envelope, Religion.

57. Below, p. 69.

58. N. Woodard to E. C. Lowe, 28 May 1854, Lancing Archives, Letters to Lowe.

59. N. Woodard to E. C. Lowe, 6 September 1883, Lancing Archives, Letters to Lowe.

60. Below, pp. 99ff.

61. N. Woodard to J. Scobell, 13 March 1851, Lancing Archives.

62. Lowe, *St Nicolas College and its Schools. A Record* . . . , p. 26.

63. S.I.C., V, p. 66.

64. Lowe, *St Nicolas College and its Schools. A Record* . . . , p. 26.

65. N. Woodard, printed letter, July 1883, Woodard Papers, Pamphlets, 1883.

66. S.I.C., V, p. 67.

67. E. C. Lowe to W. E. Gladstone, 19 November 1886, British Museum, Gladstone Papers, Vol. CCCCXIV, Additional MSS, 44,499, fol. 183.

68. These four were confirmed "with parents' consent after formal inquiries as to their baptism". E. C. Lowe to N. Woodard, Whit Tuesday, 1885, Woodard Papers, 1885 Packet, Organization.

69. Thomas Hunter contributed £200. Thos. Hunter to N. Woodard, 14 February 1872, Woodard Papers, 1872 Packet, Supporters.

70. N. Woodard to E. C. Lowe, 19 May 1860, Lancing Archives, Letters to Lowe.

71. N. Woodard to E. C. Lowe, 19 May 1860, Lancing Archives, Letters to Lowe.

72. Below, Chapter IV.

73. Above, p. 24.

74. N. Woodard to J. Scobell, 13 March 1851, Lancing Archives.

75. N. Woodard to Rev. J. Thomson, 4 January 1851, Woodard Papers, 1851 Envelope, Religion.

76. E. C. Mack, *Public Schools and British Opinion, 1780 to 1860* (Methuen, 1938), pp. 266 and 271.

77. Ibid., p. 378.

78. Woodard, *Public Schools for the Middle Classes* . . . , pp. 17 and 19.

79. Ibid., p. 18.

80. N. Woodard to J. Curtis, 12 December 1857, Woodard Papers, 1857 Envelope, School Life.

81. F. W. Cornish, *The English Church in the Nineteenth Century* (Macmillan, 1910), II, p. 85.

82. N. Woodard to the Bishop of Chichester (Gilbert), Whitsunday Eve, 1851, Lancing Archives, Letters to Bishop Gilbert.

83. N. Woodard to J. Curtis, 12 December 1857, Woodard Papers, 1857 Envelope, School Life.

84. N. Woodard to Julius Hare, 6 December 1848, Lancing Archives, Letters to Hare.

85. Lowe, *St. Nicolas College and its Schools. A Record* . . . , p. 27.

86. N. Woodard to J. Curtis, 12 December 1857, Woodard Papers, 1857 Envelope, School Life.

87. E. C. Lowe to N. Woodard, 8 December 1861, Woodard Papers, 1861 Envelope, Religion.

88. He remained at Hurst until 1863 when he was moved to Lancing. Field became Senior Chaplain of the Society and was still at Lancing at the time of Woodard's death. Edmund Field to N. Woodard, 20 March 1857, Woodard Papers, 1857 Envelope, Religion. (Italics mine.)

89. E. Field to N. Woodard, 19 January 1859, Woodard Papers, 1859 Envelope, Religion. H. G. Woods, subsequently President of Trinity College, Oxford, and Master of the Temple, was a Lancing student during the 50s. He wrote: "though it was true that boys, when preparing for confirmation, were asked by the Chaplain whether they wished to confess, no further pressure was put on them if they said 'no'." (H. G. W[oods], "A school in the making", *The Lancing Register* [Meyers, Brooks & Co., 1913], XXX.)

90. Josiah Allen to N. Woodard, undated, Woodard Papers, 1849 Envelope; Jackson Taylor to N. Woodard, 16 July 1849, Woodard Papers, 1849 Envelope, Parents and Boys.

91. G. O. L. Thomson to N. Woodard, 13 February 1881, Woodard Papers, 1881 Packet, Religion.

92. Cornish, op. cit., II, p. 84. Liddon, it is interesting to note, was asked to become chaplain at Lancing in 1859, after his resignation from Cuddesdon. (H. P. Liddon to N. Woodard, 19 February 1859, Woodard Papers, 1859 Envelope, Masters.)

93. The Bishop of Chichester (Gilbert) to E. Field, 9 January 1857, Woodard Papers, 1857 Envelope, Religion.

94. E. Field to N. Woodard, 20 March 1857, Woodard Papers, 1857 Envelope, Religion.

95. E. Field to the Bishop of Chichester (Gilbert), 5 November 1861, Woodard Papers, 1861 Envelope, Religion.

96. E. Field to N. Woodard, 28 November 1861, Woodard Papers, 1861 Envelope, Religion.

97. N. Woodard to the Bishop of Chichester (Gilbert), 1 November 1873, Woodard Papers, 1873 Packet, Religion.

98. E. C. Lowe to N. Woodard, 18 June 1865, Woodard Papers, 1865 Envelope, Religion; N. Woodard to E. Field, 1 April 1871, Woodard Papers, 1871 Packet, Religion. In the latter, Woodard wrote: "I am not prepared . . . to do anything to weaken my legal position . . . at no time are we likely to hazard the weakening of legal bonds by using our chapels for self-selected services."

99. The headmasters of the Sussex schools requested Woodard to authorize a shorter form in 1875. (R. E. Sanderson to N. Woodard, 14 July 1875, Woodard Papers, 1875 Packet, Religion.)

100. Lowe, *St Nicolas College and its Schools. A Record* . . ., p. 26.

101. E. C. Lowe, John Branthwaite, Edmund Field, A. C. Wilson: *Report of the Committee Appointed 22 June 1857 on the Religious Ceremonial of St Nicolas College* (MSS.), Woodard Papers, Pamphlets, 1857.

102. Edmund Field to N. Woodard, 29 March 1871, Woodard Papers, 1871 Packet, Religion.

103. I.e. the period between Liddell *v*. Westerton and Martin *v*. Mackonochie. (Cornish, op. cit., II, p. 16.)

104. E. C. Lowe to N. Woodard, 17 May 1886, Woodard Papers, 1886 Packet, Masters. E. C. Lowe to J. S. Bartlett, 24 October 1872, Woodard Papers, 1872 Packet, Religion.

105. E. C. Lowe to N. Woodard, 13 February 1868, Woodard Papers, 1868 Envelope, Religion.

106. N. Woodard to the Marquess of Salisbury, 14 August 1878, Christ Church, Salisbury Papers. Letters from Woodard.

107. E. C. Lowe to N. Woodard, 17 May 1886, Woodard Papers, 1886 Packet, Masters; E. C. Lowe, *A Consuetudinarium, or Guide for the Chaplains, Clerical Fellows, and other Clergy ministering in the Chapels of the College of SS. Mary and John of Lichfield*, Passiontide, 1886, Woodard Papers, 1886 Packet.

108. Lowe, *A Consuetudinarium* . . .

109. G. C. White to N. Woodard, Rogation Sunday, 1858, Woodard Papers, 1858 Envelope A, Religion. The group of clergy included Lowder and Bryan King. This group must have been the Retreat Committee of the Society of the Holy Cross, which held its first retreat in 1856, and which was violently attacked by W. Walsh in his *Secret History of the Oxford Movement* (Swan Sonnenschein, London, 1899), p. 57.

110. N. Woodard to G. C. White, Holy Thursday, 1858, Woodard Papers, 1858 Envelope A, Religion. In the 70s Woodard did allow such retreats (E. Field to N. Woodard, 12 July 1875, Woodard Papers, 1875 Packet, Religion).

111. This was certainly true of all who remained for a long time, notably E. C. Lowe, A. C. Wilson, J. Branthwaite, F. M. D. Mertens, Edmund Field. Sanderson, though he came from the headmastership of Bradfield, was at first very moderate and opposed the practice of confession (R. E. Sanderson to N. Woodard, 6 December 1861, Woodard Papers, 1861 Envelope, Religion); later he became a strong Catholic (R. E. Sanderson to N. Woodard, 27 October 1875, Woodard Papers, 1875 Packet, Religion). Henry Jacobs, Woodard's first headmaster, resigned shortly after his arrival: one reason given for this was his aversion to "auricular confession" (Henry Jacobs to N. Woodard, 31 August 1848, 1848 Envelope, Organization).

112. N. Woodard to E. C. Lowe, 28 January 1880, Lancing Archives, Letters to Lowe.

113. The future hymn-writer and author spent seven years at Hurst as a junior master. He was recommended for the position by Charles Lowder

of St Barnabas' Church, Pimlico. See, W. Purcell, *Onward Christian Soldier* (Longmans, Green, 1957), p. 54.

114. E. C. Lowe to N. Woodard, 11 March 1860, Woodard Papers, 1856 Envelope, Religion.

115. George Bampfield to "Reginald", undated, Woodard Papers, 1856 Envelope, Religion.

116. N. Woodard to the Bishop of Chichester (Gilbert), 23 January 1857, Woodard Papers, Packet D. Woodard actually took on one young man (Francis Beck) as a junior master principally to curb his Romanizing tendencies. Whether he was successful or not we do not know. (See, J. W. Beck to N. Woodard, 25 October 1854 and 31 October 1854, Woodard Papers, 1854 Envelope, Masters.)

117. E. Field to N. Woodard, 3 June 1860, Woodard Papers, 1860 Envelope, Religion.

118. Sanderson had refused to go to this meeting because of Woodard's disapproval (E. Field to N. Woodard, 24 February 1876, Woodard Papers, 1876 Packet, Religion).

119. See, N. Woodard to the Bishop of Chichester (R. Durnford), 21 September 1877, Woodard Papers, 1877 Packet, Religion; A. L. Lewington to N. Woodard, 10 September 1877; E. Field to N. Woodard, 17 October 1877; F. K. Hilton to N. Woodard, 12 November 1877. All in Woodard Papers, 1877 Packet, Religion.

120. E. Field to N. Woodard, 17 October 1877, 1877 Packet, Religion.

121. E. Field to N. Woodard, Trinity Sunday 1883, Woodard Papers, 1883 Packet, Religion.

122. R. E. Sanderson to N. Woodard, 2 January 1875, Woodard Papers, 1875 Packet, School Life.

123. Printed copy of the petition, Woodard Papers, Pamphlets undated. See also, N. Woodard to E. C. Lowe, 25 April 1872, Lancing Archives, Letters to Lowe. There are other letters dealing with the same subject from Woodard to Lowe, written in April 1872, all in the Lancing Collection.

124. C. L. Wood to N. Woodard, 17 October 1872, Woodard Papers, 1872 Packet, Religion.

125. Proof copy of "Suggestions for the constitution of a Guild for promoting Middle Class Education", Woodard Papers, Pamphlets undated.

126. Such Anglo-Catholic organizations included: The Society of the Holy Cross, the Confraternity of the Blessed Sacrament, the Oxford Brotherhood of the Holy Trinity, The Guild of the Most Blessed Saviour, and the Catholic Union for Prayer. Edmund Field belonged to all of these (E. Field to N. Woodard, 17 October 1877, Woodard Papers, 1877 Packet, Religion).

127. Chaplain Handcock to N. Woodard, 19 January 1870, Woodard Papers, 1870 Packet, Religion.

128. E. Field to N. Woodard, 9 July 1874, Woodard Papers, 1874 Packet, School Life.

129. E. C. Lowe to "Old Hurst Johnians", Mid-Lent Sunday, 1871, Woodard Papers, Pamphlets, 1871.

130. At first, R. C. Carpenter, and then his son, Herbert Carpenter. N. Woodard, *A Brief Report . . .*, p. 5.

131. Kenneth Clark, *The Gothic Revival* (Constable, 1950), p. 208.

132. N. Woodard, Printed Letter, July 1885, Woodard Papers, Pamphlets, 1885.

133. T. Helmore to N. Woodard, 31 October 1865, Woodard Papers, 1865 Envelope, School Life. See also, Ollard, op. cit., pp. 238–9.

134. N. Woodard to E. C. Lowe, 29 November 1865, Lancing Archives, Letters to Lowe.

135. Above, p. 27.

136. Below, p. 107.

137. St Michael's Bognor. *Rules and Regulations for the Internal Work and Domestic Life of the Society*, undated, Lancing Archives, Bound Scrap-book, p. 113.

138. Frances Wheeler to N. Woodard, 20 January 1875, Woodard Papers, 1875 Packet, Girls.

139. K. E. Kirk, op. cit., p. 145. I received a letter from the Lady Warden of St Michael's school on 1 November 1960 in which she informed me that there was no evidence on this subject at the school.

140. Supplement to the Lancing College Magazine, June 1891, Woodard Papers, Pamphlets, 1891.

141. E. Field to N. Woodard, 28 December 1882, Woodard Papers, 1882 Packet, School Life.

142. *Lancing Register* (Enfield: Meyers, Brooks & Co., 1913), p. 21.

143. Constance Trollope: *Mark Namier Trollope, Bishop in Corea, 1911–1930* (S.P.C.K., 1936), pp. 4 and 5.

144. Sam Brooke, *Sam Brooke's Journal, The Diary of a Lancing Schoolboy, 1860–1865*, ed. Peter Hadley (published in aid of the friends of Lancing Chapel, 1953), p. 74.

145. See, ibid., p. 110.

146. Among the clergy: John Keble, E. B. Pusey, Charles Marriott, Bryan King, J. M. Neale, J. B. Mozley, Robert Gregory, G. A. Denison, Dr Moberly of Winchester and Salisbury, Upton Richards. Among the laity: Lord Robert Cecil (3rd Marquess of Salisbury), Henry Tritton, Robert Moorsom, Lord Richard Cavendish, J. G. Hubbard (Lord Addington), Beresford Hope, and Sir T. Percival Heywood.

147. Bishop Gilbert had been Principal of Brasenose from 1822–42, and Vice-chancellor of the University from 1836–40. He opposed Isaac Williams for the Professorship of Poetry on the ground of Williams' Tractarian opinions (R. W. Church, *The Oxford Movement, 1833–1845* [Macmillan, 1897], p. 316). The Bishop's action against J. M. Neale has been noted already (above, p. 58). The Bishop regarded the two Shorehams as hot-beds of Puseyism, largely because of the activities of Woodard's vicar, the Reverend W. Wheeler. Consequently he was suspicious of any plan which came from Wheeler's curate. (See, Letters from Bishop Gilbert to N. Woodard, 1847 and beginning of 1848, Lancing Archives; see also, *Correspondence between Certain Members of the Church of New Shoreham and The Reverend W. Wheeler, Vicar, on the Subject of Innovations in the Church Services*, 1845, Woodard Papers, Pamphlets on Religious and Social Matters, I.)

148. The Bishop of Chichester (Gilbert) to N. Woodard, 29 March 1848, Lancing Archives.

149. The record of one such Visitation, on 12 March 1853, consists of two notebooks of foolscap-size paper. Both sides of the pages were used, and there is a total of 279 pages of notes. (Woodard Papers.) Mention has already been made of Gilbert's care in keeping a record of the number of confessions heard in the schools (above, p. 65). In 1862–3, he again subjected the College to close scrutiny (below, p. 81–2).

150. The Bishop of Chichester (Gilbert) to N. Woodard, 3 June 1851, Lancing Archives.

151. The Bishop of Chichester (Gilbert) to N. Woodard, 10 May 1853, Lancing Archives.

152. The Bishop of Chichester (Gilbert) to N. Woodard, 3 January 1857, Woodard Papers, Packet D, Religion.

153. Julius Hare to N. Woodard, 21 April 1849, Woodard Papers, 1849 Envelope, Religion.

154. See, N. Woodard to Connop Thirlwall, 6 April 1867, 1867 Bundle, Supporters; also see, N. Woodard, *St Nicolas College and the Rev. J. Goring and Others. A Letter to the Substantial Tradesmen, Farmers, and Others of the Employing Classes of the County of Sussex*, Woodard Papers, 1857, Pamphlets, 17.

155. *The Brighton Guardian* (12 May 1852), reported Hare as saying: "If an Evangelical objected [to the schools] because the work was wearing, as he thought a Tractarian aspect, let him join it and so give it a different colouring."

156. J. Garbett to ?, 10 December 1861, Woodard Papers, 1861 Envelope, Religion. Garbett was the successful Protestant champion in the battle against Tractarian-supported Isaac Williams for the Oxford Professorship of Poetry some years before.

157. Lord Robert Cecil to N. Woodard, 20 January 1857, Woodard Papers, 1857 Envelope, Religion; The Earl of Carnarvon to N. Woodard, 19 May 1857, Woodard Papers, 1857 Envelope, Religion.

158. Above, pp. 63f.

159. A. Escott to N. Woodard, 10 March 1851, 1851 Envelope, Religion.

160. N. Woodard, *St Nicolas College and the Rev. J. Goring* . . . , p. 25.

161. "The school buildings certainly . . . owe nothing to the landed gentry of Sussex." N. Woodard to the Marquess of Salisbury, 23 March 1885, Christ Church, Salisbury Papers, Letters from Woodard.

162. Lord Chichester to N. Woodard, 24 June 1864, Woodard Papers, 1864 Envelope, Religion.

163. H. Mackenzie to N. Woodard, 13 June 1868, Woodard Papers, 1868 Envelope, Religion.

164. *The Brighton Herald*, 2 March 1850.

165. See, C. D. Maitland to N. Woodard, 26 November 1851, and the Bishop of Chichester (Gilbert) to N. Woodard, 10 May 1851. Woodard Papers, 1851 Envelope, Religion.

166. The doubts were "founded upon certain rumours which had gone abroad and become extensively credited, that certain practices, imitative of the

peculiar discipline of the Roman Catholic Church, were carried on and required of the pupils at Shoreham". (Extract from the Minutes of the Rural Deanery of Lewes, Thursday 27 February 1851, Woodard Papers, 1851 Envelope, Religion.)

167. 26 July 1851.

168. In a report of the Hurst annual festival in *The Brighton Herald* (12 May 1855), the writer said he could discover few outward indications of Puseyism. He concluded: "But we feel none the less that it [Puseyism] is the animating spirit of the institution." In *The Sussex Express* of 25 June 1853, Woodard was described as having adopted "the principle of association for educational purposes . . . hitherto resorted to exclusively by Rome".

169. MSS. of Hewett's accusations, Woodard Papers, 1852–3 Envelope, Hewett. The College, after an official visitation by the bishop was cleared of Hewett's charges. See, *The Guardian*, 22 June 1853.

170. *The Sussex Express*, 6 December 1856. The report covers five complete columns of exceedingly small print.

171. 5 December 1856, Leading Article.

172. The Reverend John Goring, who, in 1851, had withdrawn his support from S.N.C. because of the Society's practice of Confession. In 1857, he published his correspondence with Woodard in the papers; Woodard subsequently published his *St Nicolas College and the Rev. J. Goring*. . . .

173. R. W. Blencowe to N. Woodard, March 1857, Woodard Papers, 1857 Envelope, Religion.

174. *The Guardian*, 27 November 1861. For list of Oxford Committee see, Lord Robert Cecil, Pamphlet undated, Woodard Papers, Pamphlets 1861.

175. C. P. Golightly, *A Letter to the Reverend Dr Jeune, Vice-Chancellor of the University of Oxford, in Vindication of the Handbill Distributed at the Doors of the Sheldonian Theatre on 22 November 1861* (Slatter & Rose, Oxford, 1861), p. 3.

176. Golightly, *A Letter* . . ., p. 11. See also, *The Record*, 3 January 1862.

177. *The Record*, 3 January 1862.

178. *The Guardian*, 5 February 1862; *The Daily News*, 6 February 1862.

179. *The Daily News*, 6 February 1862, Leading Article.

180. *The Record*, 13 January 1862. *The Record*, 5 February 1862.

181. E. C. Lowe to N. Woodard, 12 February 1862, Woodard Papers, 1862 Envelope, Religion.

182. *The Daily News*, 8 February 1862, 11 February 1862, 14 February 1862, 20 February 1862, 21 February 1862.

183. Woodard Papers, 1862 Envelope, Religion.

184. J. Skinner to N. Woodard, 11 March 1862, Woodard Papers, 1862 Envelope, Religion. The E.C.U. also engaged in a public dispute with Bishop Wigan which was reported in the columns of *The Guardian*, 12 April 1862; 16 April 1862.

185. *The Guardian*, 13 May 1863. The Bishop of Chichester (Gilbert) to N. Woodard, 13 May & 15 May 1863, Woodard Papers, 1863 Envelope, Religion.

186. See, *The Woodard Schools* (Church Association, 1868), pp. 14 and 33. Also M. A. J. Tarver, *Trent College, 1868–1927* (G. Bell and Sons, 1929). Below, pp. 166f.

187. W. Glubb to N. Woodard, 9 June 1864, Woodard Papers, 1864 Envelope, Religion.

188. Tarver, op. cit., pp. 4 and 5.

189. See, Letter from G.R.M. in *The Derbyshire Advertiser and Journal*, 8 February 1867.

190. See, *The Record*, 21 January 1867, Leading Article; see also, *The Derbyshire Advertiser and Journal*, 1 February 1867 (Letter from "A Layman of the Church of England").

191. N. Woodard, *Denstone Public School, In Union with St Nicolas College. A Letter to Sir T. Percival Heywood, Bart.* (Joseph Master, 1867), p. 4.

192. Sir T. P. Heywood to N. Woodard, 7 February 1868, Woodard Papers, 1868 Envelope, Midlands.

193. E. C. Lowe to N. Woodard, 23 February 1874, and 17 March 1874, Woodard Papers, 1874 Packet, Religion and Midlands.

194. A newspaper clipping in the Woodard Papers (News Clippings, undated) contains the following extract from *The Rock*: "We cannot conceive a more unsatisfactory body of men [than the trustees and supporters of the Society] forming as they do a complete Anglo-Roman clan. . . . Dr Lowe . . . is a notorious advocate of the Confessional." This was evidently written at the time of Lord Brownlow's donation of the site at Ellesmere.

195. John Henn to N. Woodard, 24 November 1887. Woodard Papers, 1887 Packet, Miscellaneous.

196. R. Moorsom to N. Woodard, 11 January 1864, Woodard Papers, 1864 Envelope, Religion.

197. Upton Richards to N. Woodard, 7 April 1862, Woodard Papers, 1862 Envelope, Religion.

198. George F. Grundy to N. Woodard, 6 February 1862, Woodard Papers, 1862 Envelope, Religion.

199. Woodard Papers, Pamphlets, undated. On the third page, reference is made to "the recent meeting in Stafford" addressed by the "late Bishop of Lichfield"; the date of this meeting was 19 October 1867.

200. E. Soward to N. Woodard, undated, Woodard Papers, undated Envelope, Religion.

201. See, Chapters 2 and 4.

202. See, N. Woodard to J. F. Sanger, 27 April 1851, Woodard Papers, 1851 Envelope, Religion; also, E. C. Lowe to N. Woodard, 28 January 1862, Woodard Papers, 1862 Envelope, Religion.

203. On 22 January 1862, F. K. Leighton (the Warden of All Souls) wrote to Woodard: "I cannot withhold my conviction that some . . . step will be necessary in order to prevent a large secession of your supporters in Oxford." (Woodard Papers, 1862 Envelope, Bishop's Investigation, etc.) The Bishop of Chichester's delay in clearing the schools of Golightly's charges brought about this secession. On 8 August 1863, Leighton wrote that "you might be able to collect some funds in Oxford, but I would not

encourage you to rely on very much amount". (Woodard Papers, 1863 Envelope, Religion.)

204. In 1881, Henry Campion wrote: "You are not supported in the county so well as you otherwise would be . . . [because] the outside public still believes that Confession is pressed upon the boys." Henry Campion to N. Woodard, 23 October 1881, Woodard Papers, 1881 Packet, Supporters.

205. R. E. Sanderson to N. Woodard, 23 January 1875, Woodard Papers, 1875 Packet, Religion.

CHAPTER 4

THE EDUCATIONAL APPROACH

1. Matthew Arnold, *A French Eton*, p. 129.
2. See, for example, Edward Baines, Jr., *An Alarm to the Nation on the Unjust Unconstitutional, and Dangerous Measure of State Education Proposed by the Government* (London: Ward and Co., 1847). For further references on Congregationalist voluntaryism, see Brian Heeney, "Opposition to State Medicine and State Education: An Historical Analogy" *Queen's Quarterly*, Vol. LXXV (Spring, 1968).
3. J. E. G. de Montmorency, *State Intervention in English Education* (Cambridge University Press, 1902), p. 108.
4. 19 George III, c. 44.
5. 31 George III, c. 32.
6. Montmorency, op. cit., p. 12.
7. Burgess, *Enterprise in Education*, p. 150.
8. Although at Cambridge Dissenters could attend, they could not graduate without subscribing to the Thirty-nine Articles.
9. 34 and 35 Victoria, c. 26 s. 3.
10. See, S.I.C., I, 131, pp. 209ff., 224ff., and above, pp. 10f.
11. N. Woodard to Julius Hare, 6 December 1848, Lancing Archives.
12. N. Woodard, Printed Letter, 12 July 1848, Woodard Papers, 1848 Pamphlets.
13. N. Woodard to E. C. Lowe, 7 May 1880, Lancing Archives, Letters to Lowe; and N. Woodard, *The Society and Schools of St Mary and St Nicolas College* (Woodard Papers, Pamphlets, 1878). See also E. C. Lowe, *Education—Primary and Secondary* (a paper read at the Church Congress, Brighton, 1874).
14. N. Woodard to Sir H. Brand, 24 October 1881, Woodard Papers, 1881 Packet, Educational Theory.
15. *Plea*, p. 10.
16. N. Woodard to C. Warrand, no date (1862), Woodard Papers, 1862 Envelope, Other Schools.
17. N. Woodard to H. J. Roby, 20 October 1865, Woodard Papers, 1865 Envelope, Educational Approach.
18. The Endowed Schools Act (32 and 33 Victoria, c. 56). There was a distinction between day scholars, to whom this provision was to be applied

directly, and boarders to whom it applied only indirectly. By insisting that a boarder whose parents desired to invoke the conscience clause must be taken in as a day boy and must be provided with his board and lodging, the application of the conscience clause was made universal.

19. The Act excluded from the Commissioner's jurisdiction endowments given during the fifty years prior to 1869. (32 and 33 Victoria c. 56. s. 14[1].)
20. *Letter to Salisbury*, pp. 10–13.
21. *Letter to Salisbury*, pp. 14, 10, and 11.
22. Peter Stansky, "Lyttelton and Thring: A Study in Nineteenth-century Education," *Victorian Studies*, V (March 1962), p. 207. Lord Lyttelton to N. Woodard, 6 December 1869, Woodard Papers, Packet E.
23. N. Woodard to Lord Lyttelton, 13 December 1869, Woodard Papers, Packet E. The "Supplemental Act" to which Woodard refers was in fact the stillborn Part II of the Endowment Schools Bill. In this measure, provision was made for government inspection of endowed schools and for government examination of masters. The agency of government was to be an "Educational Council". No such bill was ever passed. (Parliamentary Papers, 1868–9, Vol. II, pp. 347ff.)
24. G. R. Parkin, *Life and Letters of Edward Thring* (London. Macmillan, 1898), I, p. 176.
25. Ibid., p. 176.
26. Stansky, op. cit., p. 218. Sanderson was present at the first regular meeting of headmasters in December 1870, and regularly thereafter. (See, *Report of Meeting of Head-Masters of Schools Held at Sherborne on December 28th and 29th, 1870*, p. 3.)
27. N. Woodard, Printed Letter, May 1872, Woodard Papers, Pamphlets, 1872.
28. N. Woodard to E. C. Lowe, 3 December 1877, Lancing Archives, Letters to Lowe. The College of Preceptors was a body, granted a charter in 1849, devoted both to raising teaching standards and examining secondary school pupils (J. W. Adamson, *English Education, 1789–1902* [Cambridge University Press, 1930], pp. 477ff.; and S.I.C., I, p. 329). On University Local Examinations, see note 98, below. Woodard's point here is that neither would have arisen if the Church had done its job as national educator.
29. *Letter to Salisbury*, p. 5.
30. J. J. Findlay (ed.), *Arnold of Rugby: His School Life and Contributions to Education* (Cambridge University Press, 1914), p. 137.
31. A. P. Stanley, *The Life and Correspondence of Thomas Arnold, D.D.* (New York: D. Appleton and Co., 1846), p. 264. Olive J. Brose, *Church and Parliament* (London: Oxford University Press, 1959), p. 187.
32. John Henry Newman, *The Idea of a University* (New York: Image Books, Doubleday and Co., 1959), p. 87.
33. *The Brighton Guardian*, 12 May 1852.
34. E. C. Lowe, *The Image of God. A Sermon for Schoolmasters and Schoolboys Preached in St John's College, Hurstpierpoint, on the Twelfth Sunday after Trinity, 1856* (London: Joseph Masters, 1856), p.19.
35. Below, p. 165.

36. Otter, op. cit., p. 183. I have not been able to discover an MS copy of this letter in the Woodard Papers. It is fully printed in Otter.

37. N. Woodard to J. Gassiot, 12 April 1866, Woodard Papers, 1866 Envelope, Educational Approach.

38. See, N. Woodard to the Archdeacon of Manchester (G. H. Grevill Anson), 18 July 1877, Woodard Papers, 1877 Packet, Universities. See also, N. Woodard to E. C. Lowe, 16 August 1880, Lancing Archives, Letters to Lowe.

39. *Letter to Salisbury*, p. 12.

40. Prospectus, The Church Schools Company Ltd., no date, Woodard Papers, Non-Woodard Middle Class Education.

41. *The Guardian*, 27 February 1884, Letter from E. H. Plumtre.

42. N. Woodard to E. C. Lowe, 18 November 1883, Lancing Archives, Letters to Lowe. See, *The Guardian*, 13 February 1884.

43. Woodard Papers, 1883 Packet, Church Schools Co. and G. A. Denison.

44. G. A. Denison, *The School of the Church Schools Company. A Letter to the Clergy and People of the Archdeaconry of Taunton* (Oxford and London: Parker and Co., 1883).

45. "He seems to regard all acts of prudence as a sin." (N. Woodard to E. C. Lowe, 4 January 1883, Lancing Archives, Letters to Lowe.) N. Woodard to E. C. Lowe, 21 November 1883, Lancing Archives, Letters to Lowe.

46. J. G. Talbot to N. Woodard, 29 June 1883, Woodard Papers, 1883 Packet, Other Schools.

47. Adamson, op. cit., p. 358. See, *The Guardian*, 3 July 1867, Leading Article. Below, p. 166.

48. N. Woodard to J. Gassiot, 12 April 1866, Woodard Papers, 1866 Envelope, Educational Approach.

49. E. C. Mack, *Public Schools and British Opinion, 1780 to 1860* (Methuen, 1938), p. 105.

50. *Plea*, p. 15.

51. *Plea*, p. 13.

52. *Public Schools for the Middle Classes* (1851), p. 13. See p. 38 above for an account of the only day school established after 1848 (Dewsbury).

53. Pamphlet entitled *Midland Counties and Manchester Public School for the Sons of Persons of Small Means*, September 1871, Woodard Papers, Pamphlets, 1871.

54. *The Guardian*, 6 April 1870. Letter from N. Woodard. *Public Schools for the Middle Classes* (1852), p. 17.

55. *The Guardian*, 28 October 1868. Leading Article.

56. *The Guardian*, 6 April 1870. Letter from N. Woodard. *The Guardian*, 27 November 1861.

57. "Separate committees should be formed for each public school for the purpose of collecting subscriptions . . . from their old members. They would then vie with each other as to which school would contribute most; and I would also suggest that a quarterly collection should be made at the schools from the present members. If we truly profess to appreciate the

benefit of our public school education, we shall gladly try to extend it to others." (*The Guardian*, 12 June 1861. Letter from "A Public school man".)

58. N. Woodard, *To the Past and Passing Generations of Lancing Boys* (September 1884, Woodard Papers, Pamphlets, 1884), p. 3. Referred to hereafter by title only.

59. Ibid., p. 2. Although this statement was made late in Woodard's life, the same principles were clear in everything he did and said from the beginning of his educational activity. Cf. T. W. Bamford, *The Rise of the Public Schools* (Nelson, 1967), p. 37. Bamford states the conventional understanding of "public school": "The school must provide a classical education and be expensive enough to exclude the lower and lower middle classes at least."

60. *To the Past and Passing Generations of Lancing Boys*, p. 4.

61. N. Woodard, Printed Letter, June 1868, Lancing Archives, Scrap Book.

62. N. Woodard to Julius Hare, 6 December 1848, Lancing Archives, Letters to Hare.

63. Mack, op. cit., pp. 143ff, and pp. 207ff.

64. Simon, op. cit., p. 116.

65. Tiffen, op. cit., pp. 63 & 73.

66. Robert Lowe, *Middle Class and Primary Education*, p. 12.

67. Canon Moseley, *Middle-Class Education and the Bristol Diocesan Trade School* (*A Paper read at the Church Congress held in Bristol in October 1864*) (Bristol: S. E. Chillcott, 1864), pp. 4 & 5.

68. Ibid., p. 7. Of the students, Canon Moseley wrote: "The greater number of the boys are the sons of the upper class of mechanics, the rest are for the most part the sons of small tradesmen."

69. J. L. Brereton, "Principles and Plan of a Farm and County School" (1858) in Earl Fortescue *Public Schools for the Middle Classes* (Longmans, Green, 1864), p. 121.

70. *The Guardian*, 18 October 1865.

71. Albert Middle-Class college in Suffolk. Erected at Framlingham by Public Subscription to the Memory of H. R. H. the Late Prince Consort. Prospectus, May 1865 (Ministry of Education Library).

72. See, George Chandler, op. cit., p. 11.

73. *The Guardian*, 6 January 1864.

74. S.I.C., I, p. 300.

75. Ibid., p. 287.

76. Ibid., pp. 80–6.

77. Prospectus, undated, Woodard Papers, Pamphlets 1847.

78. Prospectus, December 1849, Woodard Papers, Pamphlets 1849.

79. C. E. Moberly to N. Woodard, 24 December 1848, Woodard Papers, 1848 Envelope, Organization and School Business.

80. N. Woodard to C. E. Moberly, 30 December 1848, Woodard Papers, 1848 Envelope, Organization and School Business.

81. "The course of instruction, classical and mathematical, is that ordinarily

followed in the great public schools, including French, Writing and Vocal Music" (*Calendar*, 1850).

82. S.I.C., VII, p. 137.
83. R. E. Sanderson to N. Woodard, 17 February 1869, Woodard Papers, 1869 Envelope, School Life. R. E. Sanderson Printed Letter, 18 July 1872, Woodard Papers, Pamphlets 1872.
84. N. Woodard, Printed Letter, August 1849, Woodard Papers, Pamphlets 1849.
85. E. C. Lowe to N. Woodard, 9 February 1858, Woodard Papers, Packet D.
86. Lowe, *St Nicolas College and its Schools. A Record . . .*, p. 28.
87. B. Burgis to E. C. Lowe, 20 August 1856, Woodard Papers, 1856 Envelope, School Life. "Studies seem to be conducted on the principle of, for every nine hours per working week at Chapel and prayers, about as much to Latin, three hours to French, three arithmetic and three writing" (*The Daily News*, 8 February 1862, Letter from a Father).
88. S.I.C., VII, p. 142. *Calendars*, 1871 and 1886. See also, E. Blackmore to N. Woodard, 19 February 1878, Woodard Papers, 1878 Packet, School Life.
89. *Calendars*, 1859 and 1890. See, *Calendars*, and S.I.C., VII, p. 143. Subjects in 1859 were reading, writing, arithmetic, vocal music, English, and Latin Grammar, mathematics, bookkeeping, geography, linear drawing, general history.
90. Prospectus, 30 August 1850, Woodard Papers, Pamphlets 1850.
91. James Reynolds to N. Woodard, 13 August 1851, Woodard Papers, 1851 Envelope, School Life. W. Nassau Lees, *Instruction in the Oriental Languages Considered Specially as Regards the Education of Candidates for the East India Civil Service and as a National Question* (Williams and Norgate, 1857), pp. 14–15.
92. Henry Tritton to N. Woodard, 8 February 1856, Woodard Papers, 1856 Envelope, School Life. Tritton wrote that £2,000 had been lost by 1856. See also, F. M. Arnold to N. Woodard, 30 August 1854, Woodard Papers, 1854 Envelope, School Life.
93. F. M. D. Mertens, Printed Letter, November 1865, Woodard Papers, Pamphlets 1865.
94. Ibid.
95. *Calendar*, 1871.
96. See, "The Problem of the Middle Classes", *Good Words*, 1877, p. 358. At a meeting of the Central Council of Diocesan Conferences in 1883, Mr Evelyn Hubbard spoke thus: "Our middle class boarding schools should have land and workshops attached to them; they should be really industrial schools, so that they might not only turn out clerks and book-keepers, but practical artisans and scientific farmers" (*The Guardian*, 21 March 1883).
97. E. C. Lowe to N. Woodard, Advent Sunday, 1851, Woodard Papers, 1851 Envelope, Masters.
98. E. C. Lowe to N. Woodard, 21 November 1857, Woodard Papers, 1857 Envelope, School Life. These examinations were established in 1857; similar ones at Cambridge were established in 1858. The idea of Local

Examinations (as they came to be called) was pioneered by T. D. Acland and Frederick Temple. Candidates had to journey to examination centres, and the fees were quite high. These features, together with the fact that only individual boys and not whole schools were examined, limited their usefulness in raising the academic standards of middle class schools (See, *Report on the Results of the West of England Examination, by the Rev. F. Temple, M.A. and Correspondence with George Richmond and John Hullah, Esqrs., on the Arts in Connexion with General Education, by T. D. Acland, Esq., Jun.* [J. Ridgway, 1857]; also see S.I.C., I, pp. 330ff. I am indebted to J. P. C. Roach for allowing me to read an unpublished paper of his entitled "Secondary Education and Examination, 1838–95".)

99. N. Woodard to E. C. Lowe, 24 November 1857, Lancing Archives, Letters to Lowe. The Warden of All Souls (F. K. Leighton) to N. Woodard, 9 March 1870, and the Marquess of Salisbury to N. Woodard, 26 March 1870, Woodard Papers, 1870 Packet, Educational Theory.

100. N. Woodard to E. C. Lowe, 13 May 1875, and N. Woodard to E. C. Lowe, 15 October 1880, Lancing Archives, Letters to Lowe.

101. N. Woodard to Miss Lowe, 13 September 1849, Lancing Archives, Letters to Lowe.

102. N. Woodard, Printed Letter, Lent, 1856, Woodard Papers, Pamphlets, 1856. Above, pp. 73ff.

103. Frances Wheeler, *A Scheme for the Schools of S. Michael's and All Angels in a Letter to the Earl of Strathmore*, All Saints' Day 1866, Woodard Papers, Pamphlets, 1866.

104. [Dorothea Beale], *History of the Cheltenham Ladies' College* (Cheltenham: "Looker-on" Printing Works, 1904), p. 27.

105. Isabella M. S. Tod, *On the Education of Girls of the Middle Classes* (William Ridgway, 1874), p. 9.

106. E. C. Lowe, *Middle-Class Boarding Schools for Girls in the Midland Counties*, Woodard Papers, Pamphlets, 1872.

107. N. Woodard to E. C. Lowe, 9 October 1884, Lancing Archives, Letters to Lowe.

108. E. C. Lowe to N. Woodard, 5 October 1884, Woodard Papers, 1884 Packet, Girls. E. C. Lowe to N. Woodard, 10 October 1884, Woodard Papers, 1884 Packet, Girls.

109. *Calendar*, 1871. (No list of subjects taught in the Middle and Lower divisions of the school is given.) *Calendar*, 1886.

110. *Plea*, p. 13.
"Where do you look for agents to superintend and work your National schools? To the same look, as those who will willingly undertake this more difficult and laborious task of educating the employing classes. The clergy of the Church of England have no fear of imparting knowledge to the people, of any grade." *Public Schools for the Middle Classes* (1852), pp. 16–17.

111. *Calendar*, 1859, 1864, 1871, 1884. In 1884, at Ardingly, the ratio was one clergyman to seventy boys. For an analysis of the declining number of clerical masters in public schools generally in this period, see T. W. Bamford, op. cit., pp. 54ff.

112. "The great mass of the people [by which Woodard evidently meant the middle class, broadly understood], the real life and strength of England,

occupy so anomalous a position that they can never enjoy the fatherly and friendly ministrations of their spiritual guides." He went on to give examples, one of which was that of "a printer and publisher . . . [who] stated that his clergyman had never at any time been in his house or offered to guide himself or his family in any way whatever" (*Plea*, p. 5).

113. *Letter to Salisbury*, p. 24.

114. Lowe, *St Nicolas College and its Schools. A Record*. . . , p. 18. See also, *Letter to Salisbury*, p. 24. Woodard and Lowe constantly stressed the clerical duty to teach.

115. *Letter to Salisbury*, p. 24.

116. Below, p. 113. *Letter to Salisbury*, p. 24.

117. Loose, unmarked newspaper clipping, 1853, Woodard Papers, Newspaper Clippings, 1850s and 60s.

118. *Plea*, pp. 16 and 14. N. Woodard, *St Nicolas College and the Rev. J. Goring and Others*, pp. 11 and 12.

119. Henry Jacobs, first Headmaster of Shoreham Grammar School (Lancing) and the Rev. John Braithwaite, Headmaster of the same school in the 50s, were both Fellows of the Queen's College, Oxford, (Prospectus 1848 and 1849, Woodard Papers, Pamphlets 1848 and 1849.)

120. N. Woodard, Printed Letter, 24 October 1848, Woodard Papers, Pamphlets 1848.

121. H. G. W[oods], op. cit., XXIX.

122. *Plea*, p. 14.

123. N. Woodard to Rev. Pocock, 30 October 1848, Woodard Papers, 1848 Envelope, Organization and School Business.

124. W. Purcell, op. cit., p. 55.

125. Lowe, *St Nicolas College and its Schools. A Letter* . . . , p. 5.

126. N. Woodard to George Rawlinson, 25 January 1859, Woodard Papers, 1859 Envelope, Masters. Rawlinson refused Woodard's offer despite the hope of increasing this stipend by very considerable capitation fees on boys in the headmaster's house.

127. £26 5*s* on each boy in his house, and two guineas on each boy in the school. See, "Heads of Agreement with the Headmaster of Lancing", no date, Woodard Papers, 1869 Envelope, Masters.

128. R. E. Sanderson to N. Woodard, 5 January 1869, Woodard Papers, 1869 Bundle, Masters.

129. Staunton, op. cit., pp. 302 and 303. Cf. Bamford, op. cit., pp. 127ff.

130. R. E. Sanderson to N. Woodard, 1 June 1864, Woodard Papers, 1864 Envelope, Masters.

131. R. E. Sanderson to N. Woodard, 13 December 1869, Woodard Papers, School Life. Also see, R. E. Sanderson, Printed Letter, 18 July 1872, Woodard Papers, Pamphlets 1872.

132. E. C. Lowe to N. Woodard, 19 November 1864, Woodard Papers, 1864 Envelope, Masters.

133. N. Woodard to E. C. Lowe, 20 November 1864, Lancing Archives, Letters to Lowe.

134. *Notes on Middle Class Boarding Schools and Middle Class Education, Addressed to all who have Sons at School* (Kent & Co., 1859).

135. Hugh G. Robinson, "Middle-Class Education in England", *The Museum*, April, 1861, p. 10.

136. S.I.C., I, pp. 611 and 614. See, R. Howard, *A Plea for the Establishment of Additional Public Schools in Yorkshire for the Upper and Middle Classes* (William Skeffington, 1870), p. 22.

137. See, N. Woodard, Printed Letter, Advent, 1853, Woodard Papers, Pamphlets, 1853.

138. The information about the training school in this paragraph comes from three printed documents, all of which may be found among the Woodard Papers in the envelopes marked "pamphlets":
Report of the Associate-Educational Committee of St Nicolas College, No. I, 1853 (referred to hereafter as *Report* [1853]).
Report of the Associate-Educational Committee of St Nicolas College, No. II, 1854 (referred to hereafter as *Report* [1854]).
St Nicolas College. Regulations for the Admission and Examination of Probationer Associates, 1874 (referred to hereafter as *Regulations* [1874]).

139. Lowe, *St Nicolas College and its Schools. A Letter* . . ., p. 6.

140. *Calendar*, 1854; Lowe, *St Nicolas College and its Schools. A Letter* . . ., p. 6.

141. *Calendars*, 1886 and 1890.

142. *Regulations* (1874), p. 6; R. Perry, op. cit., p. 108.

143. Lowe, *St Nicolas College and its Schools. A Letter* . . ., p. 7.

144. The *Hurst Johnian*, 1859–88. These figures are listed under "school numbers" or "new admissions". It must be remembered that some probationer associates from Hurst taught at Shoreham and Ardingly. Thus the figures in the *Hurst Johnian* might have to be slightly increased; for example, in 1871 there were two Probationer Associates at Ardingly.

145. *Calendars*, 1884 and 1888. No mention is made of the juniors in the Training School in the *Calendars*.

146. *Calendar*, 1890.

147. *St Saviour's Annals*, April 1878, p. 10.; Cf. Bamford, op. cit., p. 122.

148. In the same year five or six Associates on the foundation of the Midland Division were teaching in the Society's schools. *Calendar*, 1884.

149. E. C. Lowe, to N. Woodard, 6 February 1865, Woodard Papers, 1865 Envelope, Educational Approach.

150. Staunton, op. cit., p. 570.

151. J. H. Edmonds to N. Woodard, 5 March 1883, Woodard Papers, 1883 Packet, Masters.

152. In 1854 the College of Preceptors began to grant diplomas for secondary school teachers; in 1873 it started lectures for teachers. The Maria Grey Training College was founded in 1878. In 1879 the Teachers' Training Syndicate was founded at Cambridge; in 1883 a secondary-teachers' diploma was granted at the University of London. In 1896 the Oxford Delegacy for the training of such teachers was established.

153. E. C. Lowe, *The Image of God* . . .; *St Nicolas College and its Schools. A Letter* . . .; *St Nicolas College and its Schools. A Record* . . .

154. J. T. Coleridge to W. E. Gladstone, 12 January 1869, British Museum, Gladstone Papers, Vol. LIII, Additional MSS, 44,138, fol. 484.

155. *Letter to Salisbury*, p. 14.

156. *Calendar*, 1859.

157. *Calendar*, 1854. Any number over eight was charged £10 each. See, Lowe, *St Nicolas College and its Schools. A Report*, p. 31.

158. At Hurst, in 1858, there were ten servitors; in 1871, fifteen; in 1886, thirteen (*Calendars*). At the other schools with servitors' departments, the numbers also exceeded eight. In 1886, for example, there were twenty-one at Ardingly, eleven at Denstone, and eleven at Ellesmere (*Calendar* 1886).

159. For an example of the sort of boy accepted as a servitor, see Charles H. Christie to N. Woodard, 3 January 1861, Woodard Papers, 1861 Envelope, School Life. Christie recommended the ten-year old son of a poor widow, a servant, who had only £35 a year on which to live: "It would be a very great charity if it were possible for you to take him, as the poor woman is obliged to deny herself necessary food to maintain him." Dr Lowe wrote of a "gentleman who applied to me to receive into the servitors' school a boy whose family was utterly ruined, but highly connected, in the hope that by availing himself of the successive chances of promotion, he might struggle back again to a social position such as his ancestors had long held" (Lowe, *St Nicolas College and its Schools. A Record . . .*, p. 31).

160. Lowe, *St Nicolas College and its Schools. A Record . . .*, p. 31.

161. *The Hurst Johnian*, Vol. I (1858–9), p. 261.

162. E. C. Lowe to N. Woodard, 6 October 1873, Woodard Papers, 1873 Packet, Educational Theory.

163. E. C. Lowe, Printed Letter, 7 October 1887, Woodard Papers, Pamphlets, 1887.

164. See *Appendix B* for the parental occupations of a selection of boys in the 1860s. The fees of the school rose from 30 gns to 55 gns during the period of this study. In 1864, when the minimum fee at Lancing was 55 gns (S.I.C., XI, p. 240), that at Haileybury was £56 (S.I.C., I, Appendix I, p. 153); at Radley, £105 (ibid.); Cheltenham, 45 gns (ibid., p. 155); Bradfield, 100 gns (H. Staunton, op. cit., p. 559); Rossall, £52–£65 (ibid., p. 403); Wellington, £80–£110 (ibid., p. 405); at Rugby the minimum cost was £95 5*s*. (ibid., p. 323); at Winchester (Commoner), £105 (ibid., p. 82); and at Eton (Resident Oppidan) £144 3*s*. (ibid., p. 38). Of the twelve boys registered in 1848 whose subsequent occupations are listed in the Lancing Register, five were army officers, three were clergymen, two lawyers, one schoolmaster and one doctor (*A Register of St Nicolas College, Lancing, 1848–1900*. [Published by private subscription, 1900].)

165. Above, p. 24; S.I.C., V, p. 74. Answer to question 9649.

166. Above, pp. 32f., and Chapter 1, note 18.

167. According to the report of the Assistant Commissioner who examined Hurst on behalf of the Taunton Commission, only 10 per cent of the boys at the school had parents whose profession was given as "farmer" (S.I.C., VII, p. 105). For fees, see above, p. 33.

168. S.I.C., VII, p. 143. Also, above, p. 33.

169. H. L. Johnson (ed.), *A Register of St John's College, Hurstpierpoint* (published privately, 1914).

170. Mr Giffard, the S.I.C. Assistant Commissioner who examined Hurst, noted that "two exhibitions have been founded . . . tenable for three years and open to competition to all boys who have been at the school three years, and are not less than 16½ years of age at the time of competition" (S.I.C., VII, p. 140). Dr Lowe wrote to the Provost in 1864: "I do not see how Hurst can ever without abandoning its first ground compete with Rugby, Marlboro and Eton in scholarship. . . . Still . . . our fellows might go up with credit and graduate with honours" (E. C. Lowe to N. Woodard, 14 January 1864, Woodard Papers, 1864 Envelope, Educational Approach).

171. S.I.C., XI, p. 241.

172. "If [the headmasters] aim at making the middle schools cheaper preparation for the universities than our Lancings, our middle schools will fail to realize the object I have always supposed them to have" (E. C. Lowe to N. Woodard, 20 August 1881, Woodard Papers, 1881 Packet, Educational Theory).

173. Above, p. 33.

174. Above, p. 34. He realized that raising the fee above this amount would render the scheme "inaccessible to the description of persons for whom . . . [it] was built" (pamphlet on *Life Nominations to Scholarships at the Lower Middle Schools of St Nicolas College*, February 1878, Woodard Papers, Pamphlets, 1878).

175. *Calendar*, 1859, p. 23. Above, p. 6.

176. Mrs Wigley (*Our Home Work: A Manual of Domestic Economy* [Jarrold and Sons, 1876], p. 350) listed the budget of an engine driver (whom she described as a "highly-paid labourer"), who, together with his wife (who rented a room and sewed for her boarder) made about £170 per annum. Of this 2*s* a week was allowed for the education of their two children, and just over 6*s* a head per week for food. For a school year of forty weeks this works out to £14 10*s* for each child for board and education (deducting the board for holidays). This is not badly out of line with Woodard's charge. J. H. Walsh in his *Manual of Domestic Economy Suited to Families Spending from £100 to £1,000 a Year* (G. Routledge & Co., 1857), p. 3 made no specific suggestions except that for education and old age (savings) each family should save about one third of the amount they spend on current expense.

177. R. Perry, op. cit., p. 75.

178. Ibid., p. 42. Joseph Foster (*Alumni Oxonienses* [Parker & Co., 1888], IV, p. 1340) notes that he matriculated at Oxford in 1873.

179. R. E. Sanderson to N. Woodard, Feast of the Purification, 1881, Woodard Papers, 1881 Packet, Masters.

180. See, Burn, op. cit., p. 266; and Stansky, op. cit., p. 212.

181. See, J. P. C. Roach, "Victorian Universities and the National Intelligentsia", *Victorian Studies*, December 1959, p. 144. Woodard never mentioned this as a possibility. Lowe deplored it because it involved "separation from college life, associations and traditions, introduction to which is of infinitely greater value to the student of humbler life than to the youth of

gentle birth". (E. C. Lowe, *A Plea for Poor Scholars in the University and Colleges of Oxford Urged in a Letter to the Rector of Lincoln College*, 1867, Lancing Archives.)

182. E. C. Woollcombe, *University Extension and the Poor Scholar Question. A Letter to the Provost of Worcester College* (William Graham, 1848), pp. 3–21.

183. A Member of the Oxford Convocation, *A Letter to the Rt. Hon. Lord John Russell, M.P. on the Constitutional Defects of the University and Colleges of Oxford, with Suggestions for a Royal Commission of Inquiry into the Universities* (James Ridgway, 1850), pp. 50 and 53.

184. [D. P. Chase], *Education for Frugal Men at the University of Oxford. An Account of the Experiments at St Mary's and St Alban's Halls by the Principals of those Halls* (Oxford and London: John Henry and James Parker, 1864), pp. 6, 7, 9, and 15ff.

185. Edward Moore, *Frugal Education Attainable Under the Existing Collegiate System, with an Account of the Expenses of the System at St Edmund Hall* (Oxford and London: James Parker and Co., 1867), pp. 6, 13, and 20.

186. Lowe, *A Plea for Poor Scholars . . .*, pp. 13 and 4.

187. Charles Marriott, *University Extension and the Poor Scholar Question. A Letter to the Rev. E. Woollcombe* (Oxford: A. A. Masson, 1848), pp. 12ff.

188. Charles Marriott to N. Woodard, 16 May, 1855, Woodard Papers, 1855 Envelope, Supporters.

189. Undated circular letter, included with a printed document appealing for funds for the Keble Memorial and dated 1866 (Pusey House Pamphlets No. 71366).

190. L. A. Borradaile, "Selwyn College", *A History of the County of Cambridge and the Isle of Ely*, ed. J. P. C. Roach (*Victoria History of the Counties of England*) (Published for the Institute of Historical Research by the Oxford University Press, 1959), III, p. 495.

191. Lord Richard Cavendish to N. Woodard, Ascension Day 1870, Woodard Papers, 1870 Packet, Universities.

192. N. Woodard to E. C. Lowe, 27 March 1867, Lancing Archives, Letters to Lowe. In 1884 six boys from Lancing and one from Ardingly were resident at Keble (*Calendar*, 1884).

193. Below, 159ff. *The Guardian*, 1 November 1876.

194. In 1884 two boys from Lancing and one from Hurst were at Cavendish (*Calendar*, 1884). For Cavendish College, see J. P. C. Roach, "The University of Cambridge", *A History of the County of Cambridge and the Isle of Ely*, ed. J. P. C. Roach (*Victoria History of the Counties of England*) (Institute of Historical Research, 1959), III, p. 266.

195. N. Woodard, Pamphlet, 24 October 1848, Woodard Papers, Pamphlets 1848.

196. N. Woodard, *Public Schools for the Middle Classes* (1852), p. 19.

197. See, D. P. Chase to N. Woodard, 18 January 1858, Woodard Papers, 1858 Envelope B, School Life.

198. E. C. Lowe to N. Woodard, 14 January 1864, Woodard Papers, 1864 Envelope, Educational Approach.

199. S.I.C., I, Appendix, pp. 165 & 170.

200. Letter and Pamphlet from J. Fowler to E. C. Lowe, 23 November 1876, Woodard Papers, 1876 Packet, Universities.

201. N. Woodard to E. C. Lowe, 14 May 1879, Lancing Archives, Letters to Lowe.

202. N. Woodard to E. C. Lowe, 23 April 1879, Lancing Archives, Letters to Lowe.

203. W. B. Woodard to N. Woodard, 14 July 1879, Woodard Papers, 1879 Packet, Universities.

204. The Bishop of Ely to N. Woodard, 19 July 1869, Woodard Papers, 1869 Envelope, Universities.

205. N. Woodard to the Marquess of Salisbury, 22 August 1879, Salisbury Papers, Letters from Woodard.

206. Ibid.

207. See, N. Woodard to E. C. Lowe, 14 May 1879, Lancing Archives, Letters to Lowe. Selwyn College did attract S.N.C. boys. As early as 1884 two boys from Denstone were resident. Two years later there were three from Lancing, two from Hurst and four from Denstone (*Calendars*, 1884 & 1886).

208. *The Athenaeum*, 2 May 1891.

209. Above, pp. 34f.

210. See (Dorothea Beale), op. cit., and Mary Gurney, *Are We to Have Education for our Middle-Class Girls? or, the History of the Camden Collegiate Schools* (William Ridgway, 1872).

211. M. A. Dalvi, "Commercial Education in England During 1851–1902: An Institutional Study" (Unpublished Ph.D. Thesis, University of London, 1957), p. 332.

CHAPTER 5

THE POLITICAL BACKGROUND

1. Obviously this does *not* mean that all who comprised the middle classes were either Dissenters or Liberals. The Church of England, although strong among the upper classes, depended for its base on middle-class support (see K. S. Inglis, *Churches and the Working Classes in Victorian England* [Routledge and Kegan Paul, 1963]). That all the middle classes were Whigs, Radicals, or Liberals was manifestly untrue in rural areas throughout the nineteenth century, and increasingly untrue in urban centres during the last quarter of the century (see, Cornford, op. cit.). For a detailed study of the way in which party allegiance actually cut across the class status in Rochdale, see J. R. Vincent, *The Formation of the Liberal Party* (Constable, 1966), pp. 112ff.

2. N. Woodard, *Public Schools for the Middle Classes* (1852), p. 15.

3. Ibid., pp. 4–5 and 14.

4. The Wesleyan Methodists, of course, formed a separate case and are not included here as Dissenters. Despite Liberal grumblings and small schisms, the main body of Methodists remained Conservative under the leadership of Jabez Bunting throughout the first half of the century. After the disruption of 1849, the parent Methodist body lost over 100,000

members (E. R. Taylor, *Methodism and Politics* [Cambridge University Press, 1935], p. 167), and the new United Methodist Free Churches were founded. The leaders of the latter were usually Liberal in politics and allied themselves with the older Dissenters.

5. F. R. Salter, "Political Nonconformity in the Eighteen-Thirties", *Transactions of the Royal Historical Society*, Fifth Series (III), 1953, p. 127. There were less than a dozen Dissenting Members of Parliament.
6. The debate on Church Rates became an argument "whether we are to have a Church Establishment or not" (quoted from Archbishop Howley in Olive Brose, *Church and Parliament* [Oxford University Press, 1959], p. 55). Given this alternative the Whigs significantly clung to the principle of Establishment in the face of Radical and Dissenting demands. See also, Norman Gash, *Reaction and Reconstruction in English Politics, 1832–1852* (Oxford: Clarendon Press, 1965), pp. 72–3.
7. See Raymond G. Cowherd, *The Politics of English Dissent* (New York University Press, 1956), p. 87; and Brose, op. cit., pp. 137 and 147.
8. H. S. Skeats, *A History of the Free Churches of England*, second edn. (Arthur Miall, 1869), pp. 590–1.
9. Salter, op. cit., p. 143; Gash, op. cit., pp. 74–6.
10. Cowherd, op. cit., p. 96.
11. Lucy Brown, "The Chartists and the Anti-Corn Law League", *Chartist Studies*, ed. Asa Briggs (Macmillan, 1959), p. 364.
12. A. E. Payne, *The Baptist Union* (The Carey Kingsgate Press, 1959), p. 70.
13. Quotation from Anti-Bread Tax Circular No. 70 in C. R. Fay, *The Corn Laws and Social England* (Cambridge University Press, 1932), p. 107.
14. Asa Briggs, "The Local Background of Chartism", *Chartist Studies*, pp. 4 and 5.
15. J. F. C. Harrison, "Chartism in Leicester", *Chartist Studies*, p. 139.
16. It was endorsed by a conference of 200 Dissenting ministers (Cowherd, op. cit., p. 113).
17. The landed interest was not united in last-ditch opposition to Repeal (see, Gash, op. cit., pp. 48ff.). Furthermore there were Tories who supported the Chartists. James Raynor Stephens, the Tory opponent of the Poor Law, took part in Chartist meetings (E. Halévy, *The Triumph of Reform (1830–1841)* [Ernest Benn Ltd, 1961], p. 298). Disraeli is described by Halévy as "an eccentric Ultra-Tory with Chartists sympathies" (ibid., p. 318).
18. Sir Ivor Jennings, *Party Politics* (Cambridge University Press, 1961), II, p. 129.
19. Edward Miall, *The British Churches in Relation to the British People*, second edn. Arthur Hall, Virtue & Co., 1850), pp. 245 and 247.
20. *Church Property and Revenues in England and Wales* (British Anti-State Church Association, 1850). Pusey House Pamphlets No. 9613.
21. Vincent, op. cit., pp. 73–4.
22. B. L. Manning, *The Protestant Dissenting Deputies* (Cambridge University Press, 1952), p. 367.
23. J. L. Garvin, *The Life of Joseph Chamberlain* (Macmillan, 1932), I, p. 104.

24. J. W. Adamson, *English Education, 1789–1902* (Cambridge University Press, 1930), p. 349.
25. Above, 89. Also see, H. J. Hanham, *Elections and Party Management* (Longmans, Green, 1959), p. 119. Samuel Morley and his followers held fast to Gladstone's government.
26. Garvin, op. cit., I, p. 105.
27. F. H. Herrick, "The Origins of the National Liberal Federation", *The Journal of Modern History*, XVII (1945), p. 123.
28. Hanham, op. cit., p. 122; and Herrick, op. cit., pp. 125ff.
29. Garvin, op. cit., I, p. 130.
30. Speech by Dr Kennedy in *The Liberation Society: Tenth Triennial Conference* [1874]. Pusey House Pamphlets No. 6511, pp. 6, 49, 26, and 28.
31. Hanham, op. cit., pp. 122–4.
32. Above, pp. 99ff.
33. N. Woodard to W. E. Forster, 7 January 1870, Woodard Papers, 1870 Packet, Politics.
34. N. Woodard to J. G. Talbot, 1 January 1870, Lancing Archives.
35. N. Woodard to the Marquess of Salisbury, 25 May 1871, Christ Church, Salisbury Papers, Letters from Woodard.
36. N. Woodard to the Marquess of Salisbury, 22 August 1879, Christ Church, Salisbury Papers, Letters from Woodard.
37. N. Woodard to the Marquess of Salisbury, 22 April 1880, Christ Church, Salisbury Papers, Letters from Woodard.
38. Above, p. 21.
39. N. Woodard to W. E. Gladstone, 23 November 1856, British Museum, Gladstone Papers, Vol. CCCI, Additional MSS., 44,386, fol. 245.
40. *The Guardian*, 27 November 1861. N. Woodard to W. E. Gladstone, 21 January 1862, British Museum, Gladstone Papers, Vol. CCCXIII, Additional MSS, 44,398, fol. 46. Above, p. 67.
41. N. Woodard to W. E. Gladstone, 21 July 1865, British Museum, Gladstone Papers, Vol. CCCXXII, Additional MSS, 44,407, fol. 79.
42. N. Woodard to E. C. Lowe, 27 April 1868, Lancing Archives, Letters to Lowe.
43. T. A. Maberley to N. Woodard, 13 December 1869, Woodard Papers, Packet E.
44. N. Woodard to E. C. Lowe, 16 July 1877, Lancing Archives, Letters to Lowe.
45. N. Woodard to W. E. Gladstone, 16 June 1876, British Museum, Gladstone Papers, Vol. CCCLXV, Additional MSS, 44,450, fol. 171.
46. Roundell, Earl of Selborne, *A Defence of the Church of England Against Disestablishment*, fourth edn. (Macmillan, 1899), pp. 303 and 304.
47. R. B. McDowell, *British Conservatism, 1832–1914* (Faber and Faber, 1959), pp. 20ff. Jennings, op. cit., II, p. 60.; Diana McClatchey, *Oxfordshire Clergy, 1777–1869* (Oxford: at the Clarendon Press, 1960), pp. 210, 213, 214–15.

48. See, Cowherd, op. cit., pp. 75 and 79. Also see, W. F. Monypenny and G. E. Buckle, *The Life of Benjamin Disraeli, Earl of Beaconsfield* (John Murray, 1929), II, p. 86.
49. "The Church . . . he regarded as part of the Constitution; and the Prayer Book as an Act of Parliament which only folly or disloyalty could quarrel with." (J. A. Froude, *Short Studies on Great Subjects* [Longmans, Green, 1883], IV, p. 254. See also p. 149.)
50. A. B. Webster, *Joshua Watson, The Story of a Layman, 1771–1855* (S.P.C.K., 1954), pp. 19 and 20.
51. N. Woodard to the Marquess of Salisbury, 27 May 1880, Christ Church, Salisbury Papers, Letters from Woodard.
52. N. Woodard to the Marquess of Salisbury, 22 August 1879, Christ Church, Salisbury Papers, Letters from Woodard.
53. Founded in 1860 to "combine . . . churchmen of every shade of political and religious opinion in the maintenance and support of the Established Church" (Pusey House Pamphlets No. 73720). By 1888 it was decidedly anti-Gladstone (Pusey House Pamphlets No. 8338).
54. Walter Burrell to N. Woodard, 29 February 1864, Woodard Papers, 1864 Envelope, Politics. P. Heywood to N. Woodard, 5 January 1870, Woodard Papers, 1870 Packet, Politics. H. Meynell to N. Woodard, 29 January 1886, Woodard Papers, 1886 Packet, Politics.
55. W. R. W. Stephens, *The Life and Letters of Walter Farquhar Hook* (Richard Bentley & Son, 1878), II, p. 420.
56. *The Daily News*, 13 August 1872.
57. N. Woodard to the Marquess of Salisbury, 19 October 1880, Christ Church, Salisbury Papers, Letters from Woodard.
58. N. Woodard to the Marquess of Salisbury, 9 November 1881, Christ Church, Salisbury Papers, Letters from Woodard.
59. N. Woodard to the Marquess of Salisbury, 29 June 1882, Christ Church, Salisbury Papers, Letters from Woodard.
60. Copy of a begging letter for Lancing Chapel, undated, Woodard Papers, 1885 Packet.
61. N. Woodard to the Marquess of Salisbury, 14 October, 1885, Christ Church, Salisbury Papers, Letters from Woodard.
62. Robert Loder to N. Woodard, 18 March 1857, Woodard Papers, 1857 Envelope, Politics.
63. N. Woodard to the Marquess of Salisbury, 2 March 1874, Christ Church, Salisbury Papers, Letters from Woodard.
64. N. Woodard to the Marquess of Salisbury, 14 August 1878, Christ Church, Salisbury Papers, Letters from Woodard.
65. N. Woodard to the Marquess of Salisbury, 14 September 1880, Christ Church, Salisbury Papers, Letters from Woodard.
66. N. Woodard to E. C. Lowe, 19 August 1881, Lancing Archives, Letters to Lowe.
67. Lord Beauchamp to N. Woodard, 25 October 1884, Woodard Papers, 1884 Packet, Politics.
68. *Hansard's Parliamentary Debates*, CCXXI (1874), p. 78.

69. Above, p. 95.
70. Above, p. 57.
71. N. Woodard to E. C. Lowe, 23 January 1875, Lancing Archives, Letters to Lowe.
72. T. E. Kebbel, *A History of Toryism from the Accession of Mr Pitt to Power in 1783 to the Death of Lord Beaconsfield in 1881* (W. H. Allen and Co., 1886), p. 375.
73. McDowell, op. cit., p. 74.
74. Lady G. Cecil, *The Life of Robert, Marquis of Salisbury* (Hodder & Stoughton, 1921), I, pp. 322ff.
75. Cecil, op. cit., III, p. 268.
76. N. Woodard to the Marquess of Salisbury, 22 August 1879, Christ Church, Salisbury Papers, Letters from Woodard.
77. N. Woodard to E. C. Lowe, 21 August 1880, Lancing Archives, Letters to Lowe.
78. G. Kitson Clark, *Peel and the Conservative Party* (G. Bell & Sons, 1929), p. 154; McDowell, op. cit., p. 69; *The Oxford Movement*, ed. Eugene R. Fairweather (Oxford University Press, 1964), p. 4; John Tulloch, *Movements of Religious Thought in Britain During the Nineteenth Century* (Longmans, Green, 1885), p. 105; J. A. Froude, op. cit., IV, p. 249; Christopher Dawson, *The Spirit of the Oxford Movement* (Sheed and Ward, 1933), pp. 66ff.
79. Tulloch, op. cit., p. 87.
80. See Bodleian Library, catalogue no. *Bliss B. 421 173*. Also see, T. Mozley, op. cit., I, p. 253.
81. Georgina Battiscombe, *John Keble* (Constable, 1963), pp. 122ff. and 135.
82. H. P. Liddon, *The Life of Edward Bouverie Pusey*. Second edn. (Longmans, Green, 1893), IV, p. 199.
83. Mozley, op. cit., I, p. 253; *The Times*, 27 February 1841, pseud. "Catholicus".
84. C. Dawson, op. cit., pp. 67 and 68.
85. Tract No. 83, *Tracts for the Times*, by Members of the University of Oxford (printed for J. G. F. & J. Rivington, 1840), V.
86. [A. J. B. Beresford Hope] *The Church Cause and the Church Party* (J. & C. Mozley, 1860), p. 5.
87. Tract 59, *Tracts for the Times*, by Members of the University of Oxford (Printed for J. G. F. and J. Rivington, 1840), II.
88. R. Hurrell Froude, *Remains* (Rivington, 1838), I, p. 246.
89. Battiscombe, op. cit., p. 155.
90. J. H. Newman, *Historical sketches*. Second Series, Second edn. (Basil Montagu Pickering, 1873), pp. 340–1.
91. Liddon, op. cit., IV, p. 199.
92. Hope, op. cit., p. 38.
93. Cecil, op. cit., I, pp. 102, 120, 368.

94. N. Woodard to the Marquess of Salisbury, 14 August 1878, Christ Church, Salisbury Papers, Letters from Woodard.
95. R. Cecil to N. Woodard, 20 January 1857, Woodard Papers, 1857 Envelope, Religion.
96. Cecil, op. cit., I, p. 221.
97. Arthur Hardinge, *The Life of Henry Edward Molyneux, Fourth Earl of Carnarvon* (Oxford University Press, 1925), II, p. 13. See, The Earl of Carnarvon, *The Advantages of an Established Church* (Church Defence Institution, 1885).
98. Hardinge, op. cit., I, p. 368.
99. Monypenny and Buckle, op. cit., II, p. 656.
100. In his book on Father Mackonochie (*Martyr of Ritualism* [Faber and Faber, 1965]) Michael Reynolds asserts that Hubbard was "not directly influenced by the Oxford Movement" (p. 76). Yet, as Reynolds later points out (p. 79) many of his ecclesiastical advisers were certainly Anglo-Catholics (they included Keble himself, as well as W. J. Butler and Liddon). Hubbard's distress at Mackonochie's ritualistic excesses does not disqualify him as an Anglo-Catholic.
101. H. W. and I. Law, *The Book of the Beresford Hopes* (Heath Cranton Ltd., 1925), pp. 148, 149, 211, and 213.
102. Hope, op. cit., p. 29.
103. Law, op. cit., p. 133.
104. Charles Wibley, *Lord John Manners and His Friends* (Blackwood, 1925), I, p. 75.
105. Ibid., pp. 185 and 153.
106. Hardinge, II, p. 67.
107. L. E. Denison (ed.), *Fifty Years at East Brent, The Letters of George Anthony Denison, 1845–1896* (John Murray, 1902), pp. 45–6.
108. G. A. Denison, *Supplement to "Notes of my Life, 1879" and "Mr Gladstone", 1886* (Oxford and London, James Parker & Co., 1893), p. 22.
109. Ibid., pp. 89, 128, 129. Below, p. 147.
110. N. Woodard to W. E. Gladstone, 4 July 1856, British Museum, Gladstone Papers, Vol. CCCI, Additional MSS, 44,386, fol. 54.
111. N. Woodard to William Campion, 14 August 1856, Woodard Papers, 1856 Envelope, Politics.
112. Hope, op. cit., pp. 13, 14, 33, 34, 55.
113. E. A. T., *Alexander Heriot Mackonochie*, ed. E. F. Russell (Kegan Paul, Trench, Trubner & Co., 1890), pp. 18 and 19.
114. G. W. E. Russell, *Arthur Stanton, A Memoir* (Longmans, Green, 1917), p. 107. See also, Reynolds, op. cit., pp. 207–9.
115. F. Bennett, *The Story of W. J. E. Bennett* (Longmans, Green, 1909), pp. 250 and 251.
116. Ibid., p. 249.
117. Stephens, op. cit., I, p 155; see, W. F. Hook, *On the Means of Rendering More Efficient the Education of the People* (John Murray, 1846).
118. Stephens, op. cit., I, p. 159.

119. Stephens, op. cit., II, p. 450.
120. Stephens, op. cit., II, p. 352; J. A. Hamilton, "William Page Wood", D.N.B., XXI, p. 851.
121. G. W. E. Russell, op. cit., pp. 127, 142, and 107–8.
122. S. C. Carpenter, op. cit., p. 328.
123. F. G. Bettany, *Stewart Headlam: A Biography* (John Murray, 1926), p. 114.
124. C. E. Osborne, *The Life of Father Dolling* (Edward Arnold, 1903), p. 114. See also p. 121.
125. Ibid., p. 199.
126. Pusey House Pamphlets Nos. 13451 and 13447.
127. G. A. Denison, *Catholicity Without Establishment or Establishment Without Catholicity* (James Parker & Co., 1877).
128. The Liberation Society, *The Disabilities of Churchmen* (Pusey House Pamphlet No. 8356); A High Church Rector [T. W. Mossman?], *The State Church and National Honesty* (Pusey House Pamphlet No. 13468).
129. In the Gladstone Papers over a dozen letters from Lowe to Mr Gladstone are preserved and dated between 1865 and 1891. More were written after Woodard's death.
130. E. C. Lowe to W. E. Gladstone, 28 December 1889, British Museum, Gladstone Papers, Vol. CCCCXXIII, Additional MSS, 44,508, fol. 267.
131. E. C. Lowe to W. E. Gladstone, 20 February 1888, British Museum, Gladstone Papers, Vol. CCCCXVIII, Additional MSS, 44,503, fol. 61.
132. F. G. Lee, *The Church of England and Political Parties: A Letter to the Rt. Hon. Gathorne Hardy, M.P., D.C.L.* Second edn. (Thomas Bosworth, 1868), p. 11.
133. The Marquess of Salisbury to N. Woodard, 19 September 1880, Woodard Papers, 1880 Packet, Politics.
134. N. Woodard to the Marquess of Salisbury, 19 October 1880, Christ Church, Salisbury Papers, Letters from Woodard.
135. The obvious exception to this statement is Gladstone. According to his biographer, he was unafraid of disestablishment after 1850, and in fact feared that the establishment of the Church of England threatened the integrity of her faith (John Morley, *The Life of William Ewart Gladstone* [Edward Lloyd, 1908], II, p. 585). Yet in 1874, he sought to avert disestablishment "as long as standing ground remains", and, in 1891, he considered the Established Church "safer than it has been for a long time" (ibid., II, pp. 81 and 532). On Gladstone's political theory, and its relation to his party allegiance, see Alec Vidler, *The Orb and the Cross* (S.P.C.K., 1945) and R. T. Shannon, *Gladstone and the Bulgarian Agitation of 1876* (Nelson and Sons, 1963).

CHAPTER 6

INFLUENCE AND COMPETITION

1. Above, pp. 14.f
2. J. P. Fearon to N. Woodard, 29 November 1850, Woodard Papers, C Packet, Requests for Schools and Advice.
3. Lord Lyttelton to N. Woodard, 5 December 1873, Woodard Papers, 1873 Packet Other Scho ols.

4. Edward Fusco to N. Woodard, 25 November 1861, Woodard Papers, 1861 Envelope, Other Schools.
5. William Ford to N. Woodard, 31 May 1862, Woodard Papers, 1862 Envelope, Other Schools.
6. C. Warrand to N. Woodard, 8 June 1862, Woodard Papers, 1862 Envelope, Other Schools.
7. C. Warrand to N. Woodard, 13 June 1862, Woodard Papers, 1862 Envelope, Other Schools *and* N. Woodard to C. Warrand, no date [1862], Woodard Papers, 1862 Envelope, Other Schools.
8. R. Alliott to N. Woodard, 29 September 1881, Woodard Papers, 1881 Packet, Enquiries.
9. F. C. Pritchard, *Methodist Secondary Education* (Epworth Press, 1949), p. 191.
10. Richard Chaffer (?) to N. Woodard, 27 November, 1860, Woodard Papers, 1860 Envelope, Other Schools. See also, R. Gregory to N. Woodard, 16 May and 18 May 1867, Woodard Papers, 1867 Envelope, Other Schools.
11. Archbishop of York (William Thomson) to N. Woodard, 8 December 1864, Woodard Papers, 1864 Envelope, Other Schools.
12. The Bishop of Moray and Ross (Robert Eden) to N. Woodard, 22 June 1874, Woodard Papers, 1874 Packet, Enquiries.
13. R. P. Tours (?) to N. Woodard, 28 July 1864, Woodard Papers, 1864 Envelope, Other Schools; Theodore Thring to N. Woodard, 8, 19, 24 August 1878, Woodard Papers, 1878 Packet, Enquiries; J. D. Ridout to N. Woodard, 21 May 1866, Woodard Papers, 1866 Envelope, Other Schools.
14. T. D. Platt to N. Woodard, 31 January 1866, Woodard Papers, 1866 Envelope, Other Schools. See also, W. E. Setton to N. Woodard, 27 May 1857, Woodard Papers, London Committee Packet, Others; Charles Robinson to N. Woodard, 4 September 1865, Woodard Papers, 1865 Envelope, Other Schools; and many other letters.
15. N. Woodard to Julius Hare, 4 March 1850, Lancing Archives, Letters to Hare.
16. Edmund Venables to N. Woodard, undated, Woodard Papers, undated envelope, Enquiries.
17. R. L. Pennell to N. Woodard, 29 June 1857, Woodard Papers, 1857 Envelope, Other Schools; Thomas Morse to N. Woodard, 7 July 1860, Woodard Papers, 1860 Envelope, Other Schools; W. Woodard to N. Woodard, 5 November 1867, Woodard Papers, 1867 Envelope, Other Schools; George Gainsford to N. Woodard, 15 January 1884, Woodard Papers, 1884 Packet, Enquiries; Edward Banks to N. Woodard, 22 May 1885, Woodard Papers, 1885 Packet, Enquiries.
18. W. T. Sankey to N. Woodard, 4 December 1860, Woodard Papers, 1860 Envelope, Other Schools.
19. Above, p. 28. E. S. Armstrong to N. Woodard, undated, Woodard Papers, undated Envelope, Enquiries. J. W. L. Bampfield to R. E. Sanderson, 3 August 1875, Woodard Papers, 1875 Packet, Enquiries.
20. The Bishop of Dunedin (S. T. Nevill) to N. Woodard, 21 December 1874,

Woodard Papers, 1874 Packet, Enquiries. The Bishop of Dunedin (S. T. Nevill) to N. Woodard, 24 February 1872, Woodard Papers, 1872 Packet, Other Schools. The Bishop of Dunedin (S. T. Nevill) to N. Woodard, 5 June 1875, Woodard Papers, 1875 Packet, Enquiries.

21. The Bishop of Dunedin (S. T. Nevill) to N. Woodard, 4 July 1875, Woodard Papers, 1875 Packet, Enquiries.

22. The Bishop of Dunedin (S. T. Nevill) to N. Woodard, 4 July 1875, Woodard Papers, 1875 Packet, Enquiries.

23. The Bishop of Dunedin (S. T. Nevill) to N. Woodard, 26 October 1875, Woodard Papers, 1875 Packet, Enquiries.

24. N. Woodard to the Marquess of Salisbury, 20 April, 1887, Christ Church, the Salisbury Papers, Letters from Woodard.

25. Above, pp. 114f. J. M. Wilkins to N. Woodard, 28 August 1862, Woodard Papers, 1862 Envelope, Other Schools; also, C. H. Andrews to N. Woodard, 11 March 1874, Woodard Papers, 1874 Packet, Enquiries. N. Woodard to W. E. Gladstone, 12 December 1873, British Museum, Gladstone Papers, Vol. CCCLVI, Additional MSS, 44,441, fol. 209.

26. R. Linklater to N. Woodard, 12 May 1888, Woodard Papers, 1888–1902 Packet, Enquiries.

27. Above, p. 16. See, Diocesan School, Cowley, *Prospectus 1860 and Examination Report, 1859* (Pusey House Pamphlets, No. 692). John Slatter to N. Woodard, 30 April 1857, and 5 May 1857, Woodard Papers, 1857 Envelope, Other Schools. E. C. Lowe to N. Woodard, 19 April 1857, Woodard Papers, 1857 Envelope, Other Schools. N. Woodard to E. C. Lowe, 25 May 1858, Lancing Archives, Letters to Lowe.

28. Above, p. 50. J. W. Dover to N. Woodard, 22 December 1867, Woodard Papers, 1867 Envelope, Other Schools. Below pp. 160f. C. S. Bere to N. Woodard, 20 June 1883, Woodard Papers, 1883 Packet, Enquiries. Later, Woodard wrote to Lowe: "Mr Bere has offered me more than once the [East] Devon County School, and recently he has lowered his price to nearly one half the sum he once asked. But still I have refused it, as the property seems of no intrinsic value" (N. Woodard to E. C. Lowe, 23 January 1885, Lancing Archives, Letters to Lowe).

29. H. C. Powell to N. Woodard, 10 November 1883, Woodard Papers, 1883 Packet, Enquiries.

30. See above, p. 52. *The Guardian*, 13 June 1855. Lewis Gilbertson to N. Woodard, Palm Sunday, 1857, Woodard Papers, 1857 Envelope, Other Schools.

31. The correspondence from Egerton to Woodard, consisting of a large number of letters written in the autumn of 1859, is contained in the Woodard Papers, 1859 Envelope, Other Schools. Also see, *All Saints' School, Bloxham, 1860–1960* (Centenary Booklet), pp. 6 and 8.

32. N. Woodard to E. C. Lowe, 28 January 1880, Lancing Archives, Letters to Lowe. N. Woodard to E. C. Lowe, 28 February 1880, Lancing Archives, Letters to Lowe.

33. E. C. Lowe to N. Woodard, 23 October 1882, Woodard Papers, 1882 Packet, Enquiries.

34. Interview with Desmond Hill, historian of St Edward's School, Oxford, 11 November 1960. See above, p. 52.

35. H. Meynell to N. Woodard, 13 June 1872, Woodard Papers, 1872 Packet, Other Schools; and E. C. Lowe, to N. Woodard, 23 October 1882, Woodard Papers, 1882 Packet, Enquiries.

36. *A Plea for the Establishment of Additional Public Schools in Yorkshire for the Upper and Middle Classes* (W. Skeffington, 1870).

37. *The Guardian,* 10 June 1868.

38. H. Staunton, op. cit., p. 570.

39. R. Howard, op. cit., p. 50.

40. Percival Heywood to N. Woodard, 8 January and 26 May 1870, Woodard Papers, 1870 Packet, Other Schools.

41. Above, pp. 35 and 38f.

42. E. C. Lowe to ?, 5 January 1863, Woodard Papers, 1863 Envelope, School Life and Organization.

43. N. Woodard to E. C. Lowe, 20 May 1863, and 6 June 1863, Lancing Archives, Letters to Lowe. E. C. Lowe, *St Nicolas College and its Schools. A Record . . .*, p. 39.

44. E. C. Lowe to N. Woodard, 17 March 1876, Woodard Papers, 1876 Packet, Midlands.

45. E. C. L[owe], *Suggestions for the Affiliation of Schools With St Nicolas College,* St Chad's Day, 1877, Woodard Papers, 1877 Packet, Organization.

46. "The managers of the Leeds Church Middle Class School . . . raised the question of affiliation in July last. I am in correspondence in a somewhat similar case with Mr Bell Cox of St Margaret's, Liverpool" (E. C. Lowe to N. Woodard, 26 February 1877, Woodard Papers, 1877 Packet, Enquiries).

47. N. Woodard to E. C. Lowe, 28 February 1877, Lancing Archives, Letters to Lowe.

48. N. Woodard to E. C. Lowe, 23 January 1885, Lancing Archives, Letters to Lowe.

49. J. L. Brereton, *County Education. Accounts of the Devon and Norfolk County School Associations for 1875, with a few Remarks on the New College for Junior Students at Cambridge* (Bickers and Son, 1876), p. 3. Referred to hereafter as *County Education, Accounts . . . .*

50. J. L. Brereton, "Principles and Plan of a Farm and County School" (1858), in Earl Fortescue, *Public Schools for the Middle Classes* (Longmans, Green, 1864).

51. Earl Fortescue, *Public Schools for the Middle Classes* (Longmans, Green, 1864), p. 8. S.I.C., XIV, p. 510.

52. The occupations of the fathers of the top ten boys in the school were as follows: merchant, draper, farmer, banker, surveyor, sample taker, farmer, wine merchant, miller, wine merchant. Those of the fathers of the lowest ten boys in the school were: bookseller, farmer, bookseller, farmer, gasfitter, draper, clergyman, gas-fitter, commercial traveller, ironmonger (S.I.C., XIV, p. 510).

53. J. L. Brereton, *County Education. Accounts . . .*, p. 14.

54. See, J. L. Brereton, *County Education. A Letter Addressed to the Right Honourable the Earl of Devon* (James Ridgway, 1861). Referred to hereafter as *County Education,* 1861. See also, Earl Fortescue, op. cit.

55. Bickers and Son, 1874. Referred to hereafter as *County Education* (1874).
56. Ibid., p. 47.
57. Ibid., pp. 31 and 121.
58. Ibid., pp. 8 and 122.
59. Ibid., pp. 123 and 21.
60. Ibid., p. 124.
61. Ibid., p. 40.
62. Ibid., pp. 18ff. Above, p. 122.
63. J. L. Brereton, *County Education, Accounts* . . . , p. 6.
64. S.I.C., XIV, p. 516. C. S. Bere to N. Woodard, 20 June 1883, Woodard Papers, 1883 Packet, Enquiries. Above p. 156.
65. S.I.C., XIV, p. 471.
66. *Albert Middle Class College in Suffolk, Erected at Framlingham by Public Subscription to the Memory of H.R.H. the Late Prince Consort*, May 1865 (Ministry of Education Library, E.M. Vol. 10, 8vo. 19), p. 8. Referred to hereafter as *Albert Middle-Class College. . . .*
67. Ibid., p. 9. S.I.C., XXI, pp. 100–1.
68. *Albert Middle Class College* . . . , p. 6. S.I.C., XXI, pp. 100–1.
69. S.I.C., XI, p. 157.
70. J. L. Brereton, *County Education* (1861), p. 4.
71. Ibid., p. 17.
72. Above, Chapter 4, Note 98.
73. J. L. Brereton, *County Education* (1874), pp. 18 and 41.
74. Ibid., p. 40.
75. N. Woodard to E. C. Lowe, 18 November 1883, Lancing Archives, Letters to Lowe. In this letter Woodard referred to the Church Schools Company, also organized and financed on the commercial principle.
76. J. L. Brereton, *County Education* (1861), pp. 16, 46, 45, 47.
77. Ibid., pp. 36 and 63.
78. Earl Fortescue, op. cit., p. 153. J. L. Brereton, *County Education* (1861), p. 18.
79. S.I.C., XIV, p. 516.
80. *Albert Middle Class College* . . . , p. 8.
81. *The Guardian*, 20 February 1867.
82. S. Blackall to N. Woodard, 24 June 1862, Woodard Papers, 1862 Envelope, Other Schools.
83. E. C. Lowe to N. Woodard, 11 August 1864, Woodard Papers, 1864 Envelope, Other Schools.
84. N. Woodard to E. C. Lowe, 16 August 1864, Lancing Archives, Letters to Lowe.
85. E. C. Lowe to N. Woodard, 2 October 1865, Woodard Papers, 1865 Envelope, Other Schools. Above, p. 156.
86. S.I.C., V, p. 472. See, R. H. Hadden, *A Sermon in Memory of the Late William Rogers Preached in St Botolph, Bishopsgate on 26 January 1896*, p. 9.

87. R. H. Hadden, *Reminiscences of William Rogers, Rector of St Botolph, Bishopsgate* (Kegan Paul, Trench & Co., 1888), pp. 157 and 158.
88. *The Guardian*, 17 January 1866.
89. *The Guardian*, 20 March 1867. R. H. Hadden, *Reminiscences* . . ., pp. 166–71.
90. Ibid., p. 163.
91. *The Guardian*, 3 July 1867. Letter from the Bishop of London and Leading Article.
92. R. H. Hadden, *Reminiscences* . . ., p. 167.
93. S.I.C., V, p. 484 and pp. 475–7. R. H. Hadden, *Reminiscences* . . ., p. 162.
94. Henry Tritton to N. Woodard, 8 January 1865, Woodard Papers, 1865 Envelope, Other Schools. Henry Tritton to N. Woodard, 29 June 1867, 1867 Envelope, Other Schools.
95. Above, p. 82. Trent was opened in 1868 with fifty-three boys. See, M. A. J. Tarver, op. cit., pp. 4 and 5.
96. Ibid., pp. 5 and 7.
97. At Denstone, in 1874, the minimum fee was 34 gns (*Calendar*, 1874, Lancing Archives, Scrap Book, p. 267).
98. *Register of St Lawrence College, 1879 to 1934* (published by the Old Lawrentian Society, 1934), vi. Judging from the Register, early Ramsgate students belonged to the upper stratum of the middle class; a large number became clergy, professional, and military men. I can find no mention of specifically middle-class interest in the record of the Cheltenham school provided by Charles Williams in his *Flecker of Dean Close* (The Canterbury Press, 1946).
99. Above, pp. 15f. and p. 18.
100. S.I.C., I, p. 196.
101. Above, p. 43.
102. S.I.C., V, pp. 610–12. Robert Gregory, *Do Our National Schools Provide Education for All Whom they Ought to Train? A Letter to His Grace the Archbishop of Canterbury* (Rivington's, 1865), p. 25. Referred to hereafter as *Do Our National Schools* . . .
103. S.I.C., V, p. 622.
104. S.I.C., V, p. 613.
105. R. Gregory, *Do Our National Schools* . . ., pp. 5, 19, and 20.
106. S.I.C., V, p. 615.
107. S.I.C., V, p. 613.
108. S.I.C., V, pp. 613 and 624.
109. *The Guardian*, 21 August 1872.
110. Above, pp. 14f. H. J. Burgess, *Enterprise in Education*, p. 134.
111. Richard Chaffen to N. Woodard, 27 November 1860, Woodard Papers, 1860 Envelope, Other Schools.
112. National Society, *Middle Class Schools Committee Minutes*, 1 November 1865. Circular, Woodard Papers, 1867 Envelope, Other Schools.
113. National Society, *Middle Class Schools Committee Minutes*, 1 November, 1865, p. 47. The Minutes extend to 2 April 1879. By 1879, only £2,234

had been promised to the Middle Class Schools Fund. See, H. J. Burgess, Thesis, p. 276. Also see, H. J. Burgess, *Enterprise in Education*, p. 135.

114. R. Gregory to N. Woodard, 25 and 31 January, 1867, Woodard Papers, 1867 Envelope, Other Schools.
115. N. Woodard to E. C. Lowe, 7 May 1880, Lancing Archives, Letters to Lowe.
116. E. M. Bell, *A History of the Church Schools Company, 1883–1958* (S.P.C.K., 1958), p. 15. Prospectus, The Church Schools Company Ltd., No Date, Woodard Papers, Non-Woodard Middle Class Education Envelope.
117. *The Guardian*, 25 July 1883, Leading Article.
118. Above, p. 98.
119. *The High Schools of the Girls' Public Day School Company. An Illustrated History* (Cassell & Company), p. 4.
120. Edward Johnson, Printed Letter, 20 April 1882, Woodard Papers, 1882 Packet, Other Schools.
121. *The Guardian*, 14 November 1883.
122. E. M. Bell, op. cit., pp. 23, 38, and 39.
123. *The Guardian*, 28 August 1850.
124. *The Guardian*, 4 September 1850. Letter from W.B.H. See also, *The Guardian*, 15 February 1851. Letter from W.B.H.
125. E.g. the *Guardian*, 18 September 1850, Leading Article; the *Guardian*, 13 May 1857, Letter; the *Guardian*, 22 March 1865, Letter.
126. *The Guardian*, 8 April 1868. See also, *The Guardian*, 11 January 1865.
127. *The Autobiography of Elizabeth M. Sewell*, ed. Eleanor L. Sewell (Longmans, Green, 1907), p. 214.
128. *The Guardian*, 12 June 1878; *The Guardian*, 23 March 1881.
129. E. M. Bell, op. cit., pp. 8 and 11.
130. S.I.C., V, pp. 252–7; S.I.C., V, p. 254.
131. Mary Gurney, *Are We to Have Education for Our Middle-Class Girls? or, The History of the Camden Collegiate School* (William Ridgeway, 1872), p. 12.
132. Ibid., pp. 19 and 16.
133. S.I.C., V, p. 252.
134. S.I.C., X, p. 293.
135. Above, p. 155.
136. Founded in 1850 with forty boys, this school had 420 day boys in 1865 (S.I.C., IV, p. 489).
137. Moseley's school had ninety-eight pupils in 1864. The core of the curriculum was experimental science. Above, pp. 102f. Also see, S.I.C. IV, p. 198, and, Canon [H] Moseley, *Middle Class Education and the Bristol Diocesan Trade School* (S. E. Chillcott, 1864).
138. In the former, in 1855, there were nearly fifty boys, "sons of professional men, tradespeople, and superior mechanics" (see, C. F. Secretan, *Middle Schools. The Want of the People and the Duty of the Church* [Westminster: W. Blanchard, 1857]). The Burgh School had twenty-two boarders and twenty-one day boys in 1871 (see, Pamphlets and Prospectus, 12 June 1871, Woodard Papers, Non-Woodard Middle Class Education Envelope).

139. W. F. Connell, *The Educational Thought and Influence of Matthew Arnold* (Routledge & Kegan Paul, 1950), p. 246.
140. Quoted in Connell, op. cit., p. 246.
141. M. Arnold, *A French Eton*, p. 130.
142. Ibid., p. 37.
143. Ibid., pp. 50–1.
144. Ibid., pp. 66 and 63.
145. Ibid., p. 53.
146. Ibid., p. 98.
147. Ibid., p. 129.
148. Ibid., p. 123.
149. Ibid., p. 126.
150. Connell, op. cit., p. 255.
151. S.I.C., I, p. 15.
152. Above, p. 9.
153. *Grade I*
Commissioners: "Sons of gentlemen of independent income, Professional gentlemen, Bankers, Manufacturers, or others in large mercantile business". *Woodard* (1850–9): "Sons of clergymen and gentlemen of limited means"; by 1873 "noblemen" and "professional men" were added, but Appendix A shows that the sons of professional and businessmen were at Lancing before the Commissioners made their Report.
Grade II
Commissioners: "Sons of tradesmen in considerable business, farmers, agents, managers, upper clerks." *Woodard* (1850–9): "Tradesmen, farmers and clerks."
Grade III
Commissioners: "Sons of tradesmen in limited business, shopmen, clerks, upper artisans." *Woodard* (1859): "Sons of small shopkeepers, farmers, mechanics, clerks, and others of limited means."
See, S.I.C., I, Appendix II, p 112, and above, Chapter 1, pp. 8f., and notes 17 and 18.
154. S.I.C., I, p. 184.
155. S.I.C., I, p. 101.
156. S.I.C., I, p. 79. Woodard wrote that "The Lower Middle Class will either be our Saviour or our Ruin" (to the Marquess of Salisbury), 14 June 1871, Christ Church, Salisbury Papers, Letters from Woodard.
157. S.I.C., I, p. 603.
158. See, S.I.C., I, pp. 573, 588, 589.
159. S.I.C., VII, pp. 146–8.
160. Above, Chapter 4.
161. S.I.C., I, p. 107.
162. S.I.C., I, p. 571.
163. S.I.C., I, p. 579.
164. S.I.C., I, pp. 601ff.

165. S.I.C., I, p. 628.

166. J. B. Lee, *Middle-Class Education and the Working of the Endowed Schools Act* (Rivington's, 1885), p. 25.

167. *Report of the Select Committee on the Endowed Schools Act* (Parliamentary Papers, 1873, Vol. VIII), p. 328.

168. *Report from the Select Committee on the Endowed Schools Act* (Parliamentary Papers, 1886, Vol. IX), p. 466.

169. Ibid., p. 488.

170. *Number of Pupils Under Instruction in the Selected Schools:*

First Grade:	1868:	4,561
	1883:	8,262
Second Grade:	1868:	4,808
	1883:	9,065
Third Grade:	1868:	4,482
	1883:	10,585
Total:	1868:	13,851
	1883:	27,912

(Parliamentary Papers, 1886, Vol. IX, pp. 448–89.)

171. See, Ibid., p. 65. Evidence of Sir G. Young, Bart.

172. Simon, op. cit., p. 335. In the view of the S.I.C., "middle class" and "secondary" were virtually identical terms. Simon shows that the reorganized endowed schools were of very little use to the working classes. (Simon, op. cit., pp. 329ff. See also, J. B. Lee, op. cit., p. 36.)

173. J. B. Lee, op. cit., p. 56.

174. See Appendix F.

175. Lord Wharncliffe to N. Woodard, 3 September 1870, Woodard Papers, 1870 Packet, Other Schools.

176. *Middle-Class Education in Yorkshire* (Pusey House Pamphlets No. 7652), p. 8.

177. Ibid., pp. 17 and 20.

178. Ibid., p. 7.

179. Fragment of a copy of a letter from "C. Lincoln" to "Mr Mills", Undated, Woodard Papers, 1870 Packet, Other Schools.

180. Above, p. 168.

181. S.I.C., I, p. 196. The Science and Art Department was a government agency established to encourage the teaching of science, arts and crafts. It encouraged the provision of science classes throughout the country, and, after 1859, conducted examinations for science pupils. Success in such examinations resulted in a money payment to the schools or classes concerned. Such payments were known as "South Kensington Grants". See R. L. Archer, *Secondary Education in the Nineteenth Century* (Cambridge University Press, 1921), pp. 137 and 306.

182. R. L. Archer, op. cit., pp. 308–9.

183. *The Guardian*, 8 January 1890.

184. R. L. Archer, op. cit., p. 310.

CHAPTER 7

THE ACHIEVEMENT

1. Walter Houghton, *The Victorian Frame of Mind, 1830–1870* (New Haven: Yale University Press, 1957), p. 161.
2. Above, pp. 69, 58f., and 164f.
3. R. L. Archer, op. cit., v.
4. *Census of Great Britain, 1851. Religious Worship. England and Wales* (Parliamentary Papers, 1852–3, Vol. LXXXIX), clxxxii. Total attendances: 10,896,066. Anglican attendances: 5,292,551.
5. Ibid., clvi.
6. See, Conybeare, op. cit., p. 158. He estimates that only 1,000 of the 18,000 clergy of the Church of England were "Tractarians".
7. See above, Chapter 1.
8. J. J. Findlay (ed.), op. cit., p. 201.
9. Above, p. 174f.
10. Above, p. 102f.
11. F. Storr (ed.), op. cit., p. 79.
12. Above, p. 19.
13. Archer, op. cit., v.

APPENDIX A

St Nicolas College
Directions to Chaplains

I. You will see each boy and other Junior Member of the society, privately, at least once in every six weeks.

II. Your duty is to seek to win the children to think seriously of religious duties; to urge them to purity of heart and a conscientious discharge of their several responsibilities.

III. To those children who show a proper disposition, and who have evidently been trying to exercise themselves in religious habits, you shall give a "blessing"; but the careless and indifferent must be made to understand that you cannot bless them until they amend.

IV. Those elder boys who find the struggle of life severe, and who wish to disclose the secrets of their hearts and to obtain absolution, you shall receive under these restrictions:

1. That the consent of the parent or guardian be first obtained.
2. That the act be *voluntary* on the part of the boy (as the Church of England wishes).
3. That you ask the penitent no leading question, or suggest (*under any circumstances*) any sin by way of enquiry whether he has committed it—but that you listen simply to his own tale of woe, and to the things which prey on his conscience (as suggested by the Prayer Book). Questions, however, arising out of his confession you may ask.

V. When you hear the confessions of penitents you must do it as a religious act —with a regular form, and with earnest prayer for their amendment.

VI. Great care must be taken not to make the habits of the children artificial by forced piety; yet the infinite blessing of having the whole heart and intellect directed to the service and love of God is ever to be kept before their eyes.

New Shoreham, 1848. N.W.

[Woodard Papers, 1848 Pamphlets]

APPENDIX B

Lancing College.
The Occupation of Parents: 1864

(Taken from the Report of the Schools Inquiry Commission, Volume XI, page 250.)

The ten highest and ten lowest boys in the school order are taken as samples of the whole.

BOARDERS	OCCUPATION OF PARENT	RESIDENCE
Boys highest in school	Clergyman	Rectory near Bath
	Clergyman	Vicarage near Saffron Waldon
	Clergyman	Hammersmith
	Clergyman	Vicarage near Bristol
	Colonel in Indian Army	Kunackee, Scinde
	Clergyman	Rectory, Leicester
	Clergyman	Hastings
	Landed proprietor	Near Staplehurst
	Clergyman	Hastings
	Brewer	Near Wallingford
Boys lowest in school	Clergyman	Vicarage near Chichester
	Landed proprietor	Near Bristol
	Clergyman	Pimlico
	Clergyman	Vicarage, Isle of Wight
	Clergyman	Pimlico
	Merchant	London
	Civil Engineer	Penge
	Clergyman	Brighton
	Clergyman	Rectory near Hurst Green
	Landed proprietor	Near Tunbridge Wells

APPENDIX C

Hurstpierpoint: St John's Middle School
The Occupation of Parents: 1865

(Taken from the Report of the Schools Inquiry Commission, Volume XI, page 241.)

The ten highest and ten lowest boys in the School order are taken as amples of the whole.

BOARDERS	OCCUPATION OF PARENT	RESIDENCE
Boys highest in school	Curate	Frome, Selwood
	Bailiff	Pontefract
	Farmer	Shillingford, Oxon.
	Needle manufacturer	Redditch
	[Orphan]	Norwood
	Curate	Gidleigh, Devon
	Farmer	Staunton, Derbyshire
	Horse dealer and trainer	Middleham, Yorks.
	Newspaper proprietor	Nottingham
	Job Master	Fulham, London
Boys lowest in school	Tallow chandler	London
	Butcher	Aylesford, Kent
	Cashier	London
	Attorney	London
	Engineer	Malpas, Monmouth
	Innkeeper	Isle of Wight
	Hotel Manager	Brighton
	Builder	Gravesend
	Attorney	London
	Clerk of a London Market	London

APPENDIX D

New Shoreham: St Saviour's Grammar School
The Occupation of Parents: 1864

(Taken from the Report of the Schools Inquiry Commission, Volume XI, page 264.)

The ten highest and ten lowest boys in the School order are taken as samples of the whole.

BOARDERS	OCCUPATION OF PARENT	RESIDENCE
Boys highest in school	Master of a workhouse	London
	Publican	London
	Clerk in an office	London
	Domestic servant, butler	Chislehurst
	Gardener	Croydon
	Wheelwright	Norwood
	Builder	Brixton
	Tailor	London
	Gardener	Salisbury
	Clerk in an office	London
Boys lowest in school	Cheesemonger	London
	Father dead; needlewoman	London
	Publican	Llanover
	(Father) waiter, (mother) cook	London
	Waiter	London
	Dairyman	Anerley
	Florist	Fulham
	Builder	London
	Stationer	London
	Clerk in a pianoforte manufactory	London

There are only five day scholars, sons of a butcher, greengrocer, farmer, and captain of a coal brig.

APPENDIX E

Lambeth: Robert Gregory's Middle Class Day Schools The Occupation of Parents: 1865

IN THE UPPER DIVISION (ONE SHILLING WEEKLY):

3 bagatelle-board makers
1 baker
6 bricklayers
1 cab proprietor
4 candle-makers
9 carpenters
1 carver and gilder
18 clerks
4 coach-builders
2 commercial travellers
1 cooper
1 cowkeeper
4 engineers
6 foremen and warehousemen
1 hat maker
1 leather cutter
2 lithographers
1 pianoforte maker
1 policeman
2 porters
2 postmen
4 printers
3 publicans
1 railway ticket taker
1 rent collector
1 sawyer
1 shoemaker
2 shopkeepers
3 shopmen
1 silver chaser
2 tailors
1 wheelwright
10 widows (or no parents)
3 women separated from husbands

IN THE LOWER DIVISION (SIXPENCE WEEKLY):

2 backers
1 blacksmith
3 bricklayers
1 brickmaker
2 cabmen
5 carmen
8 carpenters
1 carriage-maker
1 carver and gilder
6 clerks
1 clockmaker
1 cooper
13 engineers
1 engraver
5 gasmen
1 gun-maker
1 ostler
1 painter
1 plane-maker
2 policeman
3 postmen
3 potters
5 printers
2 publicans
1 sailor
1 sealing-wax maker
3 shopmen
1 slater
2 stonemasons
1 tailor
1 teacher of dancing
1 tripe-dresser

1 labourer
1 lamplighter
2 millers
1 musician
3 opticians
1 upholsterer
1 ventriloquist
1 waiter
2 warders at Millbank prison
6 widows
2 women separated from husbands

(From: R. Gregory, *Do Our National Schools Provide Education for All Whom They Ought to Train?*)

APPENDIX F

Queen Elizabeth's Grammar School, Barnet
The Occupation of Parents: 1876–85

(During these years 450 boys were entered in the School; of these, 50 did not supply the occupation of their parents.)

Sons of Clergy	12	
Sons of Medical men	5	
Sons of Lawyers	11	
Sons of Army officers	10	
Sons of Civil servants	22	
Sons of Architects, Artists and Engineers	24	
Sons of Journalists & Schoolmasters	11	
Sons of Manufacturers	26	
Sons of Merchants & Wholesale Tradesmen	50	
Sons of Shopkeepers	89	
Sons of Commercial Travellers; Warehousemen; Brokers; Agents	70	
Sons of Bank managers & clerks	10	
Sons of Mercantile clerks	18	
Sons of Farmers & bailiffs	9	
Sons of Artisans & labourers	26	(partly by exhibition from elementary schools)

(From: J. B. Lee, *Middle-Class Education and the Working of the Endowed Schools Act* [Rivington's 1885], p. 51)

BIBLIOGRAPHY

The two main sources of original material used in the preparation of this book are the Woodard Papers and the auxiliary collection of the Founder's papers deposited in the Lancing College Archives. These two collections include about 9,000 letters, a great number of pamphlets, printed letters, appeals, invitations, prospectuses, and newspaper clippings. Both the Woodard Papers and the Lancing Archives collection are housed at Lancing College.

In the Woodard Papers the letters are now collected in large envelopes according to date; within these envelopes the letters are bundled according to subjects, e.g. politics, religion, school life. Thus, given the date of the envelope, together with the subject group under which a particular letter is collected, it is possible to trace any reference to the Woodard Papers in this book. Pamphlets and printed material dealing with the Woodard Schools are also to be found in envelopes according to year; newspaper clippings, drafts of statutes, etc. are likewise arranged.

Letters in the Lancing Archives collection are arranged both chronologically and according to whom they were written. Thus the two main groups of letters in this collection are referred to as Letters to Lowe (i.e. from Woodard to E. C. Lowe) or Letters to Hare (i.e. Woodard to Julius Hare). Most of the printed material in the Lancing Archives is pasted into a large scrap-book.

The collection of letters from Woodard in the Salisbury Papers at Christ Church is small but important. About a dozen letters from Woodard and a larger number from Lowe may be found in the Gladstone Papers. Other manuscript sources for this study are the minute books of two committees connected with the National Society which were kindly opened for my inspection at the Society's Westminster offices.

Of contemporary printed material other than that contained in the Woodard Papers and the Lancing Archives, the Report of the Schools Inquiry Commission and the pamphlets in the Pusey House collection have been most used. The pamphlet collection, official publications, and school histories in the Ministry of Education library were also valuable. Other material was gathered from the resources of the Bodleian Library, the libraries of the British Museum, and that of the Oxford Union.

Some nineteenth-century printed material, referred to in the notes, is not listed in the bibliography. This consists of small printed papers, often without title or author, and frequently consisting of only one sheet, which are to be found principally in the pamphlet section of the Woodard Papers; some, however, are in other collections, and to these reference is made in the notes.

The general bibliography which follows contains only works originally printed and published before 1914, except for more recent school histories and other works with a direct bearing on the Woodard schools and their competitors. Many references to recent general works are to be found in the notes.

Two gaps in the evidence on which this book is based can only be regretted. The Ardingly *Register* fails to note the future occupations of the boys listed; consequently we are denied the glimpses of the boys' careers afforded by the Lancing, Hurst, and Denstone *Registers*. In the case of Ardingly a comparison of these careers with parental occupations would have been particularly interesting. I have not been able to find very much material on which to base a boy's view of school life and religion in the early days of the Woodard schools. The school magazines are of little use in this respect, and consequently the evidence on which this book is based is principally the product of adult minds.

Manuscript Sources

The Gladstone Papers. The British Museum.

Lancing Archives. Lancing College.

The Minute Book of the Committee of Inquiry and Correspondence. The National Society.

The Minute Book of the Middle Class Schools Committee. The National Society.

The Salisbury Papers. Christ Church, Oxford.

The Woodard Papers. Lancing College.

Public Documents

Census of Great Britain, 1851. Education. England and Wales. Parliamentary Papers, Vol. XC. 1852–3.

Census of Great Britain, 1851. Religious Worship. England and Wales. Parliamentary Papers, Vol. LXXXIX. 1852–3.

Hansard's Parliamentary Debates. Vol. CCXXI (1874) and Vol. CCLXXXV (1884).

Report of the Schools Inquiry Commission, 1867–8. Parliamentary Papers, Vol. XXVIII, Parts I–XVII. 1867–8. The twenty-one volumes which comprise this report are also printed separately; the page references are identical in both editions.

Report from the Select Committee on the Endowed Schools Acts. Parliamentary Papers, Vol. IX. 1886.

General Bibliography

(With few exceptions this list is confined to works printed and published before 1914. References to modern works and to unpublished theses may be found in the notes.)

Acland, A. H. D., *Memoir and Letters of the Rt Honourable Sir Thomas Dyke Acland.* Printed for Private Circulation, London 1902.

Acland, T. D. Jun., *A Letter to William Henry Powell Gore Langton, Esq., on the Subject of the Proposed Church of England School at Taunton.* Printed for Private Circulation, 16 October, 1847. This is available in the Woodard Papers, Non-Woodard middle-class education envelope.

—— *Report on the Results of the West of England Examination, by the Rev. F. Temple, M.A., and Correspondence with George Richmond and John Hullah, Esqrs., on the Arts in Connection with General Education.* London 1857.

All Saints' School, Bloxham. Centenary, 1860–1960. Brief History of the School and Its Progress. Published to commemorate the centenary of the school, 1960.

Arnold, Matthew, *Culture and Anarchy.* 1909.

—— *A French Eton.* 1892.

Awdry, W., *An Opening Address to the Senior Members of the College of St Mary and St Nicolas, Lancing, at Their Octave Meeting for Purposes of Devotion, Business and the Exercise of a More Extended Hospitality.* London 1875. Available in the Woodard Papers, pamphlets 1875.

Baxter, R. Dudley. *National Income. The United Kingdom.* 1868.

[Beale, Dorothy], *History of the Cheltenham Ladies' College, 1853–1904.*

Bell, E. M., *A History of the Church Schools Company, 1883–1958.* 1958.

Bennett, F., *The Story of W. J. E. Bennett.* 1909.

Blackwood's Edinburgh Magazine, August 1885. Contains an article entitled "What Has Become of the Middle Classes?".

Booth, Charles, *Occupations of the People: England, Scotland, Ireland, 1841–1881*. 1886.

Boyd, A. K., *The History of Radley College, 1847–1947*. 1948.

Bradfield College Register, 1876. 1876.

Brereton, J. L., *County Education. Accounts of the Devon and Norfolk County School Associations for 1875, With a Few Remarks on the New College for Junior Students at Cambridge*. 1876.

—— *County Education. A Contribution of Experiments, Estimates and Suggestion*. 1874.

—— *County Education. A Letter Addressed to the Right Honourable the Earl of Devon*. 1861.

The Brighton Guardian.

Brighton Gazette.

The Brighton Herald.

Brooke, Sam, *Sam Brooke's Journal*. Ed. Peter Hadley. Published in Aid of the Friends of Lancing Chapel, 1953.

Burgon, J. W., *Lives of Twelve Good Men*. 1888.

Calendars of the Corporation of SS. Mary and Nicolas. The Calendars from 1850–9 are available in the Lancing archives. Subsequent issues are available at the Bodleian and British Museum libraries.

Carnarvon, the Earl of, *The Advantages of an Established Church*. 1885.

Chambers's Journal of Popular Literature, Science and Arts, Volume VI, 1857. Contains an article entitled, "Schools Cheap and Nasty".

Chandler, George, *An Address Delivered at the Opening of the Church of England Metropolitan Commercial School, Rose Street, Soho Square, 28 January, 1839*.

[Chase, D. P.], *Education of Frugal Men at the University of Oxford. An Account of the Experiments at St Mary's and St Alban's Halls by the Principals of Those Halls*. 1864.

The Christian Examiner and Religious Miscellany, Vol. XLVIII (March 1850). This American publication, available in the British Museum reading room, contains an article by "S.H.P." on "The Middle Class".

Church Property and Revenue in England and Wales. 1850.

Church, R. W. *The Oxford Movement. Twelve Years, 1833–1845*. 1897.

Clark, H. W., *History of English Nonconformity*, Vol. II. 1913.

Cole, H. W., *The Middle Classes and the Borough Franchise*. 1866.

Coleridge, J. T., *A Memoir of the Rev. John Keble*. 1869.

Conybeare, W. J., *Essays Ecclesiastical and Social. Reprinted, with Additions, from the "Edinburgh Review"*. 1855.

Cornish, F. W., *The English Church in the Nineteenth Century*, Vols. I and II. 1910.

Cranleigh School, 1865–1906. 1906. This publication is to be found in the Ministry of Education library.

The Daily News.

Denison, G. A., *Catholicity Without Establishment or Establishment Without Catholicity: A Paper Read at a Meeting of the Church League at Freemason's Tavern, 3 July, 1877.*

—— *Notes of My Life, 1805–1878.*

—— *The School of the Church Schools Company. A Letter to the Clergy and People of the Archdeaconry of Taunton.* 1883.

—— *Seventeen Reasons Why the Church of England May Have Nothing to Do With Any Manner of "Conscience Clause".* 1865.

—— *Supplement to "Notes of My Life", 1879 and "Mr Gladstone", 1886.* 1893.

Denison, L. E. (ed.), *Fifty Years at East Brent. The Letters of George Anthony Denison, 1845–1896.* 1902.

The Denstonian, 1877–1891. The School Magazine of Denstone, available at the Bodleian library.

The Derbyshire Advertiser.

Dunckley, H., *The Glory and the Shame of Britain.* 1851.

An English Catholic. *St Nicolas College Shoreham and Compromise.* Available in Woodard Papers, pamphlets undated.

The English Journal of Education.

Findlay, J. J. (ed.), *Arnold Of Rugby: His School Life and Contributions to Education.* 1914.

Fitch, J. G., *The Royal Commission of Enquiry into the State of Middle Class Education.* 1865.

Fortescue, Earl, and Others. *The Devon County School: Its Objects, Cost and Studies.* Exeter 1862.

——*Public Schools for the Middle Classes.* 1864.

Foster, Joseph, *Alumni Oxonienses*, Vol. IV. 1888.

Froude, J. A., *Short Studies in Great Subjects*, Vol. IV. 1883.

Froude, R. Hurrell, *Remains*, Vol. I. 1838.

Golightly, C. P., *A Letter to the Rev. Dr Jeune, Vice-Chancellor of the University of Oxford in Vindication of the Handbill Distributed at the Doors of the Sheldonian Theatre on 22 November, 1861.* This is available in the Pusey House pamphlet collection.

Gregory, Robert, *Do Our National Schools Provide for All Whom They Ought to Train? A Letter to His Grace the Archbishop of Canterbury.* 1865.

Grier, R. M. and F. A. Hibbert. *The Register of St Chad's College, Denstone from the Opening of the School in February 1873 to April 1904.* Published by Subscription, 1904.

Gruber, C. S., *A Letter to the Rt Hon. B. Disraeli in Reply to Certain Statements Contained in His Speech, 15 July 1874, on the Public Worship Regulation Bill.* 1874.

The Guardian.

Gurney, Mary, *Are We to Have Education for Our Middle-Class Girls? or, The History of the Camden Collegiate Schools.* 1872.

Hadden, R. H., *Reminiscences of William Rogers, Rector of St Botolph's, Bishopsgate.* 1888.

Hale, W. H., *The Designs and Constitution of the Society for the Liberation of Religion from State Patronage and Control. Stated and Explained in an Address to the Clergy of the Archdeaconry of London at the Annual Visitation, 23 May, 1861.* 1861.

Handford, B. W. T., *Lancing: A History of SS. Mary and Nicolas College, Lancing, 1848–1930.* Blackwell 1933.

Hare, Julius C., *Education, the Necessity of Mankind. A Sermon Preached at Hurstpierpoint.* 1851.

Heywood, T. P., *Reminiscences, Letters and Journals of Thomas Percival Heywood.* Arranged by his eldest daughter. 1899.

Hibbert, F. A., *A Short History and Description of Denstone College.* Undated.

The High Schools of the Girls' Public Day School Company. An Illustrated History. 1900. This is available in the Ministry of Education library.

Hill, A. H., "Middle-Class Destitution", *The University Magazine*, I. 1878.

Hill, R. L., *Toryism and the People.* Constable, 1929.

History of All Saints' School, Bloxham, 1860–1910, with Supplement, 1910–1925. Second Edition. Published at the school, 1925.

Hook, Walter F., *On the Means of Rendering More Efficient the Education of the People.* 1846.

[Hope, A. J. B. Beresford], *The Church Cause and the Church Party.* 1860.

Howard, R., *A Plea for the Establishment of Additional Public Schools in Yorkshire for the Upper and Middle Classes.* 1870.

Hurst Johnian, Vols. I–XXXIII (1858–1891). This is the Hurstpierpoint school magazine and is available in the library of that college.

Hussey, Robert, *A Letter to Thomas Dyke Acland, Esq., M.P., on the System of Education to be Established in the Diocesan Schools for the Middle-Classes.* 1839.

James, Samuel, *Some Thoughts, Observations, and Hints on Middle Class Education.* 1853.

Johnson, H. L. (ed.), *A Register of St John's College, Hurstpierpoint.* Published privately, 1914.

The Journal of the Farmer's Club, 1864. Article on "Middle Class Education". Available in the Ministry of Education library.

Kebbel, T. E., *A History of Toryism from the Accession of Mr Pitt to Power in 1883 to the Death of Lord Beaconsfield in 1881.* 1886.

—— "The Middle Classes," *The National Review*, I. 1883.

Keble, John, *Sermons, Academical and Occasional* 1847.

Kirk, K. E., *The Story of the Woodard Schools*. Hodder and Stoughton, 1937.

The Lancing Register, 1913.

Leach, A. F., *A History of Bradfield College*. 1900.

Lee, F. G., *The Church of England and Political Parties: A Letter to the Rt Hon. Gathorne Hardy, M.P., D.C.L.* Second edn, 1868.

Lee, J. B., *Middle Class Education and the Working of the Endowed Schools Act*. 1885.

Lees, W. Nassau, *Instruction in the Oriental Languages Considered. Specially as Regards the Education of Candidates for the East India Civil Service, and as a National Question*. 1857.

A Letter from One of the Special Constables in London on the Late Occasion of Their Being Called Out to Keep the Peace, 1848. Available in the Oxford Union Library.

Liddon, H. P., *The Life of Edward Bouverie Pusey*. Second edn, 1893.

Linklater, Robert, *Abolish the Mass or "The Mass in Masquerade"*. Undated.

Lowe, E. C., *The Image of God. A Sermon for Schoolmasters and Schoolboys Preached in St John's College Chapel Hurstpierpoint on the Twelfth Sunday After Trinity, 1856*.

—— *St Nicolas College and Its Schools. A Letter to the Rt Hon. Sir J. T. Coleridge*. 1861.

—— *St Nicolas College and Its Schools. A Record of Thirty Years Work in the Effort to Endow the Church of England with a System of Self-supporting Public Boarding Schools for the Upper, Middle, and Lower Middle Classes*. 1878.

—— *A Plea for Poor Scholars in the University and Colleges of Oxford Urged in a Letter to the Rev. the Rector of Lincoln College*. 1867.

A number of additional printed letters and circulars, written by Dr Lowe, are included in the Woodard Papers pamphlet envelopes. Specific references to such are made in the notes.

Lowe, Robert, *Middle Class and Primary Education. Two Speeches Delivered at the Annual Dinner of the Liverpool Philomathic Society and at the Conference on Education at the Town Hall, 22 and 23 January*. 1868.

The Manchester Guardian.

Manning, H. E., *A Charge Delivered at the Ordinary Visitation of the Archdeaconry of Chichester in July 1843*.

—— *A Charge Delivered at the Ordinary Visitation of the Archdeaconry of Chichester in July 1846*.

Marriott, Charles, *A Letter to the Rev. H. W. Bellairs, M. A., One of Her Majesty's Inspectors of Schools. On the Admission of the Children of Dissenters to Church Schools*. Littlemore, 1849.

—— *University Extension and the Poor Scholar Question. A Letter to the Rev. E. Woollcombe*. 1848.

A Member of the National Society [G. F. Mathison]. *How Can the Church Educate the People? The Question Considered with Reference to the Incorporation and Endowment of Colleges for the Middle and Lower Classes of Society in a Letter Addressed to the Lord Archbishop of Canterbury.* 1844.

A Member of the Oxford Convocation. *A Letter to the Rt Hon. Lord John Russell, M.P., on the Constitutional Defects of the University and Colleges of Oxford with Suggestions for a Royal Commission of Inquiry into the Universities.* 1850.

Members of the University of Oxford. *Tracts for the Times.* Numbers 59 and 83. 1840.

The Methodist Almanac, 1871.

Miall, Edward, *The British Churches in Relation to the British People.* Second edn, 1850.

Montague, F. C., *Technical Education. A Summary of the Report of the Royal Commission Appointed to Inquire into the State of Technical Instruction.* 1887.

de Montmorency, J. E. G., *State Intervention in English Education.* 1902.

Moore, Edward, *Frugal Education Attainable Under the Existing Collegiate System, With an Account of the Expenses of the System at St Edmund Hall.* 1867.

Morley, John, *The Life of William Ewart Gladstone.* 1908.

The Morning Chronicle.

Moseley, Canon H. *Middle-Class Education and the Bristol Diocesan Trade School. A Paper Read at the Church Congress Held in Bristol in October, 1864.* Available in the Ministry of Education library.

Mozley, T., *Reminiscences Chiefly of Oriel College and the Oxford Movement.* 1882.

Newman, J. H., *Apologia Pro Vita Sua.* New York, The Modern Library, 1950.

—— *Historical Sketches.* (Second Series) Second edn, 1873.

—— *The Idea of a University.* New York, Doubleday & Co. 1959.

Notes on Middle Class Boarding Schools and Middle Class Education, Addressed to All Who Have Sons at School. 1859.

The Nottingham Daily Guardian.

Osborne, C. E., *The Life of Father Dolling.* 1903.

Otter, Sir John, *Nathaniel Woodard: A Memoir of His Life.* John Lane, 1925.

Parkin, G. R., *Life and Letters of Edward Thring*, 1898.

Perry, R., *Ardingly, 1858–1946. A History of the School.* Published privately by the Old Ardinians Society, 1951.

Pollen, J. H., *Narrative of Five Years at St Saviour's, Leeds.* 1851.

A Practical Man, *Public and Middle-Class School Education: What It Is and What It Should Be*. 1865. Available in the Ministry of Education library.

"The Problem of the Middle Classes". *Good Words* 1877.

Purcell, E. S., *The Life of Cardinal Manning*. 1896.

The Record.

Register of St Lawrence College, 1879 to 1934. Published by the Old Lawrentian Society, 1934.

A Register of St Nicolas College, Lancing, 1848–1900. Published by Private Subscription, 1900.

Register of St Saviour's School, Ardingly. 1913.

Robinson, Hugh G., "Middle-Class Education in England", *The Museum*, April, 1861.

The Rock.

Roundell, Earl of Selborne, *A Defence of the Church of England Against Disestablishment*. Fourth edn, 1899.

Russell, E. F. (ed.), *Alexander Heriot Mackonochie* (by "E. A. T."). 1890.

Saint Saviour's Annals, 1871–1891. This is the school magazine of Ardingly and is available at Ardingly College.

The Saturday Review.

Secretan, D. F., *Middle Schools: the Want of the People and the Duty of the Church. A Sermon Preached in Holy Trinity Church, Vauxhall Bridge Road, on the Sunday After Ascension Day, 1857*. This is available in the Lancing College archives.

Sewell, Eleanor L. (ed.), *The Autobiography of Elizabeth M. Sewell*. 1907.

Sewell, W., *A Speech at the Annual Dinner of Old Radleians Held at Willis's Rooms, 22 June, 1872*. This is available in the Pusey House pamphlet collection.

Skeats, H. S., *A History of the Free Churches of England*. Second edn, 1869.

Skinner, James, *The Church and the Public School. A Sermon Preached at the Annual Commemoration Festival at St Mary's College, Harlow, Essex, with a Letter to the Rev. the President of the College*. 1861. This is available in the Pusey House pamphlet collection.

The Staffordshire Advertiser.

Stanley, A. P., *The Life and Correspondence of Thomas Arnold*. New York, D. Appleton & Co., 1846.

Staunton, Howard, *The Great Schools of England*. 1869.

Stephens, W. R. W., *The Life and Letters of Walter Farquhar Hook*. 1878.

Storr, F. (ed.), *Life and Remains of the Rev. R. H. Quick*. 1899.

The Sussex Express.

The Theological Review, 1868. This publication contains an article by "R.D.O." on "The Religion of the Middle Classes".

Thornton, F. V., *The Education of the Middle Classes in England. A Lecture*

Delivered to Members of the Mechanics' Institute, Romsey, 20 December, 1861. Available in the Ministry of Education library.

The Times.

Tod, Isabella M. S., *On the Education of Girls of the Middle Classes*. 1874.

Townsend, W. J. and others, *A New History of Methodism*. 1909.

Trent College School Lists, 1874. Available in the Pusey House pamphlet collection.

Tulloch, John, *Movements of Religious Thought in Britain During the Nineteenth Century*. 1885.

Walsh, J. H., *A Manual of Domestic Economy Suited to Families Spending from £100 to £1000 a Year*. 1857.

Walsh, Walter, *The Secret History of the Oxford Movement*. Sixth edn, 1899.

Wigley, Mrs W. H., *Our Home Work: A Manual of Domestic Economy*. 1876.

W[ood], S. F., "On Attaching the Middle and Lower Orders to the Church", *The English Journal of Education* Vol. I. 1843.

Woodard, Nathaniel, *A Brief Report on the State of the Buildings, Labours and Finances of St Nicolas College*. 1858.

—— *Denstone Public School, In Union With St Nicolas College. A Letter to Sir Percival Heywood, Bart*. 1867.

—— *A Plea for the Middle Classes*. 1848.

—— *Public Schools for the Middle Classes. A Letter to the Clergy of the Diocese of Chichester*. 1851.

—— *Public Schools for the Middle Classes. A Letter, etc*. 1852.

—— *St Nicolas College and the Rev. J. Goring and Others, A Letter to the Substantial Tradesmen, Farmers and Others of the Employing Classes of the County of Sussex*. 1857.

—— *St Saviour's Lower Middle School for the Sons of Small Shopkeepers, Artizans, Clerks, and Others of Limited Means*. 1859.

—— *The Scheme of Education of St Nicolas College With Suggestions for the Permanent Constitution of That Society in a Letter to the Most Noble the Marquis of Salisbury, D.C.L., Chancellor of the University of Oxford*. 1869.

Many additional printed letters, circulars and appeals written by Nathaniel Woodard are included in the Woodard Papers pamphlets envelopes. Specific references to such are made in the notes.

The Woodard Schools. Second edn, 1868.

Woollcombe, E. C., *University Extension and the Poor Scholar Question. A Letter to the Provost of Worcester College*. 1848.

INDEX